'94

Dear Bart Deb:

...est wishes for
...e abundant + prosperous
...97. This extraordin...
...t-off-the-press book
...great addition to your
collection.

Enjoy!
Fondly,
John   Piña

The

MARIA
PARADOX

The
MARIA
PARADOX

How Latinas
Can Merge
Old World Traditions
with New World
Self-Esteem

Rosa Maria Gil, D.S.W.
and
Carmen Inoa Vazquez, PH.D.

G. P. Putnam's Sons
New York

This book was designed to offer professional knowledge and information on the topics discussed here. The authors have modified the personal stories related in this book to protect the identity and privacy of their clients where applicable. The publisher does not offer psychological or medical services. A reader might choose to seek competent professional help after reading this book.

G. P. Putnam's Sons
Publishers Since 1838
200 Madison Avenue
New York, NY 10016

Library of Congress Cataloging-in-Publication Data

Gil, Rosa Maria, date.
The Maria paradox : how Latinas can merge Old World
traditions with New World self-esteem / Rosa Maria Gil and
Carmen Inoa Vázquez.
p.   cm.
Includes bibliographical references.
ISBN 0-399-14159-6 (alk. paper)
1. Hispanic American women—Psychology. 2. Self-esteem—
United States—Handbooks, manuals, etc.   I. Vázquez, Carmen Inoa.
II. Title.
E184.S75G55   1996   95-45587 CIP
155.8'468073'082—dc20

Printed in the United States of America

1   3   5   7   9   10   8   6   4   2

Book design by Deborah Kerner
Title page art courtesy of the Metropolitan Museum of Art, the Michael C.
Rockefeller Memorial Collection, Gift of Arthur M. Bullowa, 1973
(1978.412.257)
This book is printed on acid-free paper. ∞

Acknowledgments

Mil gracias—many thanks to the Latinas who shared their lives and aspirations with us. This book could not have been written without you. We recognize and respect your struggle and celebrate your development as women, who in most instances became *nuevas marianistas*. We are grateful that your life stories will help many Latinas to better understand their struggle and to undertake the process of change.

We are indebted to Carolyn Fireside, an accomplished writer and new gringa friend, who believed so wholeheartedly in this project that she became one of us. Carolyn's enthusiasm was contagious and her support empowering. Thank you, Carolyn, for sharing your ideas with us, and for your love for this project. Without you this book could not have been possible.

Many thanks to Barbara Lowenstein and Madeline Morel for their energy and support. Many thanks to Laura Yorke, our editor, for guiding us throughout this project.

Various friends, family members, and colleagues helped us to write this book by discussing ideas, reading early drafts, researching materials in the library, teaching us computer skills, and taking care of us: Lilliam Barrios Paoli, Isabella Bick, Marta Siberio, Alfredo Arango, Ramon Blandino, Ralph Soto, Yolanda Barro, Jaime Vazquez (your technological support has been priceless; we are truly indebted to you), Cecilia Gaston, Mari Carmen Renard, Lucy Cordoba Martinez, Carmen Torres, Joyce Weinstein, Emma Genijovich, Margarita Pizano, Lourdes Dominguez, Amalia Buendia, Julie Pistorio, Alina Clavijo, Yvette Caro, Abelardo Inoa, Denise McGreevy, Wally Martinez, and Martin Juvelier. Your love and support have helped us throughout the many months of constant struggle in the writing of this book. ¡Gracias!

Special thanks to Manuel Trujillo, our colleague, who encouraged and sought us out to write this book. His commitment to women's rights is indeed evident in his support of this effort.

Contents

The

MARIA
PARADOX

I

"Do Not Forget
A Woman's Place":

Old World vs.
New Life

Natalia, a twenty-five-year-old Argentinian-born architect raised in the United States, was in a bind. She came
to therapy torn by doubts and fears which were causing
her a lot of emotional anguish. "I hate my father! No, I
hate my entire family," she told her therapist before adding, "No, I
really love them. I even love my father, but . . . Oh, I don't know . . ."

Natalia was distraught that although she'd made the daring move
of getting her own apartment, her father still felt he had the right to
control her life. Only recently, he'd shown up unexpectedly early on a
Sunday morning, demanding to know what she'd been doing out at
two a.m. the night before. From the messages she'd played back when

she got in, Natalia knew her father had started calling around eight p.m., and called every twenty minutes until around two. At this point, she assumed, mamá must have convinced him to go to sleep. But he showed up the next morning anyway.

"I just had it. I refused to tell him where I was or who I was with," she continued. "Actually, I was with a date at a wedding in Connecticut. My sin, I guess, was not reporting my plans to the family beforehand. Why should I have? I'm a twenty-five-year-old self-supporting adult. Anyway, I'm just glad my date didn't stay over. If Papá had found a man in my apartment, he probably would have challenged him to a duel!"

But what irked Natalia most was her father's feeling totally justified in treating her like a rebellious adolescent simply because she was a woman. During the Sunday morning meltdown, he actually informed her that it was his responsibility to see to her welfare. "Furthermore," he'd bellowed, "do not forget you owe me *respeto*!" Then he'd stormed out. Now they weren't even speaking. That meant Natalia's family contact was limited to whispered phone calls with her mother, sister, and brothers—none of whom dared to stand up to Papá.

Natalia very much wanted a life of her own, both social and professional. She desperately wanted her father to be less controlling, less critical, and more loving. She wanted him to be supportive of her needs, not his own. She needed her mother to help her deal with her father, which of course her mother wasn't about to do. Now Natalia was at the point of wondering if she was going to have to fire her family permanently. But when she seriously contemplated severing her relationship with them, she got frightened and began to feel like *una mala hija*. "I want to be my own person and I want the love of my family. Why is that too much to ask?" she complained.

Natalia's dilemma is typical of what you and other Latinas face in the United States—a profound clash between women's expectations here and in your country.

Being *la santa de la casa*, the household saint whose vocation is being a dutiful and uncomplaining daughter, wife, and mother, may have been enough *para tu mamá y para tu abuela*. In any case, your mother and grandmother most probably had no choice if they wanted to be considered respectable. You, however, have choices. And while that prospect is exciting, it can also be terribly threatening.

For example, you may want to be loved, not stifled, like Natalia, but you may be afraid to set limits.

Or you may feel unsatisfied with just being a full-time housewife, but are afraid even to mention the subject of working outside the home for fear of insulting your husband's *macho*.

Or you may dream of going to law school, but doubt yourself when your mother and father unconsciously discourage you by suggesting that it will lead to your being *una solterona*, an old maid, or that it would take time away from someday being a good wife and mother.

You certainly don't want your husband and mother-in-law to treat you like a child, but you accept it because complaining to them would be a violation of *respeto*.

And you want your daughters to be every bit as empowered as your sons, but realize your entire family is pressuring you to treat your *niños* and your *niñas* differently.

Even though you feel all these conflicting emotions, you most likely have trouble expressing them. Or, like Natalia, perhaps you do nothing until you get so angry, you overreact and really cause a scene. It's because you're afraid of being considered *una mala mujer*! And not only by your loved ones, but by yourself as well.

Since you're reading this book, we assume that you, like so many of *nuestras hermanas*, are feeling the weight of this inner and outer struggle and want to resolve your conflicted emotions. Without discarding the Latin traditions you so revere, you want to become a whole person who makes her own decisions and actively strives to fulfill her dreams.

We can help you resolve, in nonthreatening ways, the split between a Latina's family and community expectations, and an individual's needs and desires. We can help you demystify a lot of needless guilt and fear, and guide you as you redirect your feelings of anger and frustration into productive energy and vibrant self-worth.

We can help because we are Latinas who were raised in *las viejas costumbres*, the old ways, and understand them all too well; because we are professional women who have managed to broker a compromise between the world of our mothers and life in North America; and because we are experienced psychotherapists with a largely Latina/o clientele—many of whose stories, like Natalia's, you will read throughout *The Maria Paradox*.

This book can be an important source of help for you if:

• you're automatically assailed by guilt and frustration and are generally feeling lousy about yourself when you put your own needs ahead of your loved ones'
• your sex and love life aren't satisfying you
• you feel typecast by a rigid, Old World belief which unreasonably views women as congenitally lacking what it takes to succeed in the world outside the home
• you're determined to shed your culturally gender-determined feelings of inferiority and become a fully enfranchised Latina without sacrificing your revered ties to family and tradition

We appreciate that the new yearnings and conflicts you're experiencing are confusing and frustrating you. After all, tradition, as enforced by your family, may be telling you that you can't be an independent-minded Latina. To many people, the very term "independent-minded Latina" is a paradox, a contradiction in terms. We heartily disagree, because in our practices we have seen many Hispanic women resolve conflicts they initially believed were irreconcilable. But in order to do so, they first had to learn that such problems can be solved only if we understand what creates them to begin with. As we see it, your ambivalence and conflicts regarding women's issues have three major sources. They can be compared to three pieces of a puzzle.

The first piece of the puzzle is *marianismo/machismo*, the traditional Hispanic gender roles. The second piece of the puzzle is the desire to acculturate, or become a member of a new culture. The third piece of the puzzle is self-esteem, or the value you assign to yourself as a human being. As you acculturate, your level of self-esteem can either "make you or break you." If it's low, you stand a good chance of falling prey to *marianismo/machismo* and acculturation stress. If your self-esteem is high, you can conquer the pressures of tradition, and change to become a self-assured, socially and emotionally well-integrated North American Latina. Our aim in this book is to help you boost your self-esteem to a new high despite clashing cultural and social pressures—and keep it there.

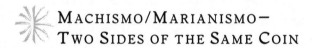 ## MACHISMO/MARIANISMO— TWO SIDES OF THE SAME COIN

So much has been written about *machismo* both within and outside the Latino community that the word has entered the English language as a synonym for oppressive male supremacy. However, it's important to be aware that *machismo* has positive aspects, too. We'll be referring to this "light side" when we feel you can use it to your advantage in improving things with the men in your life. The light side of *machismo* is personified in the *caballero*, who is a true protector in every sense of the word.

El caballero protects his wife and family from all dangers. He offers the best seat at the movies to his *dama*, stands up to give a woman his seat on the subway, carries heavy packages, always opens the door for a lady, and helps with the heavy household chores. While he is still afflicted by *machismo, el caballero* personifies the sensitive side of a man who deifies rather than denigrates his wife.

One of our purposes in this book is to show you how to bring out *la caballerosidad* in your man. Unfortunately, we will more frequently be talking about the dark side of *machismo*—not as the only side, but as the side manifested in certain behaviors and mind-sets, like those displayed by Natalia's father, which impact most negatively on our intimate relationships.

We also want to stress that living as *un macho* can be hard on a man who feels pressured to act in accordance with a rigid stereotype. We've certainly seen in our practices instances of the onus of *machismo*, when Latinos are afraid to cry or express tender feelings for fear of losing face. Clearly, gender roles carved in stone aren't in either sex's best interest. But frankly, women much too frequently are on the receiving end of a man's dark side.

Women end up in this position because the dark side of *machismo* mandates that men have options, and women have duties. It means that a man's place is *en el mundo*, in the world, and a woman's place is *en la casa*, in the home. It means that your brother is praised for being ambitious, while you are discouraged for that same quality. And it means that first your father, then your brothers, then your husband give the orders and you obey them.

But there is another side to the coin of *machismo*, which is equally rigidly enforced and deeply woven into the fabric of Latino/a life. It is called *marianismo*; it is the mortar holding antiquated cultural structures firmly in place, and it forms the core of the Maria Paradox. While discussed in academic literature—first in a ground-breaking essay written by Evelyn P. Stevens in 1973, and subsequently by such eminent academicians as Sally E. Romero, Julia M. Ramos-McKay, Lillian Comas-Diaz, and Luis Romero—as far as we know, it has never before been presented to the general reader. To us, analyzing exactly how *marianismo* affects acculturation and causes many of your personal problems is key to solving them.

While we will be focusing much of our attention on *marianismo*'s dark side, we also want to stress that *marianismo*, like *machismo*, has a light side. We'll be showing you how to access it and harness its qualities of loyalty, compassion, and generosity to fuel your empowerment and healthfully support those around you.

Marianismo: The Invisible Yoke

"No self-denial is too great for the Latin-American woman," writes Evelyn P. Stevens. "No limit can be divined to her vast store of patience for the men in her life . . . but far from being an oppressive norm dictated by tyrannical males, *marianismo* has received considerable impetus from women themselves. This makes it possible to regard *marianismo* as part of a reciprocal arrangement, the other half of *machismo.*"

Machismo has been defined by Victor de la Cancela, a Puerto Rican psychologist, as a socially learned and reinforced set of behaviors in Latino society which men are expected to follow. Indeed, if *machismo* is the sum total of what a man should be, *marianismo* defines the ideal role of woman. And what an ambitious role it is, taking as its model of perfection the Virgin Mary herself. *Marianismo* is about sacred duty, self-sacrifice, and chastity. About dispensing care and pleasure, not receiving them. About living in the shadows, literally and figuratively, of your men—father, boyfriend, husband, son—your kids, and your family. Aside from bearing children, the *marianista* has much in common with *una monja de convento*, a cloistered nun—but the order she enters is marriage, and her groom is not Christ but an all too human male who instantly becomes the single object of her devotion for a lifetime.

And what is the earthly reward for this total surrender of self, for being *una marianista*? In the Old Country, it affords a woman a level of protection as a wife and mother, gives her certain power and much *respeto* as well as a life free from loneliness and want. In today's North America, *marianismo* is the invisible yoke which binds capable, intelligent, ambitious Latinas such as many of our clients, friends, and colleagues to a no-win lifestyle.

We use the term "no-win" because *marianismo* insists you live in a world which no longer exists and which perpetuates a value system equating perfection with submission. Veneration may be the reward tendered to *la mujer buena*, but in actuality you end up feeling more

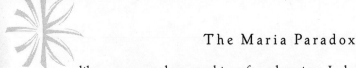

like a servant than a subject for adoration. Indeed, the noble sacrifice of self (the ultimate expression of *marianismo*) is the force which has for generations prevented Hispanic women from even entertaining the notion of personal validation. Yet such female subjugation is not only practiced today, it is —ironically—enforced by women, handed down as written in stone by our mothers, grandmothers, and aunts! We have reduced the mandates of *marianismo* to a set of iron-clad rules of behavior, ten commandments if you will.

The Ten Commandments of Marianismo

Here are the ten commandments of *marianismo*, which dictate a traditional Hispanic woman's self-esteem.

1. Do not forget a woman's place.
2. Do not forsake tradition.
3. Do not be single, self-supporting, or independent-minded.
4. Do not put your own needs first.
5. Do not wish for more in life than being a housewife.
6. Do not forget that sex is for making babies—not for pleasure.
7. Do not be unhappy with your man or criticize him for infidelity, gambling, verbal and physical abuse, alcohol or drug abuse.
8. Do not ask for help.
9. Do not discuss personal problems outside the home.
10. Do not change those things which make you unhappy that you can realistically change.

These ten commandments are *marianismo* in its purest, darkest form. But the inflexibility of these rules, like those of *machismo*, are being challenged in North America. Hispanics who have immigrated to the United States live in a society with economic needs and social and marital obligations different from those in the Old World. Consequently, attitudes and actions condemned as selfish in the Old World are more likely to be seen as self-assertive in North America.

Here is an exercise you can administer to yourself to discover how you are really feeling about things, and what you expect of yourself in many areas of your life right now. This exercise was developed by psychologists Matthew McKay and Patrick Fanning to help people determine their personal "shoulds." Since *marianismo* involves a lot of shoulds, we have adapted it so that you can determine whether many of your shoulds stem from *marianismo*.

Get out a piece of paper and write down the first should that occurs to you about each category. Don't mull over your answers. It's important that you spontaneously write down your responses. For instance, next to "Relationships: Spouse" you might write, "I should be more obedient and grateful for what he does for me," or, "I should stop pestering him when he gets home from work and just wants to quietly watch TV." After "Job activities: Efficiency," you might write, "I should start coming in an hour earlier, like a lot of other people are starting to do," or, "My office is a mess! I should get more organized!" Feel free to extend the list of your shoulds inventory to suit your needs.

1. RELATIONSHIPS
Spouse/companion
Children
Parents
Siblings
Grandparents
Uncles, aunts, and
    cousins
Friends

2. HOUSEHOLD ACTIVITIES
Cleaning
Grocery shopping
Cooking
Laundry
Maintenance

3. JOB ACTIVITIES
Relationship with boss
Co-worker
    relationships
Networking

Efficiency

Achievement and
   working toward goals

Initiative

Autonomy

Punctuality

Absenteeism

4. SELF-IMPROVEMENT
ACTIVITIES

Education

Self-help projects

5. SELF-LOVE

Appearance

Dress

Exercise

Smoking

Alcohol

Drugs

Medical appointments

Food and eating

6. FINANCIAL ACTIVITIES

Working toward a
   financial competence
   goal

Savings

Earning ability

Spending habits

7. EXPRESSIONS AND
DEALING WITH FEELINGS

Anger

Fear

Sadness

Sexuality

Love

Joy

8. RECREATIONAL AND
SOCIAL ACTIVITIES

Dancing

Traveling

Going to movies

9. POLITICAL AND
COMMUNITY ACTIVITIES

Voting

Attending meetings
   (PTA, tenants'
   association)

10. RELIGIOUS AND
SPIRITUAL ACTIVITIES

Going to church

Reading the Bible

Now that you're done, go back over your answers and label each one with the emotion which describes it best, i.e., guilt, anger, embarrassment, whatever the feeling. Next, review your answers one more time and mark the thoughts that are self-critical. Then note whether the self-criticism comes purely from your *marianismo*, or from your conflict between thinking like *una marianista* and wanting to act like a North American. An example of the former might be, "I should show my mother-in-law more respect even though she's bossy with me." An example of the latter would be: "I should apply to medical school despite my parents' disappointment with my choice of career." You may be surprised to find that your answers indicate your desire to stay the same while simultaneously wanting to change and behave in different ways. It is precisely in the desire to behave in different ways from our parents' that we confront the second piece of the puzzle, acculturation.

 ## ACCULTURATION: THE HEALTHY CHOICE

When we arrive in this country, we all go through a process of adapting to a new and often alien culture—acculturation. More technically, according to psychologist John Berry, acculturation is an adjustment that takes place when individuals from different cultures come into continuous and direct contact with, and learn from, one another.

We want to emphasize that no two cultures and no two people within those cultures go through the process in the same way or at the same rate. Some may even try to turn their backs on the new culture, while others may rush to embrace it. Either way, the truth is we simply can't avoid embracing the new culture if we want to survive and prosper. A second truth is that acculturation is experienced as a series of changes and choices which include new forms of how to live, what to eat, what language to speak, how to behave toward your relatives and peers, whether or not to follow certain patterns of behavior which pertained in the Old Country—like Natalia's father's overprotectiveness and her expected submissiveness—but which may be not useful at all in the new culture. Throughout the book we'll be examining in detail the whole spectrum of these problems—many of which are related to something called acculturation stress—as well as their resolutions.

Acculturation stress, as referred to by John Berry, is one of the negative aspects of adjusting to your new life. You can become unsure of who you are or how you're supposed to act, and that deep-seated confusion can lead to depression and frustration if it is not acknowledged to be part of a collective process, rather than the individual's fault. We've seen over and over that many Latinas view this stress through the lens of *marianismo*. When you're unsure of yourself as a woman, when you feel guilty and conflicted for straying from traditions, and what you used to do to gain approval is no longer working or is actively working against you, your confidence in yourself can be severely threatened. When something as trivial as the kind of shoes you wear to a job interview becomes vital to your self-esteem, when you're not sure whether or not to let your Angla friends even know you burn the Santería candles—the level of stress you endure is excruciatingly high and painful.

Then, too, you may feel deeply confused when you try to acculturate and are regarded by your loved ones as a traitor or archrebel, like Natalia. You may also see yourself or your man becoming rigid caricatures of your ethnic characteristics. And it's precisely here that the mandates of *marianismo* and *machismo* can sabotage you without your even realizing it. Our job here is to help you understand that acculturation brings positive change both to the open-minded individual Latina and to her cultural group as a whole.

One last important distinction we want to make here is the difference between acculturation and assimilation. Assimiliation, as discussed by John Berry, disregards all aspects of the migrant's native culture and demands total adaptation to the host society. Acculturation is a more gentle and gradual process in which, without disregarding their own culture, immigrants shift attitudes and behavior toward those of the dominant culture as a result of repeated exposure. We know of too many Latinos/as who have attempted or have been asked to attempt assimilation—with disastrous and depressing results. Sometimes, paradoxically, we see a backlash reaction, or the opposite of assimilation, with the woman becoming more *marianista* than ever. This happens because she is desperately looking for a secure basis to feel better about herself. Which brings us to the third piece of the puzzle, self-esteem.

 ## Learning to Like Yourself

Self-esteem is *la fuerza potente*, the powerful force, within yourself that is capable of enabling you to realize your fullest potential as a human being. Let us assure you that without a solid, positive self-esteem, you will be substantially limiting your chances of achieving your goals

We'd be the first to admit that the concept of self-esteem has become an American household word, not to say a cliché. It's overused and misused on the shrillest talk shows every day. Still, in its most thoughtful meaning, self-esteem has long enjoyed an honored history and remains the key to personal growth.

In the late nineteenth century, William James, the father of American psychology, published the seminal book called *Principles of Psychology*, in which he created and defined the term "self-esteem" for the first time. He argued that it is the sum of all a person thinks of as his or her own—our physical self, psychological traits, feelings, values, family, significant others, possessions, talents, and career. Self-esteem, according to James, depends on how successful we are in meeting our personal standards and expectations. For example, Natalia felt bad about herself because her maturity was being criticized and her autonomy threatened by her father—an authority figure of great importance to her, whether or not she wanted to admit it. To make matters worse, this authority figure was also challenging her common sense. In sum, all of her self-concept was under siege, making her feel ashamed, depressed, and lacking in self-esteem. While Natalia fought to hold on to her new sense of self, objecting to such treatment by a father or husband would never have occurred to older Latinas like Natalia's grandmothers. All of which was making her feel ashamed and depressed. *Para su abuela*, being obedient and submissive was a source of pride in herself.

Alfred Adler, the pioneering social psychiatrist, added to James's definition of self-esteem the components of environment and heredity. He felt that a crucial aspect of self-esteem was feeling a part of and contributing to the society to which the individual belongs. Let's view Natalia and her grandmother in Adler's context. Natalia's grandmother had felt respected and accepted as a part of her society. Because she was fulfilling cultural expectations of what a woman should be, *la abuela* felt at peace with herself. Now, however, in this new society, her self-esteem suffered. She felt that those important cultural beliefs she held so dear, such as the dictate of how a woman should behave, were being rejected by Natalia. Consequently, she felt less useful. Natalia, on the other hand, also felt rejected, because those who loved her were not accepting her new beliefs and were challenging her wisdom and maturity.

The theoreticians Coley and Mead add to the definition of self-esteem yet another component—whether or not a person's talents are perceived and appreciated by others. That means that Natalia's grandmother's self-esteem was heightened when her husband, mother, and mother-in-law acknowledged her dedication and self-sacrifice. Conversely, Natalia's desire for autonomy was dismissed by her family as being disrespectful and selfish, thus lowering her self-esteem.

It's unlikely that Natalia's grandmother was entirely satisfied with herself, in any event. Everyone who's ever lived has insecurities, things about themselves that make them feel less than competent. But self-contentment is attained by focusing on one's areas of competence and amplifying them. It's unfortunate, but through our practices we've come to see that some Latinas tend to focus on their insecurities rather than maximizing the things about themselves about which they feel surer. That's frequently because they're too sensitive and overly dependent on others' judgments of them.

We must mention here that your self-esteem can never depend only on others' opinions, because that gives outsiders control over your actions, values, and attitudes. If you allow that to happen, you'll live in anguish, depending *en el que dirán*, on what others say about you. We firmly believe that the choice of behaviors, values, and attitudes must be yours and yours alone—which is precisely why adhering to *marianismo* causes you so much trouble.

Now we would like to offer our own definition of self-esteem, taking into account the specific context of gender and ethnicity.

The Invaluable Art of Compromise

Respectfully acknowledging the wisdom of those cited above, we choose to define self-esteem as the ability to be authentic, to accept ourselves as competent, successful, worthy Latinas who love ourselves. Accepting oneself, appreciating one's own worth, is the projector which allows us to transfer the "film" of our consciousness onto the screen of the world. In so doing, we assert our rights, tell others how we wish to be treated, and proudly acknowledge that we deserve the good things life has to offer.

What challenges us Latinas is that our self-esteem can be influenced not only by heredity but also by our culture. That means that the value we place on ourselves cannot help but be impacted by *marianismo*. If Natalia's grandmother had a successful career outside the home but felt negligent in her familial role because of it, professional achievement probably wouldn't have given her satisfaction but, rather, a lot of guilt, self-doubt, and a lower self-esteem. However, the cultural expectations of a woman's role and performance change in relative terms here in the United States.

Consequently, Latinas living in the United States may need to reframe aspects of their worldviews, attitudes, behaviors, and values in North American terms in order to maintain a healthy adjustment to their new culture with little or no harm to their self-esteem. As we mentioned earlier, the integration of new cultural ideas and actions into your daily life is called acculturation. The merging of the Old World values into a competent, assertive, self-assured, and empowered Latina—into *la nueva marianista*—is what we advocate with all our hearts.

Armed with these daring new standards, we can then be assured that at the very least we have done things in a self-loving way. As such we will almost inevitably love others. In short, the self-esteem of *el nuevo marianismo* is good not only for you but for everybody else as well.

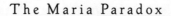

YOUR JOURNEY TO SELF-EMPOWERMENT BEGINS HERE

As we've said, our aim is to help you take those first steps away from the ten commandments of *marianismo* and move toward enhanced self-esteem—but not through rage or radical rebellion. After all, culture is humanity's way of surviving, and no one, no matter how determined, can make it solely on her own without some system of support. As Latinas who have, to some extent, moved beyond the self-defeating suppression of *marianismo* while maintaining our deep attachment to Hispanic tradition and our *familismo* (which was described by L. H. Rogler and R. S. Cooney as that close, protective, supportive, and loving connection with our families) is also the mandate to put your family's needs before your own. We feel we are qualified to show you how to grow as an individual without creating ruptures in your social structures which cannot be bridged. We will also suggest practical and what we believe are safe ways to distance yourself from abusive situations in your relationship with your mate.

We'll rehearse you in identifying the positive aspects of your native culture and teach you how to maintain and honor them. For instance, you'll learn how to redirect the maternal energy you may have always devoted to others into self-empowerment. And, best of all, we'll show you how to use classic Latina values as *personalismo*—defined by Emelicia Mizio as the ability to forge and maintain affiliations and relationships as a way of connecting meaningfully to other people—or love of community—a concept researched and referred to by Guillermo Bernal—and *sensualidad,* love of the good things in life, in ways that fulfill both you and your loved ones.

We'll direct you to finding the right kind of help if you feel you require it, whether it's psychotherapy, a support group, or a group of woman friends who get together to have fun and discuss common problems. You'll learn as well how to disentangle healthy behaviors from ineffective ones, restrictive actions from liberating choices. And we will help you single out and defuse potential trouble spots, such as school or work, where the Latina is prone to pick up a detrimental message which implies that her identity is unsatisfactory.

We hope to be able to show you that you can avoid many of these problems in the first place by being aware that what you're experiencing is a cultural clash or collision, not *una ofensa personal,* and by reminding yourself that the outdated value system to which you cling at such moments is counterproductive.

Finally, we'll steer you through the storms that arise on your voyage to self-empowerment by reminding you that change, whether it's good or bad, always entails a certain amount of emotional discomfort. It's that simple. Trying to avoid the pain provides at best a Band-Aid solution and ultimately could lead to severe depression, frustration, and exaggerated feelings of personal worthlessness.

We want to remind you here that Natalia's story, like all the stories in this book, is based on our work with actual patients. These are women who have lived with the pain of change, maintained an open mind to cultural options, and emerged empowered.

If as you read this book, you say, "*¡O sí, esa soy yo!* Oh yes! That's me," we will be gratified. And if these shocks of recognition are the first steps you take toward developing a healthy self-esteem, our purpose in writing this book will have been fulfilled.

The Chilean novelist Isabel Allende was recently quoted by the Associated Press as saying that "it took me forty of my fifty years to build my self-esteem and confidence after growing up in a strict patriarchal household." In our work with many female clients from the Hispanic community—from all walks of life and all age groups, teenagers as well as grandmothers—we have seen that with guidance, it doesn't have to take that long. In that spirit, we offer you the Maria Paradox. We feel our observations will also provide valuable insight and direction for three additional groups of readers: non-Latinas involved with or married to Hispanics; Latin-American women whose occupations or personal relationships cause them to interact frequently with North American culture; and all men—Latino or not—who want to better understand the emotional makeup of Latinas.

The Maria Paradox asks the question: Can a Hispanic woman learn to skillfully steer a course through North American society without sacrificing the Latin traditions which she treasures? Our answer is a resounding yes. Natalia would agree.

It took a lot of work with her therapist, but Natalia came to see that although she was being treated like a Latina of another generation by her father, she was actually quite a bit like him—hot-tempered and strong-willed. Once she realized that, she understood as well that nobody else in her family, including her brothers, was quite as fiery. Making peace with her father would require keeping her own emotions under control and appealing to the proud and loving side of his passionate nature.

Fist, she practiced telling herself there was no guilty party in this argument. She wasn't a bad daughter or a loose woman—that was her *marianismo* talking. And although her father's actions seemed misguided, they were taken out of love—as well as an exaggerated *macho* sense of responsibility and concern. So on a Sunday morning three weeks after the meltdown, she picked up the phone and called home. When her mother answered, she asked to speak to her father. Although this flustered her mother, she went to get him.

"Papá," she began, when he came to the phone and gruffly said hello, "I want to apologize for what you took to be my disobedience. I want you to know how much I love and respect you and how much I've missed seeing you and the rest of the family."

After a moment of silence, her father actually admitted he'd missed her too and that perhaps he had been the slightest bit out of line coming by her apartment unannounced. But, he insisted, he'd just been concerned about her welfare.

"I know, Papá," Natalia told him, "and your concern makes me feel very loved. But please believe that I live in a good neighborhood, and I don't take unnecessary chances. I only go out with men who respect me and whom I've met through friends or at work. You and Mamá raised me well. I'm very lucky to have had you as parents."

Papá, who sounded considerably more cheerful than he had, acknowledged her compliment graciously and replied he did have confidence in her. It was just that he couldn't help but be concerned that she was being properly taken care of.

"You know, Papá," Natalia replied, "you and Mamá educated me well and gave me a solid moral foundation. Now it's time I become responsible for my own needs. I am sure I will find a husband who will support my goals."

Her father confessed there was truth in what Natalia was saying, and when he asked when she was next going to visit the family, Natalia suggested that the two of them have lunch together alone.

Natalia's father had to check his schedule, but somehow managed to find a free day. And when he suggested he would take her someplace very special, Natalia replied, "No, Papá, I'll take you!"

Natalia learned in therapy that things don't change overnight and people rarely change at all. It's more a matter of *how* we change and how that change affects the way we relate to others. She knew there would be lapses and regressions in her own personal growth as well as in her new, less restrictive relationship with her family, but she appreciated that such periods were a necessary part of the healing process.

As you begin your voyage to empowerment, you too must be aware it will not all be smooth sailing. There will be times of turbulence and times when the winds of progress will seem to have deserted you. But that's life, and what is life about but change? We assure you that if you ride out the storm and wait for the winds to rise again, the skies will be brighter and the breezes more spirited than ever before.

¡*Triunfaremos!*

2

"Do Not Forsake Tradition":

___

Staying Latina vs.
Going Angla

"I'm so embarrassed, I'm mortified!" exclaimed Rosario, a twenty-five-year-old second-generation Dominican living in New York. "I wish I could ship my entire family back to Santo Domingo right now! Today! How could they do this to me? How could they put me in this position?"

Through her job with a Wall Street firm, Rosario had met a young American investment banker named Jeff and they'd been dating for six months. Her family, who were extremely traditional, especially where gringos were concerned, had been demanding to meet Jeff. Finally, feeling the relationship was going well and had a future, Rosario consented.

When Rosario and Jeff arrived at her parents' house the night of the visit, they were greeted by a crowd consisting of not only her mother, father, brother, and sisters, but also countless aunts, uncles, cousins, and family friends who may or may not have been distant relatives. Jeff shook the hand of Rosario's father and brother and nodded politely to the rest of the crew—correct social behavior to him. How was he supposed to know that everyone in the room expected a handshake and/or a personal greeting?

The evening was a disaster. Afterwards, Rosario's mother informed her that the family found Jeff *muy frío*, very chilly, and *mal educado*, badly brought up. Jeff, for his part, thought the family's reaction peculiar at best, and their code of etiquette ludicrously effusive and old-fashioned. And guess who ended up in the middle!

Poor Rosario had to put up with her mother's accusations that, by siding with Jeff—although she was actually simply trying to explain where he was coming from—she was *una mala hija*, a bad daughter, responsible for dishonoring the entire Gonzalez clan in one fell swoop. By trying to explain her family's behavior to Jeff, she was afraid she was establishing a cultural gulf between them which couldn't be bridged. Although she'd been born and educated here and felt as American as her Angla/o friends, Rosario suddenly realized she was living in two different worlds at once. Perhaps for the first time, she was confronting the complexities of being a Latina in North America. And that confrontation was making her feel torn, depressed, and suddenly unsure of who and what she was. All she could do was ask herself over and over:

- Why did I let my mother force me to bring Jeff home?
- Why didn't I know how weird my family would seem to a normal person?
- I'm one of them. Does that make me weird too?
- Would Jeff ever dare to introduce me to his family?
- Am I really a selfish, willful daughter?
- Will I be a selfish, willful wife and mother?

- Why am I feeling so bad about myself? Because I let the whole thing happen without lifting a finger to prevent it?
- Who am I really mad at—my family, my boyfriend, or myself?

Rosario's predicament isn't unique. Extensive personal and professional experience tells us that some Latinas living in North America tend to have trouble taking action. Further, this lack of self-assertion appears to be a significant component of low self-esteem. And low self-esteem is often the by-product of a cultural clash.

The psychologists Jose Szapocznik and William Kurtines have found that Hispanics tend to develop self-esteem problems if they're finding it hard to integrate two cultures. We would only add that we have clearly seen these problems in our Hispanic clientele. Unquestionably, the struggle to weave Hispanic tradition and North American innovation into a satisfying bicultural lifestyle can make for a great deal of unhappiness and self-doubt if it isn't understood and dealt with for what it is—as Rosario discovered. For the woman is at odds not only with herself but with others in both the Anglo and Hispanic spheres.

Understanding how this struggle impacts specifically on Latinas, as well as how you can reap the maximum benefits of both cultures with a minimum of discomfort and disruption, is the purpose of *The Maria Paradox* and the specific aim of this chapter. Here we'll help you learn to keep *marianismo* at bay, jump-start acculturation, and actually feel better about yourself while doing so.

Obviously, not only Hispanics have problems adapting to the North American lifestyle. Nor are Latinas the sole group coping with sexism and the male status quo. However, the pressures of immigration can sweep us up in the undertow of old values. When that happens, and *marianismo* rushes in to lower our confidence and blur our sense of self, we tend to deal with social issues in a particularly rigid, self-punishing form. Sometimes it seems that no woman in the world can be as hard on herself as a Latina.

✳ Buying into the Belief Package

What exactly does it mean to be Latina? Clearly there is no single description that fits every Hispanic woman's personality—individuals can't be reduced to cultural stereotypes, and it's not our intention even to hint at such an idea. However, we do know that certain groups share modes of behavior based on packages of beliefs—from how you dress to when you marry—that often go a long way toward defining who you are, particularly to outsiders.

These "brands" of behavior don't involve conscious choice. It's more a matter of feeling instinctively that a certain behavior is correct. Yet despite this apparent "naturalness," the way you're acting has really been dictated by society. Children learn the rules from their parents and teachers and grow up to pass them on to their own children. As the cycle continues through the generations, it evolves into tradition, into "the way things are." It's one reason why people have such a difficult time perceiving that much of their behavior is culturally motivated. But whether we acknowledge it or not, it is. And unacknowledged, the way things are can really get us into trouble—as Rosario found, to her dismay.

Conversely, it's a given that in any society you'll find an infinite range of behavior—individual characteristics and unique inner clashes between cultural expectations and personal needs. After all, human beings have an individual as well as a cultural identity.

So no, there is no single definition of what it means to be Latina, but there are critical issues and problems centering on self-esteem which we commonly share—and which are magnified by the pressures to acculturate clashing with the pressures not to change.

The Cultural Security Blanket

As regards acculturation, we would like to refer to the theory of the transitional object, developed by the British psychiatrist D. W. Winnicott. Essentially, what Winnicott discovered was that an infant becomes attached to a specific object such as a pacifier or stuffed animal as a reliable source of comfort and consolation—what the daytime TV commercials call "your child's first friend," like Linus and his security blanket in *Peanuts*. As she or he develops, the child normally progresses from the object to play. But when a child persists in clinging to the object past an appropriate age, problems may occur which often impede emotional development. Wrenching as such early separation may be, we all do separate. After all, who do you know who goes to work with a pacifier in their mouth? Or a stuffed animal tucked securely under their arm? It's believed that is because most people learn to replace the beloved object with more appropriate items, such as art, reading, or possessions that give us pleasure and security because they serve a soothing purpose. But for many people the transition is admittedly difficult, and it previews, early on, life's losses and leavetakings.

Likewise for many individuals, it's hard to let go of certain familiar behaviors when these people are going through cultural adaptation, even if the behaviors may not be useful or even remotely applicable to their new experiences in the United States. In the context of immigration, then, certain ingrained habits may function as transitional objects. But refusing to abandon ethnic traits when they are not producing the desired result should signal that what you are really afraid of losing is part of yourself.

In our new life in the United States, there is so much that is unfamiliar and frightening, even to the best-adjusted among us. When we are adjusting to the new culture, or acculturating, some Latinas might feel extremely vulnerable and especially terrified of losing the affection and esteem of loved ones, whose presence helps to anchor our sense of self. Too often, out of that fear, they regress rather than move on.

Avoiding fear will never make it go away. It must be overcome. And the secret to doing that is first to identify the fear for what it is and then to seek a solution, whether you do it alone or with support.

Do you know other people who share the fears? If you do, it's genuinely helpful if you can discuss them. Ask yourself the following questions in order to determine if you are doing things that aren't producing the desired result but that you keep on doing anyway, as a way to ease certain fears produced by cultural collision.

- Do you feel your values are often at odds with your family's? Which ones—and how?
- How nervous do you become when you have to tell your parents about something you're planning which isn't done by *marianistas*?
- Have you ever confronted those you feel will be hurt by your actions?
- Have you ever dared explain to them why you feel the need to take the action?
- Have you ever sabotaged yourself because of your fears of the cultural unknown? For example, do you steer away from predominantly Anglo stores or neighborhoods? How would you remedy that?
- Do you find yourself not giving yourself a chance to get to make Anglo/a friends? Do you tell yourself, "He or she is cold and doesn't understand my thinking," and leave it at that?
- What do you need to tell yourself in order to conquer those fears?

The people in whom you confide, whether friends or loved ones, might be much more understanding than you imagine. Go ahead—try it. If you value your family, give them a chance to prove they'll be there for you as you have been for them. Besides, you'll come to value them even more as a positive security blanket when you begin to live in two worlds.

Two Worlds, One You

Whether we consciously opt to or not, once in North America, many Latinas develop a new identity which we will call the American self. We have to develop this identity in order to survive in our new country. Only when we go back to our countries or meet an old friend do we become fully aware of the extent of these inner differences. However, until that American self becomes a natural part of us, we Latinas sometimes suppress our real selves and emotions, behave in a manner we feel is expected of us, and end up trying to act much more American than we feel or vice versa. We may go overboard about not showing emotion and come across as cold. Or, like Rosario, we may simply "forget" about aspects of our Hispanic selves, then find ourselves *en el caldo*, in the soup, because of it.

In order to understand how you're faring in your two worlds, list on a piece of paper ways you behave which you feel are culturally mandated either by Latin tradition or a North American lifestyle. For example: "I tend not to assert myself at work" could indicate you're being driven by *marianismo*. While "I resent the fact that my family is dismissive of my professional accomplishments" suggests a distinctly North American attitude. One way to make this easier is by asking your American friends how they would behave in a certain situation. It's important not to ask other Hispanics because, as we've said earlier, they may not be aware that many of their actions are imposed by Latino culture.

Next, ask yourself:

- Whose expectations am I following?
- Why do I feel conflicted? Is it because I feel trapped in an either/or predicament?
- If I'm behaving in a specific way, why am I doing it? Who am I trying to please?
- Shouldn't I be trying to please myself?

- Shouldn't I concentrate on choosing or adapting behavior I feel comfortable with?

The Bicultural Paradox and the Double Self

In the following pages, we'll be examining core conflicts and resolutions which you as a Hispanic woman are likely to experience as you confront the paradoxical position of living in two worlds at once—of having, as it were, a double self.

We will be using the term "double self" to describe two simultaneous but separate ways of behaving according to the cultural mandates you follow. For example, you may act in a very formal manner with professors or elderly persons because that is what is expected within your culture. Sometimes, on the other hand, you "do things" by North American rules because you know that this is what is required of you in order to fit in. An example of this may be to call before you go to visit a Latina friend, although traditionally it's perfectly acceptable to drop by for a visit without saying you're coming. In some of these instances, you will say, "I am not being myself." When shifting selves become your way of life, you really do feel, as so many of our Latina clients have told us, as if you had two selves.

Remember, once you leave one of the twenty-one Latin American republics or Puerto Rico and come to the United States, you may feel pressure both from within yourself and without to discard everything you are and become just like "them." The prospect of such sweeping change can be frightening and confusing to many immigrating women. In reality, it doesn't have to be at all.

It's now believed by such experts as François Grosjean that a significant percentage of the world's population is capable of functioning in at least two languages and in two cultures—and given the rapidly increasing globalism that shapes all our futures, is all the better for it. While traditional studies suggested that bilingualism was detrimental to children, contemporary Canadian studies conducted by researchers E. Peal and W. Lambert indicate that the bilingual child actually enjoys more options with which to look at the world than his or her monolingual counterpart.

According to the Bureau of the Census, by 2010, Latino/as will be the largest ethnic minority in the United States. Already we can see the tremendous growth of Spanish-language media and targeted product advertising. All of which is to say that the Hispanic presence in the U.S. is here to stay. As acculturating Latinas, we should all be aware that in economic and statistical terms, we are actually part of a burgeoning power base—and as members of a bicultural female culture, we are automatically part of a vibrant interest group. But it isn't always easy to keep that fact in mind.

More *Marianista* than a Saint

One thing's for sure. If you accept your initial cultural insecurities as an implication that there's something wrong with you personally, you'll soon find yourself in a no-win situation from which acculturating is practically impossible. That's because you may react by taking refuge in the old ways. You know that expression *más papista que el papa*—"more Catholic than the pope"? If you hide behind your heritage instead of moving on, you may become *más marianista que una santa*, more *marianista* than a saint!

Take the case of Tina, a thirty-year-old Puerto Rican, who came to Philadelphia when she was ten with her widowed father, two younger brothers, and three younger sisters. Tina's father was a hardworking man who earned his living as a longshoreman, but after he sustained a serious injury, he was unable to work at his trade and became deeply embittered. He felt that his misfortunes in America were solely due to his being Hispanic. Consequently, he instilled an exaggerated sense of ethnicity in Tina and her brothers and sisters.

Tina told her therapist, "*Papi* told me that only Puerto Ricans are to be trusted and that I should only marry a man from our country." There were other family dynamics as well, and the end result was that while some of her siblings grew up to be irresponsible and afraid of commitment, Tina went to the opposite extreme and became overly protective of her family, as well as her Hispanic identity. Here is what we mean by that.

By anybody's standards—north or south of the border—Tina was really *un desastre*, a disaster. She was trying to get a job on Wall Street, but wasn't having much success. She wanted a boyfriend, but wasn't having much luck there, either. She had given up the apartment she took when she moved to New York, as the entire family left Philadelphia. Tina moved to *el barrio* with her family, claiming that as the eldest daughter, she was needed to care for her five brothers and sisters. She disconnected the phone and was rapidly putting on weight. Drowning in depression, she passively watched her self-esteem sink lower and lower.

She was trying to be *más marianista que una santa* by adhering to all the old beliefs despite the fact that deep in her heart, she knew that they were even considered outdated by many women in her native country. But in order to ensure her father's approval, she had to capitulate in his resentment toward North American culture by behaving like the most parochial Puertorriquena. She was convinced she could remain such and still live with the times. Worse than that, catering to her father's needs instead of her own was setting up a virtually insurmountable obstacle to her own fulfillment.

Likewise, Tina was making sure she'd never meet an appropriate man, either American or Latino. To her, all men wanted was to have sex, not to love and care. Yet the very thought of having sex made her feel guilty because in her country, decent women remained virgins until marriage. When her sister had a bad experience with an Anglo, Tina immediately picked up on it as proof that as a Latina, she would never find an American man with whom she could be *simpática*. Assuring herself that she wasn't meant for the American world of work or of romance, Tina fled to a familiar environment, where no new challenges awaited her.

Of course, Tina was hiding behind the *marianista* mandate that *las mujeres buenas* must be sexually chaste. And although extreme and prohibitive in a North American context, her feelings about men were actually justified, according to traditional Hispanic cultural beliefs. After all, *machismo* maintains a rigidly enforced double standard by which men are expected to have sex before marriage and could be unfaithful afterward. If the wife of a *macho* is pregnant, sick, or unwilling to fulfill her conjugal duty, it is considered her husband's right to seek satisfaction elsewhere. It wasn't that Tina's fears were crazy, but rather that they were radically misplaced in her new country.

She was actually living out the *marianista* doctrine that women are capable of all suffering. Her case of marianitis wasn't terminal, but it was very grave.

HOW MARIANISTA ARE YOU?

Following is a list of the symptoms of "marianitis." To find out where you fit on the spectrum, first number the symptoms and feelings in order of personal priority. Next, separate them into those you can work on alone and those for which you need the help of a friend.

• Performing tasks for others when you'd rather not, simply because you feel it's expected of you
• Apologizing for acts of assertiveness—for instance, reacting to hurt or abuse, then feeling so guilty about reacting you apologize for expressing appropriate anger
• Taking actions or making statements that deep in your heart you know aren't true to your real desires—like taking on more responsibility than you can cope with because doing so makes you feel like a good person
• Putting yourself down, especially when dealing with men or superiors

- Sacrificing when it isn't called for—like letting friends or relatives crash in your apartment, even though you don't have the room
- Finding it impossible to say no to people—even when it's clear they're taking advantage of you
- Accepting relationship dysfunction—like allowing your husband to fool around because it's a wife's role to be accepting and all-tolerating
- Putting yourself and your own needs last in most situations
- Depriving yourself while going out of your way for others
- Reacting nervously to perceived criticisms because you always feel it's your fault
- Letting a man take sexual liberties with you, even when you don't really want him to
- Saying yes to a suggested restaurant or movie you don't want to go to but others do

Now make your own list of things in your life that you would like to be different. Here again, separate the ones you feel you can change by yourself and those you can't. Don't waste your time wishing you were taller or thinner. Choose behaviors you can realistically change.

The things you can change you must now view as shoulds and musts and get on with them.

The things you can't change without help require you to decide how significantly they impact your life. How much hardship do they create for you? Do they seriously impair your happiness, peace of mind, and/or centeredness? If you answer yes to these questions, face the fact that you need to seek professional help before you make a determined attempt to acculturate. We'll give you specific guidelines about how to do that in Chapter 9.

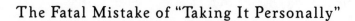

The Fatal Mistake of "Taking It Personally"

If you ever want a good life in your new country, it's imperative that you be flexible about cultural differences. The best way to do so is to not take cultural collision personally. You must constantly remind yourself that the problems you are encountering are a normal and unavoidable part of the acculturation process. It's not you the individual who's under attack, it's you as a Latina struggling to learn the rules of North American culture for the first time.

Tina, hiding behind Old World values, took every perceived slight to heart and used it against herself. Rosario, approaching the personalization problem from the opposite end of the spectrum, was haunted by the same fears of inadequacy. However, as a considerably more acculturated Latina, she had enough perspective at least to question her self-reproach.

When you're feeling personally under attack, a very important question to ask yourself is whether you need to discard the old rules or merely place them in a different context. After all, your first words, the words that nurtured and soothed you, were uttered in Spanish. Your first taffeta dress and pair of patent leather shoes, your first *fiesta de cumpleaños* and *primera comunión*, were occasions of great joy. How could you—and why should you—readily discard these treasured pieces of your past? But you must take care that you don't, without realizing it, cling to traditions that are already obsolete or dysfunctional, even in your country.

The reality is that in North America, if you try to cook like your grandmother and keep house like your mother and expect those roles to satisfy you, you're out of touch with contemporary American gender roles. Likewise, if you show up for a job interview with a prestigious corporation wearing tight, brightly colored clothes, open-toed sandals, and earrings down to your shoulders, be prepared not to get the position.

On this subject, you might find it helpful to ask your friends if they've been in situations where they sensed they were incorrectly dressed. It would be interesting to compare notes with them. We frequently trade stories with Latina colleagues about our experiences in this realm. Although at the time they happened we could never have imagined it, we laugh and laugh about them now.

Think back now on an interview or party where you yourself felt out of place. What emotions did the unease produce in you? Did you blame yourself? Did you feel intimidated? Did you feel angry and lash out as a result?

Now re-create the situation, using what you've learned in this chapter. How would you dress if the occasion happened today? What differences in what transpired might your change in outfit make?

Review your answers carefully, and you'll get a thumbnail sketch of your transcultural progress by being able to rethink old habits that no longer work for you.

Now you're ready to get down to work and begin to grow your self-esteem as a Hispanic, as a woman, and as a human being. No matter how you feel about yourself right now, we give you our word that by the time you finish this book, you will be in an excellent position to enter mainstream American culture with enhanced pride in being a Latina. But to do this, you must first learn the basics of assertiveness, trust your innate sense of what is good for you, and empower yourself to broker a cultural compromise. That's what twenty-eight-year-old Peruvian-born Ramona had to do.

The High Impact of Cultural Collision

Ramona fell in love with Peter, a North American, when he was visiting her country. In Peru, Ramona was considered to be assertive and vibrant, with a strong sense of herself. She had already been through a divorce and lived by herself *sin ningún reproche*, without reproach, from her family. Since Peter's Spanish was minimal, and since Ramona *sabía como manejarse*, knew her way around, she came across to him as independent and sophisticated.

But once Ramona and Peter married and came to the States, things changed for her. Suddenly, Peter didn't approve of the way she dressed or spoke or acted. He looked askance at her colorful cotton dresses and the dangling earrings he'd loved on her in Peru. He considered her taste in interior decorating tacky. He found her English too drawn out and flowery and couldn't stand it when she called people by endearing diminutives, like "Pedrito" or "Juanito." When she entertained Peruvian friends and celebrated Peruvian special occasions, he grew intolerant and critical.

Peter also constantly criticized Ramona for what he considered her so-called "passivity" and general inability to fit into his life in the United States. In Peru, Ramona had reminded him of an American woman, and that had been part of what attracted him to her. In the States, by contrast, she suddenly seemed very Old World.

Ramona was undergoing an acculturation crisis—with added pressure from Peter, who was demanding she abandon Hispanic tradition completely and assimilate, rather than adapt. Imagine her anguish. She was terrified of having to abandon her cultural beliefs and face the disappearance of her Hispanic self. In reaction to these fears, she clung to *marianismo* and assumed an unnaturally submissive role with Peter to ensure he would accept her.

This gratuitous embrace of *marianismo* was actually Ramona's way of feeling in control at a time when she was experiencing a vulnerability she didn't understand. She was taking her acculturative problems personally in the spirit of "The devil you know is better than the devil you don't know." From this perspective, Ramona genuinely believed that if she didn't react passively in her marriage, she would be considered *una mujer mala*, a bad woman, because she was failing to please her husband and maintain harmony in the home. As her unhappiness drove her deeper and deeper into the embrace of tradition, she was haunted by inner voices telling her that the man is always right and he is the ultimate judge of her self-worth. Needless to say, the more *marianista* she became, the more harshly Peter criticized her. Soon she was feeling chronically inadequate and depressed—blaming all her troubles on her own unworthiness, without even considering that she was being shaken by the shock waves of cultural collision.

※ BROKERING THE CULTURAL COMPROMISE

One of the first lessons a Latina must learn in her new country is that human beings can express cultural differences and still be "normal." Cultural collision—and hopefully its peaceable resolution, cultural compromise—is a virtually universal aspect of life in the late twentieth century. But this lesson is not easily learned. Rosario, for instance, felt that she couldn't be both a woman with strong Latin customs and values and a well-integrated Angla. She felt trapped by thinking she had to make an either/or choice when she really didn't.

Actually, it's such either/or choices that do the most personal damage by provoking cultural collision—instead of brokering a compromise. We can see the truth of that statement in the case of Tina, who barricaded herself inside *el barrio* and withdrew from every possible attempt to fit into the lifestyle of her new country. We can see it as well in Ramona's total switch from independence to submissiveness when faced with acculturation.

There's no denying that when cultural collisions occur in the course of a day, as they must, they can create serious communication glitches. We can be made to feel *fuera de foco*, out of focus, or even worse, that we are *menos que los demás o sin mucho valor*, inferior and lacking in self-worth. After all, your *comportamiento*, behavior, is what you are to yourself. When that *comportamiento* is challenged or invalidated by others, you feel it is you personally who is lacking. Rarely do we have the ability to instinctively separate cultural behavior from individual behavior with equanimity.

A meaningful example to bring up here concerns *simpatía*, or what has been referred to by Magaly Queralt as the Hispanic tradition of warmth, physically expressed social contact. Sylvia, a Paraguayan psychotherapist, recently attended her graduate school reunion, where she ran into a favorite Angla professor she hadn't seen for thirteen years. Sylvia impulsively moved to embrace and kiss her mentor, since this is what a *simpática* Latina does without thinking. To her surprise, the other woman immediately pulled away, because in her cultural framework, emotions are not displayed so publicly, especially toward subordinates.

Luckily, Sylvia had the professional expertise to realize that what was happening had nothing to do with her personally but rather with a cultural clash. Armed with that awareness, she was able to distance herself from her teacher. Once that occurred, she could shift naturally into a cooler, non-Hispanic mode that was more comprehensible and unthreatening to the teacher. Realizing that the situation demanded she switch from her "Latina" self to her "American" self, Sylvia successfully adapted her behavior to the particular setting in which she found herself. What she was doing was brokering a cultural compromise.

Have you ever experienced anything similar to what Sylvia went through?

Think of examples from your life when you acted one way with someone and realized afterward that you should have acted differently—when you behaved like your Hispanic self and were received with coldness or even shock.

How did you feel? Did you blame yourself? Did you tell yourself, "This person acts different from me. That's how Americans are," or did you feel inferior?

Once you acknowledged that a personal attack was really a cultural clash, did it help you to interact differently? Was the experience instrumental in making you realize the necessity of developing an American self?

Retraining + Restraining = Adjustment

If you do feel trapped between North American and Hispanic cultures, it's because you're looking at the situation in the wrong way. You'd be better off learning what Ramona had discovered: that a healthy adjustment is never an either/or process. On the contrary, it consists of gradually "retraining" and "restraining" yourself to blend two distinctly different cultural styles. As a concrete example, we've already mentioned some potential problems with the way you're used to dressing. Let's further explore the subject of the "dress code."

We all know that our choices of colors, style of shoes, hair and manicures have a lot to say about us—as individuals and as Latinas. In your new country, you may choose to continue dressing as you used to, because when you do, you feel more comfortable, more "you." However, if you wear a very bare, very floral, very mini sundress, big jewelry, stiletto heels, and long false fingernails with decals to school or to work in the winter, you'll be setting yourself apart from your fellow students and teachers or co-workers—an open invitation for them to judge you unfairly, just as they would in the job interview we described before.

You can of course, choose to wear what you wish wherever you go. But you must be prepared for the reaction you may receive from others. You must also be aware that what works in one situation may not work in another. For instance, if for that job interview you dress as your American self—in a tailored suit, small earrings, and so on—you will make a different impression, and that difference could get you the job. You may not like it, but that's simply the way things are.

Is that selling out? We have all at one time or another found ourselves consciously behaving in contradiction to our Hispanic self and felt that by "going American," we were betraying our ethnic identity. That is a textbook example of the either/or fallacy. What's crucial to successful acculturation is looking beyond either/or, assessing the particular cultural situation and determining what behavior would be most appropriate in the North American context in which we find ourselves.

Zapatitos de Charol and Palazzo Pants

It is said that Latinas overdress because when we were growing up, our uniform was those *zapatitos de charol*, patent leather shoes, and the taffeta dress. Julia, a forty-five-year-old college professor from the Dominican Republic, remembers that when she attended her first high school prom in the United States, she was the most dressed-up person in the room. During a recent vacation in Ireland, she went out one evening with a group of associates on a literary pub crawl in Dublin.

"Years had passed since that first high school dance," she recalls, "but I was still the most dressed-up person in the room. I began to feel uncomfortable, until I reminded myself that this was a legitimate part of my cultural background. So what if the rest of the group was in jeans and I was wearing palazzo pants? After all, I wasn't dolled up like Carmen Miranda or wearing an evening gown! Once it occurred to me that there was absolutely no reason why I had to look precisely like everybody else, I relaxed, my self-consciousness disappeared, and I was able to enjoy myself thoroughly."

Remember that being bicultural means accessing two modes of behavior as required by the occasion. The key to achieving this perspective successfully is being able to be you—a multifaceted individual with shades and hues that express different aspects and strengths of both cultures. Using our dress code, let's review how this works. We have learned that it is key to wear clothes appropriate to the climate, season, and occasion. However, even though you have mastered North American fashion rules, you must still develop your own style. If that style is determined by Hispanic cultural values blended sensibly with North American ones, you have succeeded in combining the best of both worlds. The key is flexibility, which in turn allows you to broker cultural compromises. That's what Julia learned.

Here is an exercise designed to help you judge your cultural flexibility.

It's important to be as relaxed as possible when doing this drill. First, remove any constricting articles of clothing such as belts or panty hose. Choose a period of time when you're not going to be interrupted. Perhaps put on some music and lower the volume on the phone and answering machine. Before tackling the questions, you may want to breathe in and out, softly and rhythmically, counting backward from 10 to 1.

Now ask yourself, "Do I feel that I have to function culturally in an either/or manner? Must I be all Hispanic or all Angla in specific instances?" If your answer is yes, list on a piece of paper or in a notebook those instances as well as the possible behavior, responses, and options you have used or could possibly have used in each of them.

When you've done that, ask yourself, "Do I feel I can trust my inner feelings about doing the right thing? Or do I question myself so much that by the time I do respond to a question or circumstances in a proper manner, it's already too late?"

If you do feel "stuck," remember to ask yourself a question which many therapists recommend to their patients, namely: "What is the worst thing that could happen if I do the socially incorrect thing?" This is a very important part of the exercise because it is so self-revealing.

Ask yourself now with total honesty, "Have I ever been embarrassed by my relatives' behavior and felt bad about myself as a result of it?" If your answer is yes, list those times you remember most vividly and explore what actions you could have taken other than simply feeling ashamed. Feelings are feelings, and you are entitled to them, but embarrassment and shame are essentially unproductive emotions. Also, keep in mind that you are not responsible for anyone else's behavior any more than you are able to change other people. You can only change yourself and the way you react to them.

Have you ever found yourself using traditional Latino/a belief values in order to avoid doing or facing something? Answering this question might require a lot of relaxation and some soul-searching because much of this behavior is unconscious, but, as we've said, bringing it to consciousness is an essential step that cannot and must not be avoided—even when you're haunted by the false guilt of betraying traditional Hispanic values such as *familismo*.

FAMILISMO AND SELF-RELIANCE

Rosario, Ramona, and Tina all had problems involving some aspects of *familismo*, which, as we've said, is the mandate to put your family's needs before your own. As we begin to acculturate, we are especially vulnerable to exploiting *familismo* in order to avoid confronting new cultural challenges. While we certainly aren't suggesting you sever your bonds with loved ones, we are saying that you should redefine them.

Familismo has always played an important role in rural societies, where reliance on others is not only critical if one is to survive because families tend to live closer to their relatives. Often there are no paid babysitters, fast-food deliveries, or taxis to take you to the airport. Therefore you have to count on relatives to help you. However, in technologically advanced societies, most people live and work some distance from each other. Loved ones can't always be depended on to be there, nor should they be. Instead of relying on a system which is inappropriate in our new cultural context, we must instead adopt a satisfying lifestyle based on *autonomismo*.

Self-reliance, the underpinning concept of what we call *autonomismo*, simply means the adoption of a lifestyle in which we can make decisions based on what is best for us without hurting others or being irresponsible. It entails putting our needs first but not selfishly. It also includes relying on others when the occasion warrants, but not automatically. After all, no one person can do everything all the time, nor should they always operate alone. Self-reliance is about taking care of ourselves in a healthy fashion.

If the concept of *autonomismo* appeals to you, ask yourself these questions:

Have you found yourself in situations where you are prevented from getting what you want by reasons that seem valid until you really think about them? For example, not saying no to relatives or friends when they ask you if they can come and visit you when you are in the middle of a job or school crisis. Or not going to a restaurant by yourself, feeling that—as a woman alone—people might look at you funny.

If you have, were you able to empower yourself to quiet the guilt-producing *marianista* voices inside you and stride boldly ahead?

But don't court disaster by asking too much of yourself as you first begin to tackle the complexities of these changes. If you've found empowering yourself too difficult to manage alone, consult a good friend whose support you can count on. Do not call upon anyone who you have reason to believe will be critical of your risk taking. If you find yourself starting to do it, lecture yourself sternly that you're sabotaging yourself. Later on in this book, we'll provide you with instructions on forming focus groups called *tertulias* with your friends. If the group you form is made up of the right women, *la tertulia* can do wonders for your self-esteem.

Of Course I Can Suffer, but Why Should I Have to?

Although we're both Hispanics and therapists, it's difficult for us to comprehend that so many Latinas who are superbly capable of succeeding don't. We have come to believe that at least in part this difficulty with making it in the United States stems from an adherence to the *marianista* inference that since women are capable of all suffering, their fate in life is to be unhappy.

Taking that suffering for granted, and accepting misery as your role in life, without even challenging its message is a sure guarantee that you will not acculturate. If you want to realize your true potential as a Hispanic-American woman, you must defy this way of thinking by recognizing it, understanding where it comes from, and ultimately making a conscious decision to discard it. We will recommend that you use a particularly effective technique called *un ejercicio de validación*, a personal validation exercise.

For example, if you constantly feel vulnerable and terrified of expressing feelings such as anger, you must search your soul for the reasons you feel this way. If it is because you grew up with the *marianista* belief that *las damas no gritan ni se comportan mal*, ladies do not shout or get angry, the following validation exercise should be of help to you. Begin by repeating it at least ten times before you go to sleep at night, and again when you wake up in the morning. Then repeat it anytime you feel your self-esteem or your resolve shrinking:

"I am entitled to express whatever feeling I may have, particularly if it is hurting me."

"I should not accept behavior from others that is detrimental to my self-esteem."

Simple as these two statements seem, when recited as prescribed they have amazing power to raise your spirits and bolster your resolve. Just try them, and you'll soon see we're right!

Here are other questions and exercises which will steer you on the path to self-worth:

Do you feel you're holding on to a restrictive past in order to maintain closeness to your loved ones?

Do you think it would help if you could start an honest, open conversation with your parents, or with anyone else who could aid you in disentangling your confusion?

Have you ever heard of the concept of self-love? How does the very idea of loving yourself make you feel? Puzzled? Embarrassed? Guilty? Eager?

Loving Yourself

A word about self-love and how you achieve it. Actually, it's not difficult to describe. The difficulty comes with first beginning to apply the concept. Here's a good way to start.

Think of a specific person, or even a pet, you feel you really love. Now ask yourself, "How do I know I love that person or creature?" You'll probably find that in regard to them, you're rarely critical and unusually tolerant. You want to give them pleasure and to avoid ever hurting them. You take pleasure yourself from giving them presents, cooking their favorite foods, celebrating their birthdays. Having them in your life cheers you up at times when you're sad, and their laughter delights you. Caring for them is not a duty but a joy.

Now, think about yourself as if you were that special someone. If you're too exhausted from a busy day to do a chore which can wait, tell yourself, "I'm going to give myself a break and do it tomorrow." If someone hurts your feelings without justification, comfort yourself by saying inwardly, "What's their problem?" Pay attention to what your feelings and your heart are asking of you, and don't judge yourself too harshly. Self-loving people always take pains to be especially considerate of themselves. Self-loving people know they can rely on themselves.

That's what Tina, the young Puerto Rican woman who refused to acculturate, learned to be through a lot of work and courage—self-reliant. As her depression continued to grow more and more intense, she got smart and began therapy. There she gradually became aware that although she refused to see it, she and she alone was responsible for changing her overwhelming unhappiness. Although she had been behaving more and more according to the dictates of *marianismo*, the result was an unbroken string of failures. Tina was refusing to be assertive because she had come to believe that such was her fate according to cultural expectations—when in fact she was simply not taking care of herself. She was actually sabotaging her employment opportunities by showing up at interviews dressed inappropriately, or by presenting herself in such a self-defeating manner that she came across as inadequate.

Some of the reasons she expressed for her difficulty in completing her degree were also complete distortions. In therapy, she learned that she was unconsciously afraid of being the only successful person in her family, which would jeopardize her fitting in.

Once she realized that she had hidden behind the *marianista* tenet of self-sacrifice because it seemed safer, the real Tina began to emerge. She started doing things for herself like going on a diet, joining a fitness class, having her nails done, pampering herself with bubble baths, and going on vacations without her family. Eventually, she could say no to things which she knew in her heart were not her real responsibilities without being overwhelmed with guilt. And as her self-esteem grew, Tina could move away from the restraints of her family and make friends. Through the support of these new additions in her life, she mustered the drive to find a job which satisfied her. Last but not least, she began dating a Hispanic-American co-worker and subsequently married him. Tina is now the proud mother of two children. She is making sure they grow up with minimal guilt—and pride in their Hispanic-American heritage. The one thing she will not allow them to do is hide behind it, as she did. She has continued to maintain a close relationship with her family, only now it is no longer restricting or dependent on anybody's part.

Overcoming Shame

Rosario, too, came to therapy, describing her conflict between North American and Hispanic-American cultural traditions as an identity crisis. In her sessions, she was encouraged to examine possible options and resolutions to her identity crisis. She began by asking herself, "Was my family's behavior with my boyfriend really weird?" Not in their culture. Then what should she have done to avoid the particular cultural collision between them and her boyfriend?

Clearly, she should have anticipated that there would be a crowd waiting to critique Jeff, so that she could have prepared him for it. That it hadn't even consciously occurred to her led Rosario to admit she was so embarrassed by her family that she put the issue out of her mind. Like all of us one time or another, she'd dealt with troublesome realities by not dealing with them at all and hoping they'd disappear. Finally, she came to see that Jeff wasn't the only one who thought her family was strange. She, too, felt that the Hispanic values and customs she shared with them made everyone, including herself, seem different.

Next she was directed to devise steps she could have taken to prevent this cultural collision in the first place. Here's what Rosario came up with:

She could have come to grips with the negative feelings she was choosing to ignore and given Jeff a clearer idea of what he was to expect when he interacted with a traditional Hispanic family. She could have explained to him that *familismo* mandates loyalty to the extended family, and that bringing a suitor home to meet dozens of relatives—all of whom are supposed to be accorded personal *respeto*—is considered a very important, almost ritualized occasion among many traditional Hispanics. She could also have tried to explain to her parents that Jeff might feel tremendously outnumbered when he saw the size of the crowd waiting for him and a little unsure of what was required of him. Informing either or both parties would have prevented a lot of hurt feelings and embarrassment.

Now that she understood what she'd failed to do, she was better prepared to cope in the future.

The most important lesson that Rosario learned from the experience was that a cultural collision had taken place to which the Gonzalez family responded by becoming ultra-Hispanic and Jeff by becoming ultra-American. Her role from now on would be to broker the compromise first within herself, then between her family and her boyfriend. She would have to be responsible for their learning about each other without belittling or labeling. Eventually, Rosario was able to congratulate herself for educating the Gonzalez family and Jeff about each other. In fact, she was thrilled to see that as Jeff loosened up, her family actually became less overbearing and far more flexible.

It's important to remember that Rosario was able to take control of the cultural collision and broker a compromise only when she understood she'd been operating from a position of shame. It also became clear that her identity crisis was ignited when she feel into the traditional *marianista* trap of blaming herself and fearing to confront both her family and Jeff.

Learning to Be Objective

Ramona, too, came to reap the benefits of *autonomismo*. At her husband Peter's suggestion, she sought help in therapy. Soon she could see that without being conscious of it, she was feeling out of control when confronted with new roles compounded by plain old-fashioned homesickness. She was also perceiving Peter's overly forceful and often insensitive coaching as a personal attack. That it had never occurred to her to confess to him that she was particularly vulnerable and ask him to be more sensitive to her needs was proof that the threat of new cultural mandates was forcing her back into *marianista* submissiveness.

Ramona didn't initially understand that adapting to a new culture carries with it implicit stress and vulnerability—and that the greater the disparity between your old and new cultural style, the greater that stress. In therapy, she was helped to see that she was employing fears and dynamics she'd brought with her from Peru that heightened, not alleviated, her vulnerability. In Peru she'd been considered *una mujer moderna*, a modern woman, who could broker the cultural compromise for Peter and help him adjust to her world. Now the tables were turned, so to speak. In the United States, Peter didn't want her taking such dutiful care of him. It made him feel as if she were mothering him.

In treatment, Ramona admitted that somewhere inside her, she knew she had to move outward in a new direction, from *marianismo* to self-esteem, before she could even begin to acculturate and learn to be bicultural, which is what she wanted. Ultimately, she achieved enough distance from her predicament so that she saw her problems were caused by cultural confusion, not personal unworthiness. Once she saw things more objectively, she could explain her thoughts and feelings to her husband, feel that she was being heard, and express her willingness to accept many of his suggestions.

Then she could broker the compromise: as she had helped Peter adjust to Peru, he could reciprocate by being her guide to North America. She was honest about acknowledging that she had a lot of changing to do, and she admitted how much she needed his support to help her through the scary moments of acculturation. With all her feelings out in the open, Ramona began her frightening/exciting journey toward becoming *una nueva marianista,* a woman at home in two worlds.

LA NUEVA MARIANISTA: THE FINE ART OF FITTING IN

You are reading this book because you, too, have chosen the path toward becoming *una nueva marianista,* whose motto is: "Women are capable of transforming suffering into self-love."

If you're smart, you'll weave together traditional Hispanic values such as *familismo* and *simpatía* with self-reliance and self-respect to create a whole new fabric whereby you enlist the support of your friends and loved ones in achieving your goals—for the betterment of everyone. Only when you sincerely believe you deserve that support will you get it. And only when you get it will you be free to stride confidently into the brave new world of possibilities that awaits you.

In concluding, we want to remind you that once we enter the United States mainland, we all go through the difficult process of adapting to North American life—unless we're totally sheltered from the world around us. But the road we take to "fitting in" makes all the difference. Either we hide behind our heritage, like Tina and Ramona, or try to assimilate and seek to "pass" as an Angla, which Rosario had unconsciously been doing—or we acculturate and strive to merge the positive aspects of two traditions into a sound foundation on which to build a healthy self-esteem.

This all-out assault on your identity is almost certainly going to happen. It's an integral part of cultural transition that you can't avoid. But you can prepare to defend yourself against it by understanding it.

We also want you to remember that even the smoothest acculturations are anything but *un juego, un manguito,* a joyride. Even moving to a new neighborhood—much less to a new country and culture—can bring on intense anxiety in anyone, regardless of gender or ethnicity.

What we are claiming, however, is that by working diligently to shed such negative instilled mind-sets as *marianismo* and acquiring enhanced assertiveness skills and greater self-assurance, you will be able to smooth out the transition—and have an exciting, eventful time while teaching yourself to be *una nueva marianista*, a successfully empowered and self-reliant Latin-American woman.

3

"Do Not Be Single, Self-supporting, or Independent-minded":

Enforcing Marianismo *vs.*
Forging a Personally
Satisfying Lifestyle

"*Como decía mi mamá*, as my mother always says—men ought to make all the big decisions!" insists Aurora, a thirty-five-year-old woman of Ecuadorean parentage who comes to therapy complaining of chronic depression. Aurora is a public school teacher. In fact, she met her Irish-American husband, Larry, when he was a supervisor in the district where she was teaching. Aurora's rather traditional mother would of course have preferred her daughter marry a Latino, but gave her consent based on the fact that her future son-in-law was a good Catholic.

Through ten years of marriage and the birth of two children, Aurora has managed to hold a job, tend to the house, and take loving care of her husband and kids. Still, she has trouble playing a major role in making family decisions. In Aurora's country, her *falta de asertividad,* lack of assertiveness, might have been accepted by her husband and made her feel like *una buena mujer.* But New York isn't Ecuador, and Larry bitterly resents Aurora's expecting him to run things. Although they're considering buying a house, Aurora refuses to tell Larry where she'd like to live or what style of house she prefers, and she's driving him crazy. In fact, Aurora's general passivity and dependency are creating a lot of tension between them.

What Larry doesn't understand is that accepting one's place in life *con resignación y pasividad* is the ultimate virtue of *la mujer perfeta, la marianista* par excellence. It simply doesn't occur to him that in Ecuador and throughout Latin America, the traditional ideal woman is expected to be dependent, submissive, and subservient to her man.

What Aurora doesn't understand is why she can't be more assertive in her marriage. She wants to—even feels it is her duty to—please her husband, and speaking up is what he's begging her to do. But she just can't. All she can do is feel depressed because, for the first time, her *marianismo* is making her feel like *una mala mujer.*

THE PASSIVITY/DEPENDENCY TRAP

Although Aurora has left her country behind, its *marianista* tradition of female passivity/dependency remains a deep-seated component of her cultural belief package. From the time she was a child, she was rewarded when she demonstrated these traits. In Ecuador she pleased her mother by devoting herself to her father and brothers and letting them make her decisions for her. But now she feels confused, angry, and depressed because pleasing her mother is seriously displeasing her husband. A New World woman on the outside, she's an Old World wife inside herself. She's incapable of assertiveness, which the psychologists R. E. Alberti and M. E. Emmons define as the ability to express and defend our feelings, thoughts, and opinions honestly without experiencing conflicts in doing so. And Aurora represents the rule, not the exception to it. Countless Latinas living in the United States still see relying on a man as a respectable woman's role in life. Consequently, they never develop their personal potential, feel much too conflicted ever to express *asertividad*, and understandably often grow depressed as a result.

Can you identify any vestige of passivity/dependency within yourself? Or do you consider yourself to be *poco asertiva*? Whatever your answer, don't be ashamed to admit it. If you can't admit it, you can't change it! By the way, if you're more *asertiva* than Aurora and believe passivity/dependency and subservience to a man are *viejas costumbres*, old-time customs, in contemporary Latin America, you're wrong. Research by the Mexican anthropologist Marcela Lagarde shows that Latin-American women continue to behave *como marianistas*. Whether we like it or not, the principles of *marianismo* remain the cornerstone of Latina self-esteem.

Now, pause and ask yourself these questions to find out how much *marianismo* you carry in your package of beliefs:

- Would I really like to hand over responsibility for my life to someone else?
- Do I prefer it when my husband or boyfriend makes all the major choices for both of us?
- Do I go along with his decisions, even if I would personally choose other options?
- Do I feel it is my husband's duty to support me financially?
- Do I believe that women without a man are losers?
- Does my dependency on a man ever make me feel angry?
- Do I go along with my boyfriend or husband because I am afraid I could make him so angry that he abandons me and I will not be able to survive alone?

If you answered yes to at least four of these questions, you are still behaving according to *las viejas costumbres*, the old ways, and may well be jeopardizing your ability to develop your full human potential. It is imperative for you to acknowledge your passivity/dependency, allow yourself to express the conflicted emotions you feel because of it, and begin the journey to self-empowerment. Crucial to that process is seeing that often you, by doing as you were taught by your mother, are functioning as your own incarcerator.

In this chapter, we'll share with you how you can feel *como una buena mujer* without having to be a doormat. We'll prove to you that as a new *marianista*, you can assume responsibility for *el timón de tu vida*, steering your own course through life. We'll help you challenge *lo que te enseñó tu mamá*, what your mother taught you—and your grandmother taught her, and your great-grandmother taught your grandmother.

To begin this voyage to freedom and genuine pride, let's look at elements of the Hispanic belief packages appropriate for other times, but not for the world we live in.

The Roots of *Marianismo*

How do Latinas get to be who they are? How were the *marianista* principles of dependency and passivity transmitted to you? How did you make them part of yourself? As we know, *marianismo* is embodied in the mother's role, and some answers to these questions can be found in the process called socialization.

Socialization is what we see as a form of cultural transmitter, a process which enables children to learn society's values, beliefs, attitudes, sex role expectations, myths, religion, and language. In most societies, the role of the mother is to teach her children, from the day of birth, the cultural commands and worldview of their society—in other words, to socialize her *niña* or *niño* so they will be prepared for coping when the young one's world expands beyond her. In Hispanic society, you'll agree, the role of the mother is engraved in stone. She is the most important agent, although not the only one, instilling in her children the principles of *marianismo* and *machismo*.

Actually, the climate for traditional gender behavior begins before birth, since, according to Marcela Lagarde, most Hispanic families frankly express a preference for male children over females. We don't claim this same gender preference is not also found in other cultures, but it is greatly exaggerated in our countries, where the desire for males is absolute, possibly because a boy is considered the proud proof of his father's virility. You don't have to be told that the birth of a girl can be considered a disappointment, especially if she has no older brothers. We're not saying that a girl is never desired, but when she is welcomed, it's frequently because she will be able to help her mother care for her father and brothers and in time her father-in-law and brothers-in-law. Clearly, this matter of gender preference can impact on the life of *la niña* long after childhood is past.

Take the case of Zulma, a Puerto Rican first-year medical student, who began therapy consumed by overwhelming anxiety and self-doubt, although you wouldn't think she had real cause to feel this way.

Zulma comes from a family of great accomplishment. Her father is a well-known San Juan industrialist, her mother a noted professor of sociology at the University of Puerto Rico, and her older sister a psychologist. Zulma always ranked at the top of her class in whatever school she attended, sometimes at the expense of her social life. Here in the United States, in a new country and in a very demanding academic situation, she was suddenly obsessed with failure. When pressed, she admitted that to her "failure" meant not being first in her class in medical school, thereby disappointing her parents, especially her father. She didn't know why she felt such strong emotions—until in therapy she recovered an extraordinary memory. As a child of about five, Zulma had overheard conversations between her mother, her aunt, and her *abuela* regarding an incident that happened when she was born. One of her uncles decided to play a practical joke on her father by telephoning him to say that his first son had been born to him. Believing what his brother had told him, Zulma's father immediately began buying his *amigos* drinks and cigars to celebrate the fact this second child was a male. When he learned the truth, he became so outraged he didn't speak to his brother for twenty years. Although she was too young to grasp all of what was being said, Zulma had understood enough to repress the knowledge but to grow up feeling generally unwanted by everybody in the family, particularly her mother and father. Indeed, when she began to recall the memories, she was overwhelmed with guilt and experienced a plunge in self-esteem.

As she got older, Zulma used academic excellence as a way to be cared about and loved. She felt that in this way she could earn her father's approval. She also used it as a way of connecting to her mother, whose emotional reserve she attributed to the same displeasure her father felt.

Zulma surmised with her therapist that to her mother she must have been a double disappointment. She had failed her husband by bearing him another girl, and in doing so, had failed herself, for she was no longer *una buena mujer.* Zulma was constant living proof of her mother's inadequacy, so she thought. . . .

We'll return to Zulma's story, but for the moment, let's delve further into the roots of Latinas' natural feelings of poor self-esteem.

BABY WANTED, BOY PREFERRED

Basic psychology tells us that during infancy the parents'—and particularly the mother's—positive feelings toward their baby girl are the foundation on which the child's feelings of self-worth will be built for the rest of her life. Do you ask yourself: Were you welcomed into the world by your family?

Did your mother want *un hijo* or *una hija?* What about your father? Do you have reason to believe he would have preferred that you were a boy? From what you've been told, which family members were glad you were a girl? Which ones were sorry?

Do you remember what toys you played with as a child? Most probably you had dolls, cooking utensils, and dollhouses, practiced sweeping the floor with a toy broom, and made play *pasteles* out of mud like the delicious pastries your mother baked. We'll bet your parents frowned on your playing with toy guns, soldiers, broomstick horses, and swords because *no eran juegos de niñas*, they weren't intended for little girls. You almost certainly were ordered to stay away from rough-housing with the little boys because it wasn't considered ladylike. The truth is, unless you had a very unconventional upbringing, you were expected to look forward with excitement and pleasure to the attainment of greater femininity afforded by playing house.

OBEDIENCE SCHOOL

An important aspect of Latina obedience training is learning to be submissive to and dependent on your parents as they prepare you to be a good, passive wife later on. *Una niña bien educada*, a well-brought-up little girl, is a model of obedience, humility, and respect for *personas mayores*, her elders, and their authority is imposed in many ways. Do you remember when you misbehaved and your mother terrified you by threatening, "Wait until your father gets home!" You learned soon enough that Father had absolute *autoridad* and Mother was totally *abnegada y resignada*, depending on Father to make the decisions and mete out punishment. By the way, if you think our claims are too extreme, here's evidence to the contrary. R. Diaz-Guerrero, a respected Mexican psychiatrist, found in his landmark research studies conducted in Mexico City that of the women he surveyed, 87 percent felt they should never challenge their mother's opinions, 71 percent believed a good wife never questions her husband's behavior, and 84 percent felt that a good wife always stands by her man, no matter what the circumstances.

No matter what you learned in childhood, you have the opportunity now, as a transculturating adult, to challenge those lessons. You no longer need to be so obedient, passive, and submissive. Now in modern times, you can take steps to become strong and take control of your own life. The first step is to become aware that you're not happy being dependent. Second, you must find constructive ways to get the point across to your man that you want to be part of the decision-making process. We know it will not be easy, because at least in the earlier stages, your new behavior may feel unnatural. And you must always be aware that people threatened by your newfound assertiveness *te van a hacer la vida imposible*, are going to make life difficult for you. And who taught you to be utterly obedient toward your parents and the men in your life? From whom did you learn your *marianismo*? The answers to those questions can be traced to a single source: your interaction with your mother.

YOUR MOTHER/YOURSELF

The most important formative relationship in your life, as we've said, is *madre e hija*, mother and daughter. Since the cultural expectations are that in Latino society, the mother is responsible for child rearing, it is clear that your *mamá* played a significant role in your development as *una marianista*. In our clinical work, the often painful *madre-hija* interaction becomes a focus of attention for many Latinas trying to overcome their early learned behaviors.

Have you forgotten *el poder*, the power, of your mother? How could you forget those times when she thought you were *muy desobediente*? And what about those battles you so often fought with her? You wanted to be independent. You wanted to go out and play with the boys, but she forbade you, out of fear that you'd become a tomboy. You wanted to study law, but she insisted that was a career only for men. She constantly claimed that only she knew what was best for you. We could go on and on, reminding you of the painful scars left by those battles, where you learned to submit unconditionally to Mamá's will.

Despite her passivity and obedience where men were concerned, Mamá was probably *un terror*, a holy terror with you, demanding strict compliance with what she felt was correct and expecting you to accept it without talking back. Of course, it was unthinkable for you to openly disagree with her wishes. If you're like many of the Latinas with whom we've worked, you may always have felt that having a controlling and demanding mother was only *your* problem. Let us assure you it's not.

A study by the social scientists N. F. McGinn, E. Harburg, and P.

Ginsburg found that the average Mexican mother tends to be strict, stern, and irritable, that she punishes with anger and discourages disagreement. The scientists also found she smothers her children with love, indulges their whims, and concedes to their desires—only so long as those whims and desires do not clash with her own. Our clinical observations strongly bear out these findings. They most likely strike a familiar chord in you, as well.

Replicating *Madre e Hija*

We can now begin to see that your early relationship with your mother has the power to shape and affect your relationships later in life with husbands, lovers, friends, children, grandchildren, even colleagues. In fact, we frequently find Latinas transferring their feeling toward their mothers onto other people in their lives.

Transference, says the psychiatrist H. Nunberg, is a fascinating psychological phenomenon dealing with unconscious feelings toward a specific person which you developed during childhood. Now, in adult life, you react compulsively and repetitively with the same childhood feelings toward another person. For example, you might not be aware how much you disliked it when your mother told you to do things and controlled many moments of your existence. Today, you find yourself intensely disliking some rather bossy man or woman without just cause—until, through therapy, you realize this person reminds you of your mother at her most overbearing.

Making this association between the present and the past is enormously liberating because the act of transference is like fighting with a ghost. It resolves nothing in your childhood, which is gone forever, but it can complicate your life in the here and now. However, once you stop transferring, the objects of your dislike will no longer wield power over you. Although they may never become your favorite people, you'll be able to deal with them in a less charged, more rational way.

Transference was a terrible problem for Ana, a forty-one-year-old Costa Rican accountant in a large municipal hospital, who wondered why she let a very domineering and controlling co-worker named Irene order her around—although they shared the same rank. While it made her furious with herself, Ana felt powerless to speak up to Irene. Only in therapy did she begin to realize that she needed Irene's constant approval and appreciation because she was replicating her relationship with her mother.

Ana worked hard at understanding this central relationship in her life and found herself asking, "What kind of mother did I have?" She began to remember how her mother would not let go of her from infancy. Her aunts and uncles told her that as soon as she started to walk, her mother had always been overprotective. As Ana's memories of childhood came flooding back, she also recalled how upset and angry her mother grew when Ana wanted to explore the world with her playmates, crying that she was *una niña mala y desobediente*. The guilt she'd felt because she wanted to separate had been enormous. Obediently, she'd learned to cook and take care of the house because Mamá said she needed to prepare herself for marriage to a good man who would require a wife with domestic skills.

Ana recounted that her mother always accompanied her to school, even when she was twelve years old, openly read her letters and diaries, demanded to meet all her friends, and dictated with an iron hand how she dressed and behaved. When she began dating, her mother insisted on chaperoning her. Eventually, she married Ruben, the Cuban-born man her mother had picked out for her. Ruben was a good man, and they had been happily married for seven years and had a four-year-old daughter. But there was one major impediment to true conjugal contentment: Mamá, whose intrusiveness Ruben couldn't stand any more than Ana could.

For her own peace of mind and the good of her marriage, Ana seriously tried to discourage her mother from taking over whenever she came to visit, but Ana found she could only keep her mother within limits part of the time. The bottom line remained that Ana felt terrible guilt at making her mother so angry, and at finding herself so angry.

She was also fearful that if she expressed her rage, something terrible would happen to her mother because of it.

If you find yourself overreacting, as Ana did with her co-worker Irene, pause and ask yourself, "Why did I behave in a way which was totally out of proportion to what the situation called for?"

When you overreact, you should regard it as a signal that there's something more going on inside your head. Every time you find out what that something is, you're honing your self-awareness: the degree of clarity with which you understand all the factors relating to a given situation. Often we're not aware that we are relating to an unconscious feeling rather than the actual circumstances at hand. But with heightened self-awareness, we can take the first step toward change. We can begin to free ourselves from the power of the past.

 ## CHALLENGING THE MYTHS OF CHILDHOOD

As adults, we have the power and potential to gain insight and initiate personal growth that we never had as children. We no longer depend on Mamá for survival and don't have to wait for her to define who we are. It is crucial for Latinas to alter the belief that our worth was determined in childhood and that it is impossible to change it. We need to move forward in this new country of ours, where self-definition is the task of the healthy adult. We need to challenge the myths of childhood.

Therefore, you must learn to understand how much of your definition of yourself and your worth is an accurate reflection of what you are and how much is a product of circumstances and other people's misperceptions. Only through healthy separation can come a truly liberating compassion and forgiveness. However, that's not always easy.

That said, we want to make it clear that you should not use blaming your mother as an excuse for inertia—any more than you should disregard the fact that, given cultural considerations, she felt she was acting lovingly and in your best interests. Instead, you must tell yourself, "I am an adult now, and I don't have to act the way I did when I was a child." What you have to do now is called separation.

Separation and Individuation: Moving Beyond Blame

Separation and individuation are challenging steps for any young child but especially daring for little girls, according to the French psychoanalyst Christiane Olivier. Separation is the ability of children to put emotional and physical distance between their mothers and themselves. Developing as an individual distinct from Mamá is termed individuation. Ana was able to separate from her mother only when she began to see herself as a grown-up who was in charge of her life and responsible for her actions. As such, she could see clearly that her needs had changed since she was a little girl in Costa Rica. She no longer required her mother to tell her what to do or to be her main role model.

She learned that part of her task as an acculturating Latina was to sort out and discard from her belief package ineffective behavior which she acquired from her mother's orthodox *marianismo* and replace them with more accurate, positive observations she'd arrived at independently. As a result of gaining insight into her relationship with her mother, she has also learned to treat her own four-year-old daughter differently. In *nueva marianista* fashion, she has come to believe a mother can be firm without being controlling and intrusive. Keep in mind that *la cadena de tu vida*, the chain of your life, can be changed if you become aware of the past missteps that marked your relationship with your mother and the current overreactions which signal you're still affected by them.

MAMÁ DEAREST

Regina, a forty-eight-year-old Cuban, was simply unable to set limits and draw lines in the sand with her mother, Leonor, who lived with her. Regina's American husband, Ben, and fourteen-year-old son,

Charlie, also had to put up with Grandmother's constant demands. In due course, Regina's marriage became strained because of the older woman's interference in running the household and Ben's resentment toward Regina for doing nothing to stop it.

Regina, of course, felt terrible pangs of *marianista* guilt when she imagined showing her mother the disrespect of telling her what she, Ben, and Charlie felt. She was furious with her mother and wished she would leave, but the second she let the anger surface, she developed terrible *jaquecas*, migraine headaches. From childhood, Regina remembered her *tía-abuela*, her mother's aunt, saying to Doña Leonor that to wish harm to another person is a mortal sin. Regina felt she would be punished for having negative thoughts about Mamá. In therapy, she even expressed the notion that *las jaquecas* were God's punishment for her evil thoughts about Leonor.

We would be surprised if you didn't know that in some situations or others, relating to Mamá can be troublesome, to say the least, and full of mixed feelings. Yet some Latinas can only see the negative side of their mothers, while ignoring positive traits because they are so enraged. Furthermore, it's important to remember that often the things you detest about yourself are aspects of your personality which are closest to hers. Once you can come to terms with this, your shared traits can actually serve as a bridge for improving your relationship. Developing a close relationship with your mother is especially important if you want her support. This support may include what may seem to your family a shockingly unconventional lifestyle—living alone and deciding not to get married.

THE OLD-MAID COMPLEX

As you know, *la mujer sola*, whether she's single, divorced, or widowed, has no valid place in Latin American society because a woman's role is to be a wife and mother. Too often, women who choose to be alone are regarded as outcasts. However, there are many North American women who are alone by choice and are accepted by society. Once you begin the acculturation process, you'll see there are many options women in the United States can choose, but you, as a Latina, may feel intense anxiety when you think about them, because you know that following a nontraditional path will almost guarantee you absolutely no support from your loved ones.

That was the dilemma of Lucia, whose chronic sadness and dissatisfaction with herself brought her to therapy. The thirty-five-year-old daughter of a middle-class family of Medellín, Colombia, and a graduate of a prestigious religious high school and university, she accepted an important post at United Nations headquarters in New York City—only to meet with her family's furious disapproval because she had chosen a career over marriage and children. Lucia felt tremendous anger and guilt whenever she called her mother, because she always got a lecture about her unwillingness to fulfill *la tradición familiar,* the family tradition, of marrying *un hombre bueno* and becoming a housewife.

Lucia was the only female sibling in the family who was single and self-supporting. Time after time, her oldest sister, who was a wife and mother of four, scolded her for not marrying one of the wealthy men who had proposed to her. To add fuel to the fire, Lucia had lived with an Italian diplomat in New York for six years without marrying him. They had eventually split up when he was permanently reassigned to Italy and Lucia didn't want to relocate. The breakup didn't improve things with her family. To them, the damage had already been done.

As her therapy progressed, Lucia began remembering things from the past. She mentioned that even as *una niña,* she'd had an independent streak which was the bane of her parents. She recalled her mother complaining about her willfulness at the dinner table, and her father's replying, *"Tú la criaste!* You raised her!" Not only was all this said as if Lucia weren't present, but her mother never raised her voice in her own or her daughter's defense. As the years passed, Lucia's whole life became a determination to be as little as possible like her mother. As she rejected eligible bachelor after eligible bachelor, her mother even told her it would be better if she had been a nun—anything but *una solterona,* an old maid.

The result of all this was that Lucia's father hadn't spoken to her in years, and her mother was beside herself because she considered her daughter a "loose woman," with total disregard for the respect she owed her elders and the family. In her family's eyes, Lucia was also a sinner because she had an independent mind and exercised her right to choose what she wanted from life.

Lucia's actions challenged the status quo and the principles of dependency and submission of the *marianismo* ideology. But it must be said she was paying a heavy price for her courage. When she came to therapy, she complained of chronic vulnerability, guilt, anger, and self-belittlement. A medical doctor she knew diagnosed her correctly as *la solterona;* a woman alone, with neurotic complaints. Lucia was suffering from the Old Maid Complex.

Lucia made her choices knowing she would be cut off from a lot of valued tradition, including *familismo,* but she felt strongly that she had a right to be what she wanted to be. To her, a woman should be able to play the multiple roles of mother, wife, and professional, and she objected strongly to the narrow definition of who she was as viewed by her culture. As we have seen, in Latin American countries, women are defined according to the rules of *marianismo,* which in turn is defined by the rules of *machismo.* And these traditional rules pigeonhole both men and women, leaving them unhappy and unfulfilled. In North America, women like Lucia are daring to defy conventions which no longer apply, undergoing the pain of change and becoming *nuevas marianistas*—able to be fulfilled in both the workplace and the home.

However, if you're going to make this transition, there is a very crucial, very scary step you're going to have to take: confronting her.

Confronting Mamá

We want to stress here that Hispanic tradition doesn't encourage daughters to confront their mothers, because it can be interpreted as *falta de respeto.* Regina, the forty-eight-year-old Cuban whose own mother, Leonor, was making her so upset, knew this. But in the end, she didn't let it stop her from conveying her feelings to Mamá. It wasn't easy. She spent a lot of time in therapy working on it. First, she had to become aware of her anger toward her mother and the fear that it would overwhelm her, making her lose control and do something horrible. Once she acknowledged the anger, Regina was surprised to learn that underneath it lurked ambivalence, despair, betrayal, fear, sadness, guilt, powerlessness, and poor self-esteem.

She came to realize that Leonor's continuous criticism not only diminished her self-worth but enhanced her need for Leonor's approval—which, of course, never came. This discovery was a breakthrough for Regina because it enabled her to understand on an emotional level the connections between her need for her mother's approval, her poor self-esteem, and the anger she felt when her mother withheld praise. "No matter what I do," Regina would say repeatedly, "it's just not good enough for my mother." But every time she said it, she was making the situation worse. In fact, her low opinion of herself made her perceive even mild criticism from her mother as a full-scale attack.

Regina's most important action was to begin giving herself credit and approval as a wife and mother. She accepted the fact that her sense of self-worth could not hinge on her mother's seal of approval. In therapy, Regina was also helped to perceive her mother more realistically by reflecting on the cultural context in which the older woman grew up. Slowly, it all came back to Regina—her mother's stories of how difficult it had been for her when she was raising Regina and her brother. Although Leonor had been totally dedicated to her children, her husband was extremely critical of her mothering skills and claimed she wasn't doing enough for his *niños*.

Then there were the stories of Regina's late papá's never taking her mother out because *su deber era criar los hijos*, her duty was to care for her little ones, leaving his wife with only the church and her family as outlets. Although Regina had never discussed with her mother the fact that her father kept a mistress, it was a well-known family secret.

Still, years later, her father always referred to his wife as *una mujer santa*, who was not only the best mother in the world but a woman of compassion who put up with his infidelities.

When Regina's father passed away and her brother expressed no interest in inviting their mother to live with him, she followed the traditional cultural expectation that the daughter is responsible for taking care of aging parents—despite the fact that she had never gotten along with Leonor and that their relationship had worsened after Regina married an Anglo. Thinking of her father's and brother's disinterest, she reflected with astonishing understatement, "The men in my family haven't been very supportive of my mother and me."

As Regina thought over what she'd just said, she began to get a better understanding of her mother's own troubles and even to feel empathy for her—quite a change from the overwhelming anger she'd felt before. Suddenly she was seeing her mother not *como una bruja*, as a witch, as she had in the past or as the *marianista* saint her father had praised, but as a lonely woman who was constantly being put down, throughout her married life. Regina could now get in touch with feelings of compassion, gratitude, even of commonality with Doña Leonor.

It's key for you, too, to access feelings for your mother other than the anger of which you're so afraid. Like Regina, you will almost certainly find that many of your emotions are positive, since no relationship is all black or white. When you finally are able to achieve an emotional balance, you will feel, as Regina did, that a heavy weight has been lifted from your heart.

We have worked with many Latinas who are unable to see that their mothers actually loved and admired them. If your relationship with your mother is difficult, it is up to you to first understand and then break the vicious circle that holds you both captive. This is how the vicious circle operates: Your poor self-image increases your need for your mother's approval while intensifying your belief that she generally disapproves of you. Consequently, you get angry and disparaging. At the same time, your self-respect plummets because your dealings with Mamá are always colored by anger, of which you are afraid.

Regina, seeing these patterns working in her relationship with Leonor, worked very hard on building up her self-esteem through verbalization and visualization exercises and affirmations. Higher self-esteem made Regina feel more comfortable telling her mother when she was upset with her, as well as when she identified with her.

Leonor, in turn, slowly began to acknowledge her daughter and praise her for her professional achievements and even her skill in the kitchen. Then came the day when she announced to Regina that she had shown wisdom in selecting such a good and loving man as Ben, even if he wasn't Cuban. "Your papá," she told her, "didn't make me feel good about myself, and I do not want the same thing for you."

From Regina's story, you can see that it is possible to find a way to feel emotionally connected to your mother and experience both the affection and irritation which are equally normal parts of any intimate relationship. Let's now revisit the other women you met in this chapter to see how their confrontations with Mamá turned out.

Mother/Daughter: From Adversaries to Allies

Remember Zulma, the medical student plagued by the knowledge that her father had wanted her to be a boy? During a visit to Puerto Rico, she decided it was time to confront both her mother and her father. When Papá invited her to visit one of his factories to advise him on health care services for his employees, Zulma felt she had a God-given opportunity. After the tour they stopped for a drink at a nearby café. Summoning her courage, Zulma began to share with her father how her awareness of his reaction to her birth had unconsciously made her feel inadequate all her life. She went on to explain that her overachieving as a result of that low self-esteem was now causing her both physical and emotional problems. She also informed Papá that she intended to talk frankly with her mother about the same issues.

Zulma's father was surprised by his daughter's admissions and admitted that he'd done a very silly thing as a young man. He was very happy to have her, he exclaimed, and he would be just as happy no matter how successful she was in her studies. But he urged Zulma not to be too hard on her mother. For the first time, Zulma would become aware of how incorrectly she had interpreted her mother's emotional distance.

Now her father confessed that all through Zulma's childhood, he'd had a mistress—probably because it was the *macho* thing to do. Whatever the reason, the affair had made his wife tremendously unhappy. At last Zulma was beginning to see that her mother's reserve was the result of her own tremendous sense of unworthiness and sadness that she couldn't satisfy her husband sexually. "The affair is all in the past," her father continued. "Your mother is *una buena mujer*. I asked her for forgiveness, and she granted it to me. I am as happy to have her for a wife as I am to have you for a daughter." As he embraced Zulma, her father added, "But if you ever have a son, be sure you raise him differently than my mother did. That's where I learned that foolish *macho* behavior that has hurt you and your mother, two women I love with all my heart!"

Zulma's confrontation with her father had gone better than she could ever have hoped, but she still had the conversation with her mother ahead of her. When Mamá herself suggested they go shopping together, Zulma was taken aback. As they drove to the shopping area, her mother told Zulma that her father had shared their conversation at the café. Consequently, she wanted to have a similar discussion with her. Zulma had been anxious about this, assuming her mother would be angry and rejecting after her father spilled the beans. Once again, she was wrong.

Mother and daughter never got to the stores but instead went to the beach, where Zulma spoke quite frankly about how rejected she'd felt as a child. In no time they were both crying, but her mother surprised Zulma by telling her how sorry she was and that Zulma was completely justified in feeling angry. She explained that she had indeed loved her and her sister, but that her own concerns about losing her husband and raising her daughters in a single-parent home should there be a divorce had prevented her from expressing the love she felt.

"I want to do it now," she told Zulma, hugging and kissing her. "And I, like your father, will continue to love and respect you whether you're first or last in your class!"

As time passed, Zulma's self-esteem continued to grow. She learned to balance her time despite the pressures of medical school, was among the top twenty-five graduates in her class, and began dating Paul, an American pediatric resident who supported her professional and personal goals for advancement. Today, Zulma is a highly success-ful Manhattan pediatrician in private practice, Paul's wife, and the mother of two children with extremely loving and indulgent grandpar-ents in Puerto Rico.

And Ana, whose inability to express her anger toward her mother was causing her to act out and be bullied by a bossy co-worker? Gradually she learned through treatment to express her resentment without doing her mother irreparable damage. She began to say to her-self, "I didn't turn out so bad. Look at all I've accomplished!" After ad-mitting she both liked and valued herself, she began to stand up to her mother without feeling she was *mala*. And when she did, always with the words "Mom, I really love you and want to understand you better," her mother revealed a startling secret from the past.

Mamá's first child, a girl, had died at birth. Subsequently, she bore three boys, but wanted a girl very badly. When Ana was born, Mamá made *una promesa* to God that she would make sure nothing bad hap-pened to her beloved *hija*, the answer to her prayers. All through Ana's childhood, her mother had been terrified that she, too, would die. She had never outgrown that fear, even though Ana was an adult with a family of her own.

Ana told her mother she understood the dread, but that Mamá needed to acknowledge that God had allowed Ana to grow to healthy adulthood. "Mamá," she continued, "now you've got to let go of some of your control for the sake of my family." She then told her how help-ful therapy had been for her and asked if the older woman would like to talk to someone about those fears that wouldn't go away. Tearfully, her mother admitted that she would. Ana consequently contacted a nun who was a psychiatric social worker at her mother's church, and Mamá began to see her. As allies, both in therapy, Ana and her mother both grew in marvelous new directions. Ana became more assertive, and Mamá became less bossy. Now Ana had the emotional strength to begin dealing with her overbearing co-worker, Irene.

Since she felt more confident about herself, she rehearsed different scenarios, using visualization exercises, for confronting her co-worker. Finally, the day arrived when Ana could firmly tell Irene to stop being so bossy. What satisfaction she received from establishing new boundaries in both relationships! The following year, Ana's new sense of self-esteem paid off, and she was promoted to a supervisory position. Guess who reported to her? When Ana told this to Mamá, the older woman replied with a haughty toss of the head, "Well, now we'll really show Irene who's boss!"

Lucia, whose family regarded her both as a loose woman and as an old maid, finally came to see that she, too, couldn't make peace with herself until she worked things through with her mother. The best time to do it, she and the therapist agreed, was during Mamá's coming visit to New York. They also worked out a very clever plan for initiating the confrontation *con mucho respeto*. After her mother arrived, Lucia wrote her a highly personal letter, making sure the tone was as noncombative as if she were writing to a friend.

The therapist and Lucia felt that writing such a letter would be the most effective approach, giving her more control over her feelings and emotions than if she just blurted them out. Down deep, Lucia was coming to realize she loved her mother, who was a victim of the way her traditional society treated women and hadn't had the choices her daughter had.

Lucia presented the letter to Mamá in person, along with a dozen red roses, her mother's favorite. Seeing the roses, the older woman exclaimed, "But today isn't Mother's Day!" Lucia replied, "Every day is Mother's Day, and in addition we're celebrating the reunion of two good *amigas*, Mamá! Then she gave her the letter, which began,

"*Queridísima Mamá y amiga*"—Dearest Mother and friend—and ended, "*Con respeto y admiración, tu hija y amiga.*"

As her mother read the letter, she started to cry, and for a moment Lucia was afraid she really was going to reject her. But to her surprise, Mamá finished reading, got up, went over to her, and embraced her, saying, "Let's talk. No matter what you choose to do with your life, you will always be my daughter!"

It took courage for Lucia to put her feelings on paper, and her mother recognized that and respected her for it. By reaching out in that way, Lucia had opened the door for two Latinas of different generations to talk heart to heart as allies about their commonalities and differences. And Mamá did in fact become Lucia's ally. With a grin, Lucia told the therapist that her mother had returned to Colombia the leading defender of Lucia's independence—even supporting her daughter when she began traveling to Third World countries in her new job as chief executive officer of a humanitarian relief agency. In fact, her husband commented, "What happened to you in New York? You've become Lucia's defense attorney!" To which her mother replied rather mysteriously, "Oh, only a woman could understand . . ."

Six Steps to Mothering Yourself

These success stories of acculturating Latinas struggling with *marianismo* as expressed in the relationships with their mothers and others close to them suggest certain commonalities. Following are six crucial steps to mothering yourself, recommended by Victoria Secunda in her book *When You and Your Mother Can't Be Friends: Resolving the Most Complicated Relationship in Your Life:*

> Step 1: You gain insight into your relationship with your mother.
>
> Step 2: You determine how your mother's relationship colors the way you relate to others.

STEP 3: You identify the actions your mother used to control you as a child, and perhaps still uses now that you are an adult.

STEP 4: You become aware of your own feelings in response to your mother's controlling behavior.

STEP 5: You explore mutual ground and develop alliances with your mother.

STEP 6: You establish the actions you need to take to diminish your mother's power over you and change your relationship with her.

We cannot stress too often that as adults we are no longer powerless in relation to our mothers. Indeed, we have the freedom to define our self-worth independent of our childhood experiences. Some Latinas still feel unable to assert themselves in their mother's presence and are afraid to enter into a dialogue based on equality with them, because they feel such an act would be *una falta de respeto*. Nonsense! We live in a different epoch, often in a different country, than our mamás did. In fact, you might be surprised to find that your mother actually welcomes the chance to talk to you about how different things were when she was a girl. You'll never know if you don't try.

A note of caution: Before you even begin a conversation with your mamá about your own childhood, have a fantasy discussion with her in your head. You might even want to do it in writing. Prepare yourself for all the possibilities—anger, clashing perceptions, refusal to answer, defensiveness, or claims of *falta de respeto*. This rehearsal will help you deal with your anxiety, fear, and guilt and will also prepare you for whatever difficulties may ensue. Here again, as you move away from *marianismo* and try to forge a life pleasing to you rather than to your *mamá*, be prepared for a lot of unpleasantness.

New Rules for a New World

The increasing number of Latinas in North America who are household heads, divorcées, widows, and professional women—according to the U.S. Census—suggests clearly that more and more women are challenging the *marianista* ideology. The opportunity to play these new roles, however, has caused trouble in the family.

There's no denying that when you first realize your needs are as important as anybody else's and articulate it, you probably will meet with conflict. Conflict may not be easy for you to handle because your dread of abandonment gets in the way and causes you to back down. If when you read these lines, your stomach tightens or you feel *dolor de cerebro,* literally "pain in the brain," you must prepare yourself to get strong enough to fight your natural inclination to flee. However, as we see in our clients, many Hispanic women are developing effective coping mechanisms to help them adjust to their new environment without altering their goals. They are learning to address these conflicts and to help others in need of support.

You have the chance to change your circumstances by becoming aware of your needs and wants, allowing them to surface, and acknowledging your desire for growth as a healthy woman, not to be twisted no matter what your family says. Ask yourself these questions to test how independent you are:

- Do I believe I have the power to choose?
- Do I see alternatives to developing my internal resources?
- Do I avoid thinking, taking action, and assuming responsibility for myself?
- Do I believe that my need for nurturing and intimacy are indicators of my lack of independence?
- Do I prefer to be with men instead of women because they give me a clearer sense of who I am and what I'm worth?

Don't become upset if the results tell you things about yourself you didn't want to hear. Just remember that change is always possible as long as you want it. And you can't really want it until you see the problem clearly and confront it directly. But once you do, you can begin rewriting the "script of your life"—a term used by P. J. Caplan in the book *Don't Blame Mother: Mending the Mother/Daughter Relationship*.

Rewrite the Script of Your Life!

Remember the fairy tale you were told as *una niña, el cuento de la Cucarachita Martina?*—recently revisited by the Puerto Rican writer Rosario Ferré. If you sit down and think about it, the cultural expectations of this children's story, which our *abuelas, mamás, y tías* repeated so many times, convey a very powerful *marianista* message.

The little cockroach Martina, you'll recall, found a nickel and after much thinking used it to buy powder so she'd look pretty and find a husband who would take care of her. Cucarachita rejected the marriage proposals made by the dog, the cat, and the rooster because they were arrogant, insensitive, and authoritarian. They all barked, hissed, or crowed, "*¡Aquí mando yo!*—I give the orders here!" when Cucarachita asked what they would do on their wedding night.

Finally, Perez the mouse seduced her by his loving, sensitive, and fair-minded behavior, since most Latinas at heart long for a man with these attributes. But as Cucarachita was cooking a stew for the wedding feast like a good *marianista*, Perez the mouse couldn't wait to taste it, fell into the *olla*, and drowned. Therefore we don't know whether he would have fulfilled Cucarachita's expectations, but little *marianistas-in-training* who hear this tale certainly get the impression that although they aspire to a loving marriage, *el destino* will deny them the chance and will instead saddle them with *un mandón*, a bully!

It's always been true that the rules of society are taught to our children through fairy tales. But now, in the United States, women are beginning to question their subservient fate. Perhaps Latinas can begin to break the cultural link by rewriting the script of *La Cucarachita Martina* and create a story where men and women live together in gentleness and harmony.

Can you imagine how wonderful it would be to tell stories *a tu hija* which would not perpetuate the negative aspects of *marianismo*, instead focusing on the opportunity to be independent, assertive, and active without losing your self-respect? Admittedly, rewriting the script of your life is harder than rewriting a fairy tale—but it will brighten your existence and strengthen your self-worth in the real, exciting new world around you.

Remember Aurora, whose struggle to please her husband by being assertive and her mother by being passive/dependent began this chapter? Through therapy, she developed the courage to rewrite the script of her life.

First, Aurora worked on reevaluating what femininity meant to her and began to separate her own definition and desires from those of her mother. She was the first one to admit her luck in having a husband who was cheering for her to change. Because of Larry's support, Aurora was able to begin making small decisions, such as choosing the restaurant when the family went out to eat. She made the decision, and nothing terrible happened. In fact, everybody had a good time, which gave Aurora confidence to assert herself again. Soon she was actively involved in searching for what she could now admit was her own dream house.

But the problems with her mother still needed to be resolved. Fighting the dread that Mamá wouldn't love her if she became more independent, Aurora began to respectfully disagree when the occasion warranted it. One such instance occurred when she and her mother were discussing the new house and Mamá insisted she was behaving like a shrew by being so outspoken. Aurora was able to respond that Larry hadn't become angry when she told him she wanted a Tudor house. In fact, he welcomed the input. In this way, she proved to Mamá that things were different between husbands and wives in North

America, and saw for herself that once gain, her disagreement didn't precipitate disaster.

Then came the big test: the Communion of one of Aurora's children. Mamá was insisting she herself choose the outfits, the restaurant, the guests. Summoning all her reserves of strength for what she thought might be a big battle, Aurora suggested that she appreciated the offer of help but thought she could handle the tasks by herself. "Mamá," she said, "*así me veo muy apurada, tú eres la primera persona que voy a llamar.*" If I get stuck, you'll be the first person I call. Although her mother was surprised, she went along, the event was a success, and everybody was happy.

As she continued to outgrow her *marianismo*, Aurora's relationship with Larry improved until they both felt they were partners in a healthy, interdependent marriage. A few years later, she called the therapist to report that she'd been promoted to a supervisory position in her school district. She wanted to thank her, Aurora said, because it was clear her new assertiveness had contributed to her advancement. Perhaps best of all was the day when Aurora and her mother went to pick up the car at the garage on their way to go shopping. When a male employee ignored them in order to wait on a man who'd just come in, Aurora spoke right up and insisted she was first in line. The attendant immediately went to get their car. As they walked to it, Mamá put her arm around her daughter's shoulder, gave her a hug, and announced, "We women really stand up for ourselves, don't we?"

Our work with Latinas has shown us that your goal should never be disconnecting from Mamá, although the advisability of total severance has been argued in the psychological community for decades. To us, it is imperative that you establish and maintain connectedness by becoming assertive, exploring mutual ground, and developing an alliance with your mother rather than doing battle with her. In so doing, you will find your truly empowered self and pave the way for other meaningful alliances with your own daughters and granddaughters.

In the past, the *marianista* dogma, which was designed to reinforce *machismo*, led many Latin American women to depend on the traditional rules for raising and restricting their daughters. However, mother-daughter support, women's support of each other, should now give you the strength to rewrite the script of your life. We're sure that with that support you can face the pain and longings in your own and in your mother's past and move beyond them as you shape a far better and more openly loving future for you both, for your daughters, for Latinas, for all women.

4

"Do Not Put
Your Own Needs First":

*Selflessness vs.
Self-Fullness*

Ernestina, a thirty-two-year-old Colombian-American, was ready to explode because her husband's younger brother, Nestor, had shown up in New York from Colombia one day out of the blue and moved right in. That Ernestina and her husband, Gilberto, didn't have the space was not a consideration. Nestor simply camped out in the living room. To make matters worse, he drank heavily and liked to party, which meant he habitually came home at all hours, bellowing loudly and spoiling for a fight.

The final straw was that, drunk or sober, he treated Ernestina like a servant, not as his brother's wife. But when she finally mustered the courage to complain to Gilberto, he insisted *que era su deber de hermano ayudar a Nestor a levantarse*, that it was his familial duty to help Nestor to establish himself, no matter how he behaved, and that as his wife, it was hers, too.

Ernestina did not speak up again, realizing that as a good *marianista*, she was obliged to honor her husband and his family. When a friend asked why she hadn't been able to stand her ground with Gilberto, she replied, "*¿Qué puedo hacer? Él es el hermano de mi esposo y es mi deber ayudarlo.*" What can I do? He is my husband's brother and it's my duty to help him. This despite the fact that doing her duty was making Ernestina miserable, putting tremendous strains on her marriage, and playing havoc with her self-esteem.

WHEN RESPECT AND SELF-RESPECT COLLIDE

You may remember that in Chapter 1, we cited Alfred Adler's definition of self-esteem, which embraces not only an individual's acceptance of self but also his or her willingness to contribute to the social interest of the group. From this premise, we can understand why people strive to participate in communal needs dictated by cultural values in order to enhance their feelings of self-worth—and that we all try hardest to follow those cultural dictates accepted by the majority, as Ernestina did.

You may also remember that in Chapter 2 we referred to the conflicts between cultural values and personal needs you may experience when you're acculturating. If you become too "Angla," you risk losing the esteem of the Hispanics in your life—who include your loved ones. Being judged as worthy by significant others is undeniably important, but in Ernestina's case, the fear of losing that intimate *respeto* had pushed her backwards into the *marianista* trap of abnegation, humility, and sacrifice.

In this chapter, we'll show you how *marianista* perfectionism coupled with cultural collision reveals itself in your everyday interaction as selflessness—and how selflessness is integral to your beliefs regarding your role as a female in your relationships with the males in your life. You'll see how your *marianismo* impacts on self-worth and allows you to let a spouse treat you badly, a mother-in-law badger you, a co-worker take advantage of your lack of assertiveness. We'll also give you direction and provide examples of women who have fought the inner battle for "self-fullness"—and won.

Sandals in a Snowstorm

It's clear that cultural dictates quite often exist for the practical purpose of survival. At times they can be very clear, at other times less so—but they are deeply ingrained in people's personalities and are regarded as everyday, commonsensical requirements for group "membership." For example, it's not abnormal to wear lined boots and a heavy coat when it's snowing. Wearing sandals and a bathing suit under the same conditions would seem at the very least impractical. Conversely, appearing at the beach in a fur coat on a sweltering August afternoon would be viewed as equally abnormal or inappropriate.

A cultural dictate which made sense for millennia was the expectation that, given the fact that a baby's main source of milk is the mother's breast, women would be the primary caretakers of children and of their family in general. From a practical point of view, we can see the revelance of the mother's presence in the development of the child's self-esteem. That means, as we've already discussed, that the socialization process—which affects self-esteem throughout the infant's lifetime—evolves primarily out of an individual's relationship with mother. As children begin to move beyond the exclusive mother-infant relationship and individudate, their self-esteem is affected positively or negatively by other family members, as well.

Next, the individual ventures out into the world. Now self-esteem is also affected by the attitudes of the group, be it a school class or the kids in the neighborhood. If those attitudes are perceived by the individual as negative, they exert a negative influence on the sense of self which can often be difficult to change. When you think of an immigrant as a cultural "child" venturing out into the world for the first time, you can understand why acculturation is so difficult to achieve. In a way, it's like reliving a painful part of childhood—with you as the small, innocent boy or girl and the new culture as vast and threatening beyond measure. In such a climate, any negative feedback reverberates on our self-esteem with exaggerated resonance.

If we examine general North American attitudes toward Hispanics, we discover many unflattering stereotypes that can't help but affect the way we feel about ourselves—although in actuality the negative stereotyping is often caused by cultural collision. For example, if you turn down a college scholarship or a good job opportunity in another state because you are the primary care giver of an ailing parent, you may be perceived as either too involved with or overly dependent on your family. Likewise, if you decide to move in with your family after your divorce because you have two children and a job and need the in-house child support, you may also be regarded as socially inadequate and incapable of taking care of yourself.

Sometimes the pressures aren't caused by external reactions but follow from your inner values, which can also cause confusion and psychic discomfort. When, like Ernestina, you get caught in a combination of low self-esteem and self-imposed, overly exaggerated cultural obligations, you can be overwhelmed with sadness.

Latinas and Selflessness

Over and over in our practices, we observe the tremendous tension stemming from having to juggle two distinct and often opposing value systems. We've discussed it at length in earlier chapters. As we've said before, many self-esteem problems have little to do with culture, but we want to stress again that frequently these conflicts are sharpened and intensified when an individual is trying to live in two worlds at once. It is only natural that any Latina newly exposed to different cultural views through television, school, work, or her *amigas* will begin to question herself. This self-doubt possesses a dimension the woman may never before have experienced. It is called alienation, and it carries with it a constant sense of worthlessness and sadness. Once a Latina is gripped by a sense of not belonging, of not fitting in or being understood, she may try harder and harder to give to others, to be as *marianista* as possible, so that she will feel *más buena*, more worthy as a woman.

We know that Latinas tend to define ourselves as *buenas* or *malas* based on how well we do things for others—because ingrained in our hearts and minds are the *marianista* values passed down over the generations by the people we most respect, love, and admire. When we look at the Latin woman's caretaking qualities, we are confronted with the compulsion to be selfless. For the Latina, selflessness really means not being there for yourself. This, of course, is part and parcel of the *marianista* motto, reinforcing the idea that women are capable of bearing all suffering—as the *marianista* attitude toward motherhood so clearly shows. But for women acculturating to a new society, an identity crisis ensues when *desinterés*, or selflessness—a very natural part of yourself—abruptly begins to seem *muy extraño*, very strange indeed.

William Jones, the great thinker we mentioned earlier, felt that whatever goals we choose for ourselves become one of the measures of our self-worth. Clearly then, if an acculturating Latina opts for New World goals, such as having a career, and her family berates her for such ambitions, her sense of self-worth is going to suffer greatly. But even if the goals we choose are dictated by cultural as much as personal preferences, not living up to them makes us feel unworthy. For instance, a mother can display superb child-caring skills 80 percent of the time but still feel she is *una mala madre* when her mother-in-law criticizes her for not having made *la compota*, the baby food, by hand, or for not being *una buena ama de casa*. Likewise, when Nestor complained to his brother that Ernestina wasn't showing him the proper respect and Gilberto reprimanded her for it, she felt like a failure according to the laws of *marianismo*. Granted, she was experiencing a cultural collision between Hispanic expectations of female dependency and subservience to her men and her anger at being treated like a doormat, but that only intensified her unhappiness with herself.

Latinas and the Need for Approval

Part of the problem is that self-worth is also tied to approval. This explains why for many Latinas the need for approval is very, very strong. It is also what makes us become more dependent on others than we should be.

Dependence on someone else is a necessity of life. We have to depend on those we love and trust for support, care, affection, and in order to feel better when we're going through difficult times. But positive dependency, like so many things in life, is a matter of degree. Consequently, if we look to these same people to validate our sense of personal worth and to do things for us that we should do for ourselves—such as decision making about issues that affect us personally—then our relationship with them is *enfermiza,* or unhealthy. We would probably all agree that a person is overly dependent if she or he regularly subordinates his or her own will to another and is unable to make independent or mutual decisions.

It is crucial for you to be able to distinguish when you're relating to your significant others mutually from when you're acting dependently in an unhealthy manner. By the way, this dependency can flow from them to you. But in this instance we will refer to your dependency on them. You depend on others to validate you, to make you feel okay about yourself. Also, without realizing it, you may be encouraging your children and husband or partner to expect you to be reciprocally responsible for making them feel good. Unless you do everything for them, *no te sientes una mujer completa,* you don't feel whole. But in truth, to achieve that wholeness you and only you—not those with whom you have relationships—must be the force driving your self-esteem. We'll see how to accomplish this later on, but first let's look at some examples that illustrate clearly how trying to be selfless coupled with the need for approval can have very destructive results.

DOÑA QUIXOTE

Maria, a twenty-eight-year-old Dominican-American, always dreamed of going to school and becoming a nurse. Instead, she married Pedro, who was determined to go to medical school. After they emigrated from the Dominican Republic to New York, Pedro was able to achieve his dream bankrolled by Maria's salary as an executive secretary. Once he became a doctor, Maria expressed the desire to stop working and realize her own ambition of becoming a nurse. Pedro had no objections, even to her hiring a housekeeper—as long as she did all the domestic planning and continued to provide him with fresh-squeezed orange juice in the mornings, make sure he had clean clothes in his closet, and be a "trophy" wife who always looked like a fashion plate.

Like a good *marianista*, Maria obliged her husband by becoming everything to everyone. It is to her great credit that she was able to get her nursing degree and secured a position which she loved. As she advanced steadily in her career, Santa Maria continued to be the perfect wife and housekeeper. Then a series of events occurred which would send her to therapy. Around the time that Maria gave birth to a baby girl, Pedro's father died, and it was decided that his widowed mother would come to live with them. The woman was intensely critical and highly demanding, and she wouldn't leave Maria alone.

But what was the young mother to do? She didn't feel she could complain to her husband, because in all probability he would simply get upset and insist that honoring his mother was part of being *una buena esposa*. What was particularly galling to Maria was that her husband had brothers and sisters who were willing to take in their mother, but Doña Eva insisted on living with her darling Pedro and behaving like a queen—even monopolizing the bathroom in the morning when everyone else in the family had to get to work or school.

Next, Maria was offered a wonderful work opportunity in

Philadelphia, which she had to refuse because Pedro's practice was in the New York area.

Maria was clear in her mind about wanting her career, but she shared with many other women in this book a sense of guilt that spilled over into many areas of life. That's because they all depended on others to define their self-esteem and self-worth based on their fulfillment of certain traditional roles. We have repeatedly acknowledged that some of the problems described are shared universally by women of every ethnic persuasion. But we know from professional experience that having to be the ideal woman in order to feel good about yourself is widespread among Latinas. Maria is a perfect example.

Maria was becoming increasingly unhappy, depressed, and anxious. Despite that, she never complained to Pedro because she felt that selflessness was her duty. Every *marianista* bone in her body told her every time she felt imposed upon or disappointed in her own desires that she was being the worst thing a Latin wife and mother can be. She was being selfish.

"I know how crazy this sounds," she told her therapist, "but I would just feel so selfish asking my mother-in-law to leave." When asked what was so bad about being "selfish" in a situation where she was being psychologically and verbally abused, she insisted that the therapist *simplemente no la entendía,* just didn't get it. First she cited as a role model her grandmother, who had sacrificed for the good of her family to the point of sainthood. "And I," Maria continued, "I'm not even able to support my husband when he wants to take care of his mother."

The fact that her grandmother's selflessness happened in a time and place remote from Maria's life didn't seem to occur to the young woman. What she finally could understand is that she was trying to be her grandmother. "And," the therapist added, "your mother-in-law and your mother!" In point of fact, Maria was trying to be a good wife and mother, a trusting friend, a perfect hostess, and all the rest of the roles assigned to her in the *marianista* package. "From now on," her therapist quipped, "I'm going to call you Maria Doña Quixote because you're trying to fulfill the impossible dream!"

THE PLACE WHERE SELF-FULLNESS BEGINS

If you find yourself caught in a bind between selflessness and selfishness, if you realize that doing your duty is making you feel bad about yourself but that not doing it overwhelms you with guilt, you've got to step back and try to assess objectively what's going on. The old saying has it that a journey begins with a single step. For you, that's literally true. That first step back is where your journey to self-fullness starts.

Look at it this way: Every situation consists of a series of circumstances. What you have to do is examine them.

When you do things solely for yourself, how do you feel? If you never, or rarely, do so, make an effort right now to list the things you dream of doing for yourself alone.

¿Hay alguna cosa que en este preciso instante tú verdaderamente disfrutaría? Is there anything you can think of this very minute that you would genuinely enjoy? Contemplate it and your feelings toward even thinking about it. If you feel guilty, you need to have a dialogue with yourself. Bearing in mind that your goal is to be accepting of yourself, list five reasons why you deserve to do this activity.

Be as imaginative as you like and let your fantasies run free. Of course, if you choose activities which are realistically within your grasp, you may not have to wait as long to attain them. But in any event, fantasies, especially when written down, can tell us a lot about ourselves.

Now list several activities you do for others that you genuinely dislike—such as supermarket shopping or always being the one to get up to tend to the baby in the middle of the night. How do you feel about doing these things? Are you falling into the trap of believing they are your sole responsibility? Remember, they are only if you think they are. Do not use your mother as a role model, because her cultural conditioning was different, and who's to assume she was any happier about these issues than you are?

Can you tell yourself how you react to criticism about things you regard as your sole responsibility? Around whom does this responsibility revolve? Your husband? Your mate? Your boyfriend? Your children? Your mother? Your mother-in-law?

Now take a blank piece of paper and write down areas where improving your performance would make you feel good about yourself. Examine them one by one and ask yourself, "Why do I feel this way? Who wants me to improve my performance—me, or someone else?"

Of course, it's always possible that, given the support and nurturance you get from a significant other, acceding to his or her demands may well be worth the personal sacrifice. But you have to understand that if you don't feel the request is justified, doing it anyway in order to please someone else won't make you feel good in the long run. Instead, you must ask yourself what compromise you can work out to make the situation more tolerable for everyone concerned, including yourself.

Should Maria have asked Pedro if he would speak to his mother about waiting to use the bathroom until they left for work?

Should she have conveyed to Pedro the difficulty involved in dealing with her mother-in-law's constant demands when there were relatives who could have helped take some of the pressure off Maria by inviting Doña Eva to stay with them for limited visits—perhaps on a rotating schedule?

Or should she simply have continued to obey the rules of *marianismo* and put up with her mother-in-law's demands and derision with a silent sigh?

If you believe, as Maria initially did, that you must be selfless because you'll be better loved and viewed as a better person as long as you put others' needs before your own, *tú sólo estás buscando líos*, you're only asking for trouble. In contemporary society, the price you'll pay for hiding behind your *marianista* selflessness is never feeling truly secure in that love. That's because it doesn't come from within you, but from others.

It is really true that loving yourself is a prerequisite to receiving love from others—as well as fully giving it. To call a self-loving person selfish is not only misguided, it's genuinely unhealthy. Look at Clara.

Recognizing Selflessness

Clara is a Nicaraguan social worker in her late thirties, whose husband, Roberto—an engineer—lost his job and was unemployed for two full years. Although she was now the sole support of the family, Clara turned her paycheck over to Roberto every week to help him maintain his *macho* by continuing to manage the family finances. Unfortunately, he dipped freely into the money to bankroll the lifestyle he'd enjoyed when he was working. Whether he was adding to his CD collection, buying expensive art, or going out for the evening *con sus amigos*, he refused to acknowledge the need to make sacrifices until he was employed again.

Although Roberto's behavior was extremely upsetting to Clara, she didn't say a word to him because *marianismo* mandates you do not challenge male authority and must always stand by your man. Instead, she tried increasingly harder to cut down on her own expenses, stopped buying clothes, and gave up going to the movies *con sus amigas*. Of course, when her two small children needed something, she bought them the very best. It was only herself she denied. Eventually, Clara developed a stomach ulcer and became chronically sad and weepy. At the suggestion of her medical doctor, she came to therapy—but didn't even know she was anxious and depressed, or that her anger and self-imposed victimization were making her physically sick.

Like Maria, Clara felt it was her duty to stand by her husband. After all, she insisted, he was feeling bad about himself because he'd lost his job and was no longer the family's provider. And she had grown up with the belief that men always need to be taken care of—as well as with the *marianista* tenet that women are born to sacrifice. Since childhood, Clara's role model had been her mother, whom she considered saintly. Widowed at thirty, she had never remarried. Clara proudly recounted that her mother had been so totally dedicated to her and her brother and sister that she rarely left the house except to go to church, to the market, or occasionally to visit relatives. But that sense of "blind" devotion which Clara so admired in her mother was the very same emotion which was, in a different context, causing her such grief.

If we think of Maria and Pedro's mother, of Ernestina and her brother-in-law, of Clara with her insensitive husband, as a group, we see they share the theme of selflessness at the expense of sinking self-esteem. Every one of these women allowed herself to be victimized and exploited. Every one of them believed, as *marianismo* told her, that suffering and sacrifice was her lot in life.

Perhaps you're in a situation similar to Clara's, Ernestina's, or Maria's. Take whatever predicament involving selflessness is bothering you presently. Are you telling yourself, "*Tengo que ser buena.* I am duty-bound to be good"? Imagine you are a friend of yours. Hold an inner dialogue with that friend and make sure she is understanding and noncritical. Allow your imaginary friend to tell you you shouldn't put up with any situation which makes you feel like a victim.

After you've completed this exercise, go to an actual person, your *mejor amiga*. Make sure, of course, that this best friend is also understanding and noncritical. After you've spoken to her about your problem, compare this actual conversation with your imaginary one.

Hopefully, what you'll learn from these exercises is that by being selfless, you are unconsciously following a rigidly defined cultural norm which could be making you extremely unhappy. You'll also come to realize that you have options and models other than the ones you've chosen in the past. There's no doubt that in your new country, new challenges and choices are being offered you. And these include the chance to develop your sense of self-fullness.

As you read through the rest of the stories in this book and find one that you strongly identify with, make a point of analyzing the problem before you read the solution, then devise your own solution. After you've done that, read the rest of the vignette and see how close you came to what the woman was actually helped to do. Following is a brief story illustrating both the woman's problem and how she solved it, so that you can practice the above exercise.

• • •

Josefa, a Cuban-American, needed a lot of hard therapeutic work before she could ask her eight-year-old daughter and thirteen- and fifteen-year-old sons to help out with the extremely time-consuming task of handling the bills at a grocery store she and her husband owned in Queens, New York. Her husband, Manuel, was a hardworking man who had emigrated to New York from Spain. In fact, he was the stereotypical workaholic immigrant. His industry had turned their little store into a thriving supermarket, and he'd expanded into other areas of enterprise, including a food delivery service. Josefa didn't understand why Manuel refused to hire outside help or install a computer setup and fax machine.

Indeed, as the family business became larger and more successful, Josefa could hardly handle the growing mountain of work which managing the bills required. That task alone consumed as much as seventeen hours a day. In addition, she had other business-related duties to attend to, as well as all the chores required of a conscientious Latina wife and mother. There was no question that Manuel put as much time into the business as Josefa did, but he didn't have to keep house and see to the kids' needs.

When Josefa came to therapy, she was on the point of physical collapse and very depressed. But when asked to think about what she could do to change things, she quickly replied, "Hire an accountant," then added she felt it was a waste of time to mention this to Manuel. Deep inside, not being able to handle the accounting made her feel inadequate. Nevertheless, the therapist pressed her to explore short- and long-term solutions in her sessions. Eventually, with the plans formulated, Josefa had proof that she could come up with a plan to make her life easier. She also realized she was assuming responsibility for everyone's happiness at the expense of her own.

Rather than try to approach Manuel directly, Josefa discussed the situation with relatives in other businesses, who brought the suggestion to her husband. Only then did she realize that Manuel hadn't taken the action because he was afraid outsiders would steal from him. She further came to appreciate that he was following the traditional Spanish cultural dictate that businesses should be family-run.

Now that Josefa had achieved some emotional distance between her own needs and her *marianista* compulsion to be totally devoted to her husband and his business, she was able to discuss matters with her husband rationally and put her time to better use. She was then able to start doing good things for herself, such as taking a few days off from the store to go shopping or have lunch with friends. She even allowed herself to sleep late every now and then. One day she was able to confess in therapy, *"¡Mi vida está más llena!"* My life is really more fulfilled! Without a doubt, taking care of yourself is the best antidote available for depleted self-worth.

It will come as no surprise that initially when Josefa started making changes with her family, her husband and children felt she was being selfish, not self-full. Her way of dealing with that was to gather the family together and get all of them to air their views without getting angry. When her husband accused her of being lazy, she calmly responded that she couldn't continue her previous grueling schedule indefinitely. "If I continue like this, I'm going to get sick and not be any good to anyone," she explained.

She went on to tell her family that she was working two full-time jobs, as a shopkeeper and as a homemaker, a task which is humanly impossible to do. Then she asked them to help her out by making their own breakfasts on weekends and allowing her a little time off from the store at regular intervals—as well as from the kitchen at night. The kids, she suggested, could work up a rotating schedule themselves so that they could all do "store duty" and "dinner duty" when it best fit into their school schedules. What Josefa was doing was empowering herself.

Like Josefa, you must learn to feel responsible for—and entitled to—your own happiness. This isn't easy for many Latinas since, here again, empowerment is another concept that doesn't exist in Hispanic culture. In fact, we've asked many of our colleagues throughout Latin America to translate "empowerment," and we all agree there is no word for it. If there were one, it would be *empoderamiento*, but as you'll probably agree, it doesn't convey the same weight in Spanish. In any event, the Latina in North America must understand that she has choices, realistic ones. She must realize she can negotiate solutions. She should not fear asking for help with domestic chores from her husband, mate, and/or children—or from a housekeeper, if finances allow it. If both she and her husband work, day care is a strong possibility. The danger here is that many Latinas are too perfectionistic to ask for these kinds of help.

Don't be one of them! Grow comfortable acknowledging that there are limits to your time and energy! Failing to do the impossible does not make you *una mala persona*. Indeed, defining yourself as a "good" person doesn't have to depend on sacrifice or on stretching yourself so thin that eventually you can't be any use to anyone. Remember, you can still maintain many of the beautiful traditions of our culture within your family, but you don't have to do it so alone, and you don't have to become a martyr in the process. We'll deal in depth with this issue of being everything to everyone in Chapter 8 and prove to you there are wonderfully workable solutions to your seemingly unsolvable problems.

Egotism—or Empowerment?

Remembering that she had a right to take care of her needs was key to Maria's ultimately getting her mother-in-law out of the house, without starting a war. In the process, Maria also learned that Pedro's cultural expectations were very traditional, very *macho*. It wasn't his fault that he assumed his wife would show his mother the proper respect. He'd learned his behavior since childhood, just as Maria had. Once she could distance herself enough to appreciate her husband's predicament, she could begin to empathize with his position and factor it into whatever solution she devised.

Maria explained to Pedro that she knew he was himself a prisoner of his mother's demands, and she acknowledged how difficult assuming responsibility for Doña Eva's well-being must be for him. Surprisingly, he responded by telling Maria how much he appreciated her understanding his predicament. Soon he was sharing with his wife how angry he became when his mother was whiny and hypercritical. Before long, husband and wife were united in trying to find a solution to what they both regarded as a major domestic dilemma.

You should note that Maria turned Pedro from her adversary into her ally by approaching him calmly and without anger—with sympathy for him instead of antagonism or desperation. She learned that the bottom line in getting what you want from others is understanding what they feel—and why they do it. Once Maria and Pedro confronted together the *macho* mandate that an only son must assume responsibility for a widowed mother, he could admit he didn't want to, especially since his sister was more than willing to take Doña Eva. In fact, he confessed that he needed Maria on his side if a solution was to be worked out. For the first time, Maria could maintain some objectivity and not slip into the *marianista* mode of behaving like her grandmother.

Maria and Pedro called a family meeting with Pedro's sisters. Without anger or accusations, they suggested that all the siblings examine the problem with their mother and come up with possible solutions together. When some of the sisters insisted their mother be humored in whatever she wanted, Maria knew they were behaving according to traditional *familismo* and didn't take their opinions personally.

With Pedro backing her, Maria explained to her in-laws that having had to defer to her mother-in-law's chronic demands for three long years while holding a full-time job, managing the house, and being a good mother to a growing daughter had put more stress on her than she could handle. They proposed that since Pedro's older sister had the room and had offered to take in Doña Eva, that alternative should be presented to the older woman. At that point, Maria and Pedro could assure her that the move was only temporary, until Maria's daughter was older. Lo and behold, when the plan was presented to Doña Eva, she went along with it. Once she was living with her daughter in a larger space, she herself realized she was happier and could still visit her son periodically.

It is a tribute to Maria's new ability to think rationally without blaming others, and to involve all interested parties in the decision-making process that the mother-in-law problem was solved so amicably. Never make the mistake of feeling you must solve problems yourself, especially when the solution requires others' input. If you do, you're shortchanging, even undercutting yourself significantly. Once Maria appreciated the difference between selfishness and self-fullness, the impossible dream became reality.

Granted, the concept of selfishness means different things to different people. However, we took an informal survey of women we know to try to arrive at a working definition. We found that almost universally, selfishness has a negative connotation. For the most part, it was defined as being overly concerned with oneself, seeking pleasure, or ensuring your own well-being at the expense of others. The definition also tended to include an all-or-nothing element, since it stressed satisfying yourself at all costs. Actually, we see selfishness a little differently. While there are countless people who thoughtlessly use others to get what they want, there are also many who possess what we call positive selfishness, or self-fullness. These people are motivated by healthy self-love.

What exactly does it mean to be self-full—as opposed to self-fulfilled? When we take the word apart, we see it means allowing yourself to have a sense of inner satisfaction. Think of the difference between feeling hungry and feeling satisfied. Which would you prefer? Self-fullness permits you to take care of your needs by sorting out what is fair for you to do for others and what others should be doing for themselves. It implies responsibility for providing yourself with a sense of comfort, peace, and happiness as opposed to constant sadness.

In summary, self-fullness means first being aware of your needs, then sorting out the reality of those needs to prepare to fulfill them. It mandates thinking of yourself without guilt or blame. Thinking and

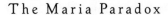

giving to yourself does not mean hurting others in the process. It means you are making sure you care about your own quality of life. It also means to allow or ask others to help you.

Maria was able to make her life more bearable and her self-esteem healthier by making the following moves, which you should take good note of:

1. She confronted the fact that cultural beliefs were putting terrible pressure on her and her family.
2. She defined just what those beliefs were and the specific negative effects they were having on everyone concerned, starting with herself.
3. She realized she was taking sole responsibility in situations which should have been shared emotionally and physically with others.
4. She acknowledged her right to be self-full and acted on it.

Let's now investigate how Clara learned to consider her own needs and get her unemployed husband, Roberto, to be more sensitive to them. Before she could truly begin to act out of self-fullness, she first had to understand her identification with her mother and then to initiate a candid conversation with her. To Clara's surprise, her mother confessed she regretted never having remarried. Now that her children were adults with families of their own, she felt extremely lonely in her home. However, she added, staying single was her destiny, and had she married again, the match would have been harshly disapproved of by her relatives and friends. Last, she urged Clara *a no seguir en sus mismos pasos,* not to follow in her footsteps, but to think of herself and her own needs and desires. Clara's mother was giving her permission to be self-full.

At last Clara felt entitled and empowered to confront Roberto and ask him to take responsibility *en no ser un botarate,* for not being a spendthrift and for helping around the house now that he had the time. She did this gently, suggesting that she needed his support. By catering to his *macho*, she got her point across. First Roberto began to chauffeur the children to school, lessons, and birthday parties. This was a small start, but Clara made sure to express her appreciation to him. Armed with that appreciation, he gradually began helping around the house, even attempting to do some of the cooking—always with Clara's appreciation as a reward. Clara also knew that, in truth, Roberto wasn't cut out for housework and would do anything to get out of it. Which he did. In record time he found a new job!

Now back to Ernestina, the woman with the freeloading brother-in-law. Nestor's outrageous behavior, coupled with her husband's inability to understand her objections to it, persisted for the next few years, as Ernestina's self-worth steadily declined. Eventually, Nestor did move out—to live with his brother Gilberto who had left Ernestina for another woman. That's when she started her voyage of renewal.

When Gilberto first walked out on her, Ernestina fell apart, often feeling victimized, lonely, and despondent. Then *se levantó*, she picked herself up, and started being good to herself—taking bubble baths, going out to dinner and the movies with friends, taking long walks and bicycling with her kids. She also accepted the fact that she was entitled to be angry, and subsequently used that anger to energize herself. She reached out instead of allowing her husband's and brother-in-law's behavior to destroy her. She didn't blame herself for Gilberto's leaving her for another woman. She placed the blame squarely where it belonged, on him, and decided to go on with her life.

Is Ernestina's bravery unusual? Probably not. We know of many Latinas who rise to tragedy and muster the courage to do whatever it takes to survive and become self-full. We'd be the last to deny that the process takes an enormous amount of work, but the results are more than worth it. The case of Ernestina is a beautiful example of a woman's strength. Note that she employed part of the *marianista* motto that women are spiritually superior to men and added a new definition to it: Women are spiritually superior to men and capable of changing their own suffering.

When asked how she did it, Ernestina said, "I had no choice. I have three children." But she must be given enormous credit for venturing into divorce with two boys and a daughter. She got a job at a cargo airline before filing for the divorce, so she was sure her family would have an income whatever happened. Regardless, many of her relatives blamed her for "destroying her marriage." "In that respect," she added, "I guess I wasn't a hundred percent successful. But I'll tell you that first I thought of my children but then I began to think of myself."

Ernestina was fortunate to have a loyal group of women friends, who supported her every step of the way. "It was difficult at first," she remembered, "but I kept telling myself that it was more difficult to put up with my brother-in-law's unspeakable behavior, and what I made myself admit was my husband's philandering. I prayed a lot and did good things for myself. But most important, I created a mantra and stuck to it. 'You can do it. You can stop this abuse. You can do it,' I said, I don't even know how many times a day." (See page 111, where a mantra is explained.)

Once Ernestina acknowledged she deserved a lot better than she was getting, she began to feel a healthy sense of entitlement. She stopped being selfless and became self-full. She put aside the cultural stereotypes which had previously dominated her. Refusing to define her worthiness in terms of what a good *marianista* wife and mother was, she now thought instead of what was beneficial for her children and herself.

Ernestina is an average human being who learned to believe in herself.

Do you believe in yourself?

Are you afraid to believe in yourself?

What do you regard as your inner strengths?

Try saving some quiet time in which you write down your good points as well as your sources of support. Try not to allow any negative thoughts to creep into the process, and don't use the excuse that you have no good points. Keep thinking until you come up with at least five things you admire in yourself and as many sources of support as you can muster.

Ask yourself, "Isn't it better to go through rough times for a while with the support of family, friends, or psychotherapy than to remain in a painful and unhealthy situation?"

❋ YOU ARE YOUR CHOICES

Empowerment can only be acquired through the choices you make. If you don't make any, you have no control over your life and consequently no power. So don't allow yourself to cling to the negative aspects of *marianismo* at the cost of your own self-worth. Try some of the methods we recommend throughout *The Maria Paradox*. Hopefully, doing so will give you a new sense of control, and will make you feel the freedom and enthusiasm of being your own person at last.

Also, look at the cultural dictates presented in this book and see which ones are helpful to you and which are making you miserable. Then create your own options, which include retaining the concepts that are supportive and helpful to you. For example, a *macho* dictate is responsibility for the woman. Turn it to your advantage, *abandonándote a la merced de tu macho*, throwing yourself on your man's support, when necessary. Use it in a new way by making him feel that giving you what you deserve is part of that responsibility. Remember, a key aspect of self-fullness means learning to negotiate with significant others.

Don't ever lose sight of the need to give to yourself. Become your own mother by listening to your feelings, believing in them, giving yourself permission to rest when you're exhausted. That's what you'd do for your children. Now do it for yourself! If the weight of your duties becomes overwhelming, ask for help. And never forget that you must have the courage to confront what is making you unhappy before you can begin the journey to the highest level of self-fullness. If anybody has earned it, you have.

5

"Do Not Wish for
More in Life than
Being a Housewife":

━━

*The World of Work vs.
the World of Home*

A forty-two-year-old Colombian-American friend of ours named Sonia was, until a recent career advancement, deputy commissioner of a New York City governmental agency. Sonia was with the agency for twelve years, moving up to become *la mano derecha*, the right-hand person, of her boss the commissioner. Many colleagues felt she actually ran the place, since the commissioner was a political appointee without Sonia's managerial experience. Among her duties were labor negotiations, interdepartmental relations, and representing her boss at after-hour functions, as well as meeting with labor unions. Clearly, she was delegated substantial responsibility, which she handled with extreme professionalism and competence.

But Sonia didn't get that far without having to grapple with some very painful personal choices. She remembers vividly the constant conflicts with her mother and with her husband, a successful Latino attorney, when she announced she was going for a master's degree in business administration and would no longer be a full-time housewife. She also recalls the guilt she felt about not always being there for her teenaged daughter.

However, Sonia realized she wasn't happy being only *una mujer de su casa*. In addition to being a wife and mother, she knew she needed a career to feel fulfilled, and she intended to have one. In order to get what she felt she deserved, Sonia had to do battle with her husband, her mamá, but most especially with herself. She says she'll never forget the intensity of the deep-seated doubt and guilt she had to endure before she could move beyond *marianismo*, have the career, and maintain a healthy self-esteem.

Conflicted like Sonia or not, Hispanic women are joining the American workforce in steadily increasing numbers—as the following statistics dramatically prove.

According to figures provided by the Census Bureau and the Department of Labor Women's Bureau, the labor-force participation rate for Hispanic men and women, 67.4 percent, is higher than for all whites (66.2 percent) and for all African-Americans (63.8 percent). Hispanic women achieved a milestone in the late eighties when, for the first time, 50 percent of Latinas sixteen years and up were employed—3.6 million, to be exact. Forty-one percent were concentrated in the technical, sales, and administrative support occupations such as computer operators, secretaries, bookkeepers, teachers' aides, registered nurses, and social work assistants; 21.7 percent were employed in the service occupations, among them, child care work, waitressing, and household cleaning; and only 15.7 percent served as managers and professionals.

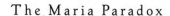
By the year 2000, it is projected that 5.8 million—a stunning 57 percent of the Hispanic female population in North America will be working. And an untold number of us will be burdened with culture- and gender-based career conflicts.

In this chapter, we'll discuss with you the inner conflicts many Latinas experience because of work-related issues—among them, the competing demands of family and job. We're going to give you examples from our clinical practices of Hispanic women who have successfully resolved these conflicts and brokered a compromise between home and career. We'll help you learn to navigate through these dual worlds as they did, including learning to be assertive without being aggressive, keeping the male status quo at bay, turning traditional Latino/a behaviors to new advantage, and dealing with the anxieties and rough patches that change always brings. Like these women, you'll be learning to modify or relinquish the principles of *marianismo* in favor of self-esteem. The process is worth every ounce of determination you put into it—but it's not going to be simple or easy. In terms of *marianismo*, you'll be heading straight into the eye of the hurricane.

WHEN SUCCESS EQUALS FAILURE

Let's take our friend Sonia as an example of what we mean. When her mother and husband condemned her for wanting to continue her education at what they perceived to be the expense of her roles as wife and mother, Sonia had to fight hard to maintain her self-esteem. If she hadn't battled against *marianista* tradition, success would have made her feel like a failure because she would have accepted her family's views of her as a less than perfect wife and mother.

Think about it. To many, many Latinas who are pursuing careers outside of homemaking, *el triunfo en el trabajo*, success in work, is a mixed blessing. The more successful they become in the North American world of work, the less successful they feel as Hispanic women. Too often they unknowingly find themselves in the grip of an identity crisis.

Remember Rosario, the young woman with the Anglo boyfriend and the traditional Hispanic family in Chapter 2? Eventually, her cultural conflicts became severe enough that she began therapy, claiming she was having an identity crisis. Let's explore now what that really means. The *Dictionary of Behavioral Science* defines identity as the way the individual orients him/herself to the external world—in other words, the outward expression of yourself, the "me" which is recognized and responded to by family members, friends, colleagues, and associates. In a society like North America, which is founded on the work ethic, identity is most widely and seriously defined through work—which is to say that our jobs go a long way to making us feel good or bad about ourselves.

Many Latinas first enter the workforce when they enter the United States, which means that during the overwhelming changes that accompany emigration, work-related problems and conflicts tend to be overlooked. It is at this stage that Latinas feel conflicted between the *marianismo* mandate to stay home and the economic reality of needing to work outside the home. This is especially unfortunate because it is in this venue that the clash between Old World values and New World expectations has some of the strongest impact and repercussions on a Latina's sense of self. She craves the automatic respect and support of *familismo*, yet she badly desires the status and respect in the workplace which was unthinkable to her mother and to her grandmother. She isn't sure how assertive she wants to appear in either sphere. She doesn't know whether co-workers look down on her for being shy or her family for being tremendously rebellious. Through no fault of her own, she is in crisis because her identity becomes a blur.

As a Latina in North America, in what situations do you feel the most uncertain about who you are?

What are your three greatest dreams for yourself? Can you express them to your loved ones?

Is there anyone you can talk to when your dreams clash with your expectations, or economic necessity comes up against tradition?

It's vital to remember that a majority of the millions of working

Latinas are doing so out of economic need. Either along with or instead of a man, they are assuming *el rol de proveedor*, the role of the breadwinner. In nineties North America, they are feeling pressured to cast aside traditional *marianista* self-stereotyping in order to safeguard their family's welfare. However, far too frequently their men have not assumed any of the homemaking functions—either because the woman doesn't feel comfortable asking or because the man sees the idea of housekeeping as not in keeping with *un macho*'s role. It is this precarious balancing act between being a wage earner and a nurturer that is saddling us with a whole new burden of guilt, anxiety, and depression.

How many women in your family go to work or college? How are they regarded by their relatives? How do you feel about them?

Let's look at it this way. *Marianismo* demands that we take care of the children and run the household and feel happy to do it. While our husband's place is outside the home providing for the family, ours most decidedly is not. Even to this day, it's all too true that whether or not they become corporate VPs, many single and/or childless Latinas are devalued. They have not lived up to what was expected of them. *¡Son menos mujeres!* They are behaving like men!

And let's face it, today in North America being a full-time mother doesn't get the very high premium it may get in your country. Anglas have been joining the labor force en masse since the seventies, and by the eighties the multiple-earner family became the norm. There has also been a rapid escalation in the number of families maintained by mothers with preschool children who, out of necessity, have to work, sometimes at two or more jobs. Even more surprising, a recent Gallup poll published by *The New York Times* revealed that North American wives now share equally with their husbands in supporting the family—with 48 percent of the women surveyed reporting they provided at least half the combined income.

The bottom line is that whether out of need or desire, the North American woman works. If you want to be *una marianista* in good standing, North American society may have only a marginal place for you. Latinas must learn that professional competence is every bit as acceptable a source of female self-esteem as being a good wife and mother.

Fear of Success

That said, we have both found that Latinas rarely come to therapy consciously expressing anxiety about wage earning. Instead, they usually begin by talking about marital difficulties or problems with children or other family members. It's only in the course of treatment that work-related issues begin to emerge. Take the case of Cecilia.

"My marriage is my top priority. I guess I'm just old-fashioned," she began. Cecilia—a twenty-six-year-old Mexican woman married to an American physician and living in New York—was anxious and depressed because she felt she was inadequate as a homemaker. "I'm a perfectionist," she continued, "and I really punish myself if I don't do things well." In Mexico City, a maid had done the cooking, cleaning, and marketing under her mother's supervision, so Cecilia had never had to learn those skills. Now, without even her mother's direction, she was drowning in a sea of self-condemnation.

Like many Latinas, Cecilia tended to focus on what she perceived as her faults and minimize her professional strengths, intellectual capacities, and career ambitions—all considered cardinal sins in the *marianista* dogma. She also repeatedly undervalued herself by assuming there was "something wrong" with her. In actuality, by feeling helpless and inadequate, she was using *marianismo* to hide more pressing problems from herself. But as her identity crisis built, the real nature of her conflict began to surface.

Although educated as a medical anthropologist, Cecilia had never worked in the field. Now, after two years in New York, she was feeling the first stirrings of wanting more from life than being a perfect wife. She wanted a job. "If I'd stayed in Mexico City, I'm sure I wouldn't be having these feelings," she confessed. "I'd have just stayed home, like other women of my class. But things are so different here." Once she accepted the fact that North American wives worked outside the home as a matter of course, Cecilia abruptly changed her mind. All at once, she felt unrecognized and disrespected because she didn't have a career. She even began to feel envious of her husband, George, and suddenly found herself wanting to compete for respect with him. Cultural conflicts were lowering her self-esteem and blurring her self-image. Still, in one particular way, Cecilia was very lucky. She had the support of an understanding man. George, from the outset, had said he would support her in any career choice she made.

When Your Man Is Part of the Problem

We appreciate that for many Hispanic women married to Latinos, and for Anglas with Latino partners, things may be much more complicated than they were for Cecilia, whose husband was on her side. We must never forget that the Latino man has been raised to believe it's his birthright to have a woman waiting for him at the end of the day—with a bright smile and a hot meal. When that deeply ingrained pattern is disturbed or altered, he may feel his whole world has collapsed.

In addition, especially if immigration has put more job stress on the man, he may feel vulnerable about his *machismo* and be harsh in his resentment of his wife's wanting—or needing—to support him financially. If a man's *machismo* is threatened, he may respond by making his woman behave in a more subservient fashion, to bolster his own flagging self-esteem.

The case of Cindy, a forty-five-year-old North American, comes to mind here. She was referred to therapy by Dr. Perez, a Colombian physician, who was a friend of her fifty-seven-year-old Cuban husband, Carlos, after she'd been complaining of depression, insomnia, and stomach problems. Carlos accompanied Cindy to her first session, although he was clearly less than thrilled to be there. Cindy and Carlos had been married for ten years. They had met at the large Manhattan advertising agency where they still worked. In fact, Cindy reported to Carlos. It was the second marriage for both, and they both had grown children and were grandparents.

When they'd first met, Cindy had instantly fallen in love with this attractive Latino who was always *un caballero* during courtship, showing a concern and forcefulness that made her feel secure and loved. Now, though, he had become irrationally jealous and tremendously possessive, demanding she cater to his every whim and obey him at all times. If she so much as had a conversation with a male co-worker at an office party, Carlos would accuse her of flirting. If his dinner wasn't on the table exactly when he wanted it, he would bellow that she wasn't doing her wifely duty. His shirts were never ironed properly, according to him, and the house was never neat enough. Cindy was beginning to feel both bullied and inadequate.

If Cindy's story strikes a familiar chord in you, we feel it is imperative that you seek a support system outside the family: in a therapeutic relationship, a support group, or dialogues with your *comadres*—women friends who are not family but who share trust, confidence, and loyalty, and who help one another.

Ask yourself:

• How do the men in my life—father, boyfriend, husband, brother—feel about my educational and career goals?
• Have they encouraged me?
• If so, were they willing to do household tasks traditionally performed by women?
• Have they discouraged me?
• If so, what did they say?
• How did their negativity make me feel?
• Did my feelings affect my life choices?
• Did I consider that their resentment might stem from insecurities of their own?

On that score, it might interest you to learn that data gathered from the 1990 census by Robert Brischetto in *Hispanic Business* shows that for the first time, there were more professional Hispanic women than Hispanic men—although the women were still underrepresented in higher-paying professions. In fact, the number of professional Hispanic females doubled during the 1980s. However, while traditional female occupations such as teaching account for nearly half of all these women, the greatest growth ratio has been in professions traditionally overrepresented by men.

Brischetto, using a "growth ratio" formula (meaning the number of professionals in 1990 divided by the number in 1980), reported that Latinas had a 4.7 growth ratio among mathematicians and computer scientists, 3.2 among lawyers and judges, 3.1 among social scientists and urban planners, and 3.0 among engineers, architects, and surveyors. These data suggest that Latinas are moving rapidly into professional positions, which strongly implies that on a personal level they are being confronted with new and dynamic conflicts between *marianista* principles and American career expectations. Take Mercedes, for example.

Grace under Pressure

A thirty-five-year-old Cuban-American, Mercedes worked at a prestigious San Francisco law firm but wasn't happy. "If I want to make partner," she complained, "I must behave like a man and kill off anybody who gets in my way." Her words ring true to women of all backgrounds and aspirations. It does seem that what it takes to get ahead is measured in such male attributes as aggressiveness, competitiveness, analytical thinking, task orientation, power seeking, impersonal relationships, and invulnerability to feedback.

For many Latinas like Mercedes, adopting these male attributes leads to a conflict between being a success and being a woman. Maybe because of that fact, we've observed that many Latinas avoid competitive situations in their jobs even at the cost of their own career advancement. Perhaps you remember that when you were a child, the females in your family scolded you for fighting with your brother, saying, *"Las niñas no pelean con los hermanos"*—Little girls aren't allowed to fight with their brothers. This translates into the rule that women must not compete against men, certainly not in the business world. Traditionally, the only acceptable form of competition has been with another woman for the love of a man.

Ask yourself:

- What does being a woman in a man's world mean to you?
- How do words like "aggressive," "competitive," "ambitious," and "power-conscious" make you feel?
- What qualities about yourself give you the most pride?
- How much satisfaction do you derive from your career success?
- Do you feel guilt or anxiety when you find yourself competing with a co-worker in the workplace?
- If you could, would you prefer to stay home and take care of the children rather than work in the business world?
- How would you feel if, in order to succeed in your career, you must keep late hours at night and could see your children for only half an hour before they go to bed?
- If you ever terminated a personal relationship because it interfered with your career goals, how did you feel?
- Do you feel that in order to succeeed in your career you have to give up your role as a wife and mother?

 ## GLASS CEILING VS. STICKY FLOOR

It's difficult to deny that a majority of women, regardless of race or ethnicity, face job discrimination solely on the basis of gender. This is what is meant by the "glass ceiling," a term signifying that fewer qualified, competent women have the top jobs and sit on corporate America's boards of directors than their male counterparts. In fact, *The New York Times* recently reported the findings of a federal commission which studied barriers to promotion in industry and found that despite three decades of affirmative action programs, the glass ceiling continues to block women and minorities from senior managerial positions.

Women in general constitute less than 5 percent of senior executives in industries across the country, according to the federal commission's findings. But the underrepresentation of Latinas in management positions is even more discouraging. In 1988, the Department of Labor found that Latin women constituted only 1.6 percent of all employed managers. Which is to say that for Latinas the path upward is profoundly rocky. In addition to gender discrimination, they must face conflicts created by their culture and drilled into them since childhood—like *marianismo*.

This double bind is best explained by Nelly Galan, a highly successful, thirty-one-year-old Cuban-American media entrepreneur. Galan, who divorced her Latino husband when she was twenty-two, explained in the pages of *The New York Times Magazine* that "in the circle of my family, I'm not accomplished because I'm not married, and I don't have a kid." Galan illustrates perfectly how *marianismo* clashes with career ambitions. The many Latinas who want to shatter the glass ceiling, like Nelly Galan, must deal with a radical reversal of priorities in which, suddenly, husband and children are not only not the be-all and end-all, they are relegated to second place after job and profession.

Further, in order to occupy the executive suite, Hispanic women must display such traits as ambition, competitiveness, assertiveness, independence, and the willingness to work many hours outside the home in a self-disciplined manner—great on a résumé but a possible invitation to rejection if you want a Hispanic husband as part of your life package.

As you can see, it is even more difficult for Latinas to take on the status quo, because they are fighting a war on three fronts as they grapple with pressure from the corporate world, Hispanic culture, and their own divided selves. Clearly, any Latina with managerial ambitions must be especially highly focused, determined, and very brave to battle *contra viento y marea*, against all odds.

THE HIGH COST OF SUCCESS

Let's again refer to our friend Sonia. Her story of pursuing a career in civil government over the objections of her family is one of self-discipline, hard work, and the emotional scars sustained in breaking out of the *marianismo* mold.

Sonia's husband simply refused to accept her for what she was. He also couldn't see himself assuming any of Sonia's household tasks, because according to him, his law career demanded every second of his time. Ultimately, they divorced. That was five years ago, and since then she's dated many men, but really hasn't wanted to get serious. "I traded my successful, Latino ex-husband for a big job," she jokes, then adds more seriously, "I'd like to be able to have it all—a loving and supportive man, more time for my teenaged daughter, and a top executive job. *"¿Por qué los hombres pueden tenerlo todo, y las mujeres no?"* Why can men have it all, and women can't?

Sonia was gratified when her hard work and sacrifice resulted in an appointment as an assistant secretary of a federal agency in Washington. However, before she left her city job, she was asked by her boss, the commissioner, to help interview and select her successor. A white male was eventually chosen for the position—at $15,000 more than Sonia had been making! The commissioner offered the lame explanation that married men merit larger salaries because they have wives and children to support.

This type of upper-echelon job discrimination applies not only to Latinas. In fact, figures from the Department of Labor show that by the late eighties, American women employed as executives, administrators, and managers working full-time had median earnings of $21,874, while their male counterparts made $36,150.

The Sticky Floor

At the other end of the employment spectrum is another barrier for Latinas—the "sticky floor" of low-paying, low-level jobs in state and local government. Professors Sharon L. Harlam and Catherine W. Berheide of the Graduate School of Public Affairs at the University of Albany recently found that 63 percent of Latinas nationwide are stuck in this category. In fact, compared to other racial and ethnic groups, Latinas are the most likely to be secretaries, clerks, typists, toll collectors, and dispatchers—all essential but undervalued occupations with little prestige and less room for advancement.

Take the case of Lucia, a twenty-eight-year-old Puerto Rican who has worked as a bridge toll collector for seven years. She remembers all too well how hard she worked to pass the civil service exam, as well as the loving support of her husband, Jose, also an employee in a state agency. Lucia has always received excellent evaluations from her male boss, so she naturally assumed he was satisfied with her job performance.

However, twice her supervisor has denied her application for a promotion. The first time he told her she would have trouble supervising a group of fifteen men. The second time, he informed her that she was too "emotional" and wasn't tough enough to control the men who would be working under her.

It will come as no surprise that Lucia instinctively interpreted both denials as her problem. On the one hand, she was angry with herself. On the other, she felt that perhaps she should be happy with what she had since she wasn't capable of achieving more. Lucia, like many other Latinas, was opting for the *marianista* path of blaming herself for her miseries instead of taking a clear-eyed look at the preconceptions and prejudices built into the status quo.

SHATTERING THE GLASS

It's worth reminding ourselves at this point that the tenets of *marianismo* as recounted by Evelyn Stevens describe the ideal woman as dependent, self-sacrificing, submissive, humble, with little desire for autonomy or mobility. Can you imagine that list of attributes in a résumé, job description, or want ad?

So, once you've decided *marianista* expectations are undermining your career goals, you need to behave like our friend Sonia and resist self-criticism at any cost. She put up quite a struggle against her guilt about being an ambitious woman with managerial goals. Still, there were plenty of times when she was feeling particularly conflicted and would think to herself, "You should stay home taking care of your daughter. *¡Tú eres una mala madre!*" To silence the condemning voice inside her, to raise her spirits and strengthen her resolve, her therapist suggested she create a mantra. A mantra is a form of meditation consisting of a few sentences which you devise yourself, memorize, and recite over and over whenever you feel bad for not behaving like your mother, mother-in-law, or grandmother. You can say the mantra as many times as you need to until the critic inside is silent, and leaves you be.

The mantra must include an element to remind you of the original need that created the particular *marianista* expectation in the first place, as well as the reason that particular dictate no longer fits you or your situation and must be modified.

This was Sonia's mantra: "Staying home is a leftover expectation. Now I work to pay for my daughter's college education. I also love my job, and I am very good at it. I am a good mother for safeguarding my daughter's future and taking care of myself, too."

Sonia's conflicted emotions are far from unusual. Latinas with the low self-esteem produced by *marianista* guilt frequently have trouble maintaining clarity about themselves. They must work hard at maintaining an objective view of their life and work situations without retreating into *marianismo* when assertiveness is the issue.

So, bearing that in mind, how do we Latinas begin to shatter the glass ceiling and raise ourselves off the sticky floor? First of all, we must become aware that the workplace system exists to maintain the status quo, which in turn maintains male superiority—to the detriment of both women and men.

Many Latinas know intellectually they are competent, but emotionally continue to feel inadequate and powerless. If you can identify in yourself such devastating, debilitating feelings, try to keep in mind that the workplace system has been created specifically to make you feel that way. Keep in mind as well that the men around you didn't invent the status quo. They are victims of it too.

The first step you must take, then, is to acknowledge this reality, because until you do, you're part of the status quo and *tu peor enemiga*, your own worst enemy. The second step is to learn to compete.

Positive Competition

In our practice we see Latinas every day who have been trained from infancy not to compete professionally. That's why women like Mercedes, who wanted to become a partner in her law firm, perceive competition as a form of aggression and use such violent metaphors for ambition as "killing off anybody who gets in the way." After all, females are taught to be *sacrificadas*, automatically self-sacrificing, so they often feel guilt rather than satisfaction when they win a promotion. On top of that, they may feel that by succeeding, they'll appear "castrating" to men. But in this area, as in so many others, those negative feelings are based on old rules which no longer apply.

Let's challenge these assumptions, one by one. First of all, unless you never want to leave your house, you're going to confront the need to compete. But if you compete fairly, you and your "opponent" both have the same opportunity to win. You do not have to *usar juegos sucios*, or play dirty, to get what you want. In fact, you'll find your most effective weapons to be your skill and knowledge—and your belief in your own abilities—which enable you to do a superior job.

We know positive competition works because both of us have engaged in it and remained sensitive to our colleagues. Granted, *clavar el cuchillo en la espalda*, stabbing someone in the back, is considered the law of the corporate jungle, but it doesn't have to be. We as Latinas have the unique opportunity to infuse competitiveness with the fairness, honesty, and honor it had in olden times. The crucial point is convincing ourselves that we are legitimately entitled to success. That's how we become empowered.

However, empowerment can create problems of its own. If you've never been in touch with your own power, it's not only difficult to know what it feels like, it may actually feel very uncomfortable. No matter! Assertiveness may not be natural to you, but it can be acquired. And the higher you climb in the corporate ranks, the more opportunity you'll have to wield power in a positive manner.

Have you ever asked yourself:

- Do I feel powerful? Do I want power? Do I fear power? And why?
- What exactly does power feel like? Good? Uncomfortable? Exciting?
- In what area of my life have I most often felt those feelings—home, school, or work?

Many Latinas feel torn about professional responsibility because they think their only empowerment option is to imitate male behavior at work. Are you one of them? Are male values and behavior the only model for success you can imagine in the corporate world?

Who are the people you most admire at work? Are they men? Are they women? What makes them outstanding?

Be as honest in your answers as you can because they'll teach you a lot about yourself, your friends, and how to get in touch with your individual and collective inner strength. You'll also be in a better position to compete, as every woman must, for your right to succeed in the workplace.

Dealing with Criticism

Once you are ready to compete positively, you will have to learn how to withstand criticism. Learning how to respond healthily to criticism is a cornerstone of career success. Here, for instance, is a common predicament: Your boss denies that he's giving better assignments to another male co-worker than to you, who deserve them. While it's essential to confront your superior, you must be prepared for the way he will most likely react—by denying your accusation, telling you you're being supersensitive, and disarming you with criticism.

Susana, a thirty-three-year-old Venezuelan-American who works as a stockbroker, was struggling to withstand criticism without feeling a failure. In fact, it was those very feelings of inadequacy and failure that sent her to therapy. In her sessions, she recalled her mother's criticisms when she was growing up, those of one of her college professors, and now of her boss and her boyfriend.

Susana recognized that she experienced criticism as a powerful weapon directed against her, because it aroused her own internal critic whose job, as the voice of *marianismo,* was to make her feel nonsuccessful. She had to ask herself if she really was a failure and whether she was perceiving reality accurately. Was there any truth to her boss's criticism? And how could she tell? In turn, Susana's sessions focused on learning how to handle criticism while averting self-blame and self-doubt. Her goal was to be able to accept responsibility for her behavior without having it lower her opinion of her own worth.

One of the lessons Susana took to heart was not to take all criticism personally. There were many factors, she came to see, that could contribute to an accusation which had nothing to do with her or her performance—from her superior's having a bad day to possessing bad interpersonal skills. Once she'd mastered that, Susana could begin working on tactics for handling criticism. She first grasped three losing moves people make when being criticized. As adapted from psychologists McKay and Fanning's work on self-esteem, here are the three negative responses people make to criticism: (1) they become defensive; (2) they immediately counterattack; (3) they retreat.

Here are the three winning moves, also adapted from McKay and Fanning, which Susana began using to withstand criticism: (1) relax and just try to hear the person; (2) clarify the criticism; (3) agree partially with the criticism and give back the rest.

From the time she learned about herself and acknowledged her fears, Susana was able to be more assertive and productive in the career arena. Self-knowledge is always your most powerful weapon in the battle for success. Dr. Jean Baker Miller, in her best-selling book, *Toward a New Psychology of Women*, defines power as the capacity to produce change. Here again are the steps to job empowerment:

Get the correct reading of the workplace situation.

Fight the urge to take discrimination—and on a smaller scale, criticsm—personally.

Begin to fight for your rights and win!

The Secret Shame

Sometimes, though, your battle can take a terrifying turn. That's what happened to Mildred, an attractive twenty-five-year-old New York international banking analyst of Puerto Rican parentage. She originally came to therapy at the suggestion of her doctor, who suspected her migraine headaches had some psychological links. Stylish and well educated, Mildred chose to live by herself in Manhattan, although she had been invited to move in with her unmarried brother, a physician who lived outside the city. She had dated several men and was now seriously dating Alfred, a thirty-year-old Puerto Rican engineer.

The migraines, along with depression and anxiety, had begun about half a year earlier. Although Mildred talked freely about her life, she became guarded when the subject of intimacy was introduced—a notably ineffective behavior which is not uncommon in Latina clients. It was only when she felt secure in therapy that she disclosed her secret shame.

Six months before, a new manager was assigned to her section. The man, whom we'll call Mr. Smith, was a middle-aged Anglo with a photograph of his wife and children prominently displayed on his desk.

Immediately, Mildred "felt funny" whenever Smith asked to see her in his office. With difficulty, she admitted she felt that every time he looked at her, he seemed to be undressing her with his eyes—but she didn't dare ask female co-workers how they felt about him. Things escalated rapidly, until, after she'd repeatedly turned down his invitations to lunch, he began to use obscene language with her. When she pleaded with him to stop, he accused her of seducing him and wearing provocative clothing. He threatened to block her upcoming promotion to senior analyst unless she capitulated to his desire. Mildred, remembering her mother talking about *las mujeres de la vida*, the prostitutes, in La Perla section of Old San Juan, wondered if maybe Smith was right and she was one of them.

Mildred felt trapped. She had worked four long years for the promotion and desperately wanted it, but not at the expense of surrendering to Smith. She considered telling her brother or her boyfriend but was afraid that they would overreact and cause her more trouble than she was already coping with. From out of nowhere, she began flogging herself with *marianista* recriminations: Her father had warned her that a woman's place was in the home, not the bank; if she had been married, her husband would have defended her from her harrasser; and on and on.

 ## Your Fight Against Harassment

Many Latinas who have been sexually harassed feel uncomfortable admitting it. The very idea that they would be sexually approached makes them feel, as Mildred did, that they are indeed *las mujeres de la vida*. Sexual harassment is denigrating to all women, but for Latinas, it is an invitation to silent misery.

The low status, both socially and economically, of Latinos in the United States, where we can experience discrimination on the basis of ethnicity and gender, adds one more crushing dimension to the harassment issue. We believe that sexual harassment of Latinas is so prevalant because their general employment status is low and because bosses too often regard them as a captive labor market, especially if they are in this country illegally.

Often, harassers make accusations of professional incompetence and poor work attitudes against their victims. Mildred is a perfect example of what a powerful weapon such an accusation can be. Her self-confidence was utterly shattered by Mr. Smith's unfounded attacks on her professional skill—and by her inability to exercise control over her own career advancement. "You know," she said in therapy, "it wasn't easy for a Puerto Rican woman to get a Wall Street position. The men there think we're all stupid, and I had to work doubly hard to demonstrate that I'm every bit as intelligent and able as they are." Only through working toward empowerment in her therapy was Mildred finally able to take action.

However, Mildred was distressed by the harassment experience in another, more troubling, area—Mr. Smith's remarks that there was something unnatural about her for not wanting to have sex with him. "I thought all Spanish girls were hot," he told her, and when that didn't work, he went so far as to accuse her of being a lesbian. Her family had constantly teased her about not wanting to be a "typical" Puerto Rican woman, and Mr. Smith's barbs were causing her old doubts about her femininity to resurface.

In time, Mildred would acknowledge that she and only she could define her femininity. With a little distance, she could divorce her boss's actions from her own past experience and correctly appreciate that he was deliberately attempting to make her feel more vulnerable. Mildred is not the only Latina who has endured this inner struggle in the face of harassment, for it's been instilled in us that a man is superior, knows best, and must be pleased at all times. However, it is crucial to keep in mind that we contemporary Latinas have options that were not available to our mothers and grandmothers—and chief among them is the right to choose with whom we share physical intimacy.

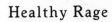

Healthy Rage

Mildred began to feel empowered and to overcome her migraines only when she learned to deal with the suppressed anger that was contributing to them. Anger is admittedly an exceptionally difficult emotion for many Latinas to recognize, express, and handle in a positive manner. Since anger directed at men is a *marianista* taboo, they react to anger with diminished self-worth. If you have difficulty in this area, as Mildred did, it is important for you to learn to give yourself permission to feel justifiedly angry when an aspect of your self-esteem is threatened.

In order to get in touch with her healthy rage, Mildred was given the following assignment: For a week she was to make a list of every situation in which she felt angry—such as failing to achieve success when she expected it and perceived social rejection.

As a result, she learned to link her anger directly to challenges to her self-esteem. She came to see that instead of expressing her fury at Smith, where it belonged, she was turning it inward on herself. Consequently, she was feeling depressed and unconsciously using the headaches as a form of punishment *por ser una mujer*, simply for being a woman.

Next, she practiced expressing her newfound rage in therapy sessions so she would learn how to handle it before she tried to express it to Smith. She was told she could rant, rave, weep with full intensity. Eventually, she mastered the art of giving herself permission to experience strong feelings and began to be less and less afraid of coping with them. Remember, if you're upset and don't get those troubled emotions out of your system, you'll continue to experience emotional distress, not to mention physical discomfort.

Fighting Back with Everything to Lose

Latinas have a lot to lose by daring to protest harassment. However, they also have the most to gain—in terms of greater self-esteem—when they seek help and file complaints against the perpetrators. We guarantee you that you'll feel better about yourself if you direct your anger, self-doubt, powerlessness, and depression outward where it belongs. Stand up to your harasser and fight the abuse. You'll be pleased to find that what began as a very negative experience ended up by giving you greater mastery over your own destiny.

However, such a victory is not achieved without a struggle. And there are certain areas where that struggle is particularly threatening to the Hispanic woman. According to the United Nations, there are no Latin-American countries where sexual harassment is considered an illegal act. That's because most of their civil codes contain a provision called *patria potestas*, which mandates male authority over women and children. Based on the principle of *imbecillus sexus*—which regards all women as defenseless and stupid—*patria potestas* reflects the *marianista* tenet that men are superior to women.

Whether or not we consciously adhere to *patria potestas*, we've all been indoctrinated with it. Which means that it may be especially scary for a Hispanic woman to actually accuse a man under the law. In domestic violence cases, for instance, Latinas appear to be particularly unwilling to report spousal abuse. The same reticence appears to be true when the issue is sexual harassment. Why is there a conspiracy of silence among Latinas?

Many women are afraid to tell their families about abuse or harassment because they feel too ashamed. Others fear jeopardizing their family's income or losing the college scholarship or foundation grant. And let's face it, sexual matters in general aren't easy for Latinas to discuss. We tend to feel ashamed, guilty, humiliated, cheap, degraded, embarrassed, demeaned, afraid, powerless, complicit, and intimidated by the subject of sexual harassment.

You may wisely choose not to mention the harassment to the men in your life if you can anticipate their response. If a man is very jealous, he may accuse you of flirting or of being unfaithful. If he is prone to violence toward others, confessing the incident to him could only add to your troubles. If this is the case with you, seek other sources of support immediately! Talk to friends, a community mental health

center, a legal aid society, your priest or pastor, a sympathetic family member, *una espiritista, curandera,* or *santera,* even a private or public employment office where you could be advised as to the course of actions that you might take.

You Don't Have to Take It Anymore

At this juncture, we must remind you that the rules of the Old Country quite possibly no longer apply to you. In your country, women may be capable of all suffering. In the United States, you don't have to take it anymore. This is the conclusion Mildred came to.

When Mildred gained sufficient self-knowledge to stop blaming her *marianista* self for Mr. Smith's actions and redirected her feelings where they belonged—onto Mr. Smith—her migraines disappeared. As she became increasingly reassured about her femininity, she began to mobilize herself into action. She took many of her female colleagues into her confidence. It didn't take long to discover that many women at the bank, both Latinas and Anglas, had been victims of some form of harassment but were afraid to talk about it. In fact, some had also been approached by Mr. Smith. Now that they were able to share, they realized the extent of the problem for the first time. Mildred also shared her experience with her boyfriend and her brother, who indeed became upset, but not violent as she had feared.

Backed by the men in her life and her friends at work, Mildred notified Smith's superiors and demanded that the company take action against him. When the company did nothing, Mildred hired a lawyer who initiated litigation. Although the case is still in court, Mildred has emerged from her secret shame a stronger, more self-possessed and empowered Latina who believes she is her own best advocate.

Whether your work-related problem is balancing home and career, battling the male status quo, shattering the glass ceiling, or freeing yourself from the sticky floor, the key is always to remember this: The problem is not yours, it's theirs. But only you can take action to solve it.

Please do not consider taking action without the moral support of a therapist, a support group, or your friends. The *marianista* idea that a woman is capable of all suffering and must fight her battles alone is not only counterproductive, it is an invitation to needless misery.

 ## REDEFINING AMBITION

In closing, let's revisit some of the Latinas we met in this chapter to see how they first gained objectivity, then proceeded to balance traditional Hispanic values with American enterprise.

Remember Cindy, the American woman who was having tremendous problems in her marriage to Carlos, a Cuban with whom she also worked? She began treatment with a Latina psychotherapist who helped her to see that immigration had put Carlos through an identity crisis of his own, which was also affected by the fact that he was not the sole support of the household. The more he felt his *macho* role reduced in North America both as the absolute ruler of the home and as the single wage earner, the more he reverted to the old ways and became increasingly domineering. Cindy considered herself fortunate that even though he refused to come to therapy, he let her go.

Eventually, Cindy's sense of self-worth improved sufficiently that she was able to take steps toward equality. First, after informing Carlos that she thought his being her boss at the office was adding pressure in the home, she requested a change of department. There, she developed relationships with co-workers which helped her feel less isolated and more independent. Appreciating that a Latin man needs a male confidant under these trying circumstances, she solicited the help of their friend, Dr. Perez, who worked with Carlos on being more aware of his American wife's needs. But the biggest victory was getting her husband to agree to her hiring a cleaning woman so, as she told him, she could spend more time with him.

What Cindy learned about *marianismo*, that women are always supposed to be there for a man, helped her to engineer change. She also learned that starting with relatively small changes—like getting a cleaning person—is important because it acclimates the other person to accepting bigger ones. She remains somewhat unsure about what the future holds for her and Carlos, but at this point still wants to continue to try. And if she changes her mind somewhere in the future, she knows that there are options open to her.

Susana, the young Venezuelan-American stockbroker who was having a lot of trouble taking criticism, finally got smart, gained self-knowledge, and began confronting the things she needed to change in herself in order to succeed in business. After a while, she learned to be assertive—when appropriate—effortlessly. As her self-confidence grew, so did her job level. Eventually, she was appointed head of the Caribbean international department of her brokerage firm. When asked what advice she would give to other ambitious Latinas haunted by *marianista* fears of success, she replied, "Don't be afraid to change! Work hard at it and make yourself endure the rough times because, believe me, they pass, and then, well . . . the pleasure you get from accomplishment is worth every bit of the pain you had to live through to achieve it!"

When we first encountered Cecilia, the Mexican-American married to an American doctor, she was driving herself crazy because she saw herself as a failure as a housewife. Cecilia represented a classic case of distorted self-image because she magnified her weaknesses and minimized her assets. It was difficult for her even to get in touch with her real desire, to get a job, because her assertiveness was cringing behind her *marianismo*. Eventually, at her husband's urging, she started psychotherapy.

In order to help Cecilia integrate both her positive and negative qualities into wholeness, the therapist gave her an exercise in which she was told to list her positive and negative personality traits, then grade them.

Taking the test was a breakthrough for Cecilia. She was very surprised by how much she did indeed like herself. She gave herself particularly high marks for intellectual capacity, interpersonal skills, physical appearance, and academic excellence although she scored lower on daily-living tasks, on how others perceived her, and on femininity. You might want to try this exercise yourself.

As a result of her response, Cecilia started to question her *marianista* principles. Eventually, she came to accept the fact that her career desires were not a distortion of "normal" femininity but, rather, acceptable needs for fulfillment and recognition that her marriage and emigration had brought into focus. Now she could free herself to pursue activities which were personally gratifying, not culturally mandated. Luckily, her husband was not only very supportive but also quite successful, which meant that when she chose to have children, Cecilia would be able to stay home with them while they were little and put her career on hold. She was well on the way to enjoying the best of two worlds.

Lucia, the Puerto Rican bridge toll collector who felt she was suffering gender job discrimination but was haunted by fears of her own inadequacy, also began therapy. Through the sessions, she came to understand that her supervisor saw all women, not just her, as emotional and incapable of managing men. Once she was able to put some distance between her self-esteem and her situation, she was able to choose a course of action—in this case, going over the head of her immediate supervisor. It took some time for her to make this step. After all, for twenty-eight years she had bought the *marianista* notion that women are not meant for the workplace. That she took this step at all is a tribute to her personal courage and the strength of her marriage, for her husband was with her every step of the way. By the way, after demanding a review of her job performance, she was granted the promotion. Her immediate superior, when called in to evaluate her work, even had to admit she deserved more responsibility.

And what about Mercedes, who dreamed of becoming a partner in her law firm but feared she couldn't act with the necessary killer instincts? In therapy, she came to appreciate the crucial difference between aggressiveness and assertiveness. Assertiveness, she learned, was about feeling good and competent while aggressiveness was about acting out self-doubt through force.

Another important insight of Mercedes' involved the traditional Latin cultural value of *personalismo*—as stated before, described by Emelicia Mizio as the ability to make and keep relationships and thus connect meaningfully to other people. Once she reframed *personalismo* as networking, Mercedes was able to bring substantial business to her firm through the cordial, warm relationships she formed with Latin businesses in the Midwest, California, and Latin America.

Without stabbing anyone in the back, Mercedes was made a junior partner and given total responsibility for heading the newly created international department, with major emphasis on GATT, the new trade agreement involving Canada, the United States, and Mexico. She truly believes that in the next decade, she will become one of the top corporate lawyers in the country—without having to imitate the male model of success.

In closing, we'd like to return to the story of our friend Sonia, who chose her career in government over a traditional Latin marriage. She and her daughter, Alexa, live in a beautiful house in Washington, D.C. Next fall, Alexa will be going away to college, where she intends to study corporate law and eventually work at a multinational firm. Sonia knows the beautiful house will seem very empty without Alexa, but she supports her daughter's ambition and drive every step of the way. They often discuss the price Sonia had to pay for choosing a full-time profession. "It would be wonderful, darling," she tells Alexa, "to have an executive job, a loving and caring man, and a brilliant and beautiful daughter. But I have two out of three, so how could I not feel happy with myself?"

That's not to say that Sonia has given up hope of marrying again. She continues to date but feels that having a man is not essential to her self-esteem. She doesn't feel like less of a woman when the relationships don't work out, and no longer uses the principles of *marianismo* as a measure of her worth.

All these women learned certain lessons that enabled them to become what they wanted without the constraints of tradition. We have made a list of eight mandates to bear in mind as you work toward your own empowerment:

1. Decide that your professional role is a priority for you.
2. Work at strengthening your self-esteem.
3. Feel confident with your self-image.
4. Learn to deal with your family's objection and Latino men's rejection.
5. Derive great satisfaction from your intellectual life.
6. Feel comfortable with short-term intimate relationships.
7. Overcome feelings of abnormality when you don't comply with traditional Latina gender roles.
8. Become part of a support network of friends and/or colleagues that provides emotional nourishment.

Power Plays

In this chapter, we've shared with you the experiences of women who have boldly asked themselves, "How does my professional self fit within the context of *marianismo?*" They admitted to themselves that their work life often conflicted with their family life, that job discrimination and sexual harassment were not their fault, and that to succeed they had to acquire a whole new set of effective behaviors, including autonomy, independence, self-sufficiency, assertiveness, and competitiveness. To their surprise, they discovered that professional success did not make them feel less worthy as Latina women. In fact, their self-esteem soared.

The stories of these women should inspire us all. As an ambitious Latina determined to succeed in your new country, your goal, like theirs, must be to allow yourself the inner freedom to feel affirmed and effective in multiple but integrated roles as wife, mother, and competent worker. We must all affirm our right to become empowered, to make a full contribution to society and realize our intellectual potential without feeling guilty, selfish, or unfeminine.

6

"Do Not Forget That Sex Is for Making Babies— Not for Pleasure":

▭

Old World Marriage vs. Real-Life Passion

Dora, a thirty-one-year-old architect born in New York of Colombian parents, came to therapy with marital problems that were making her depressed and unhappy. She'd been married for five years to Juan, a forty-year-old Chilean physician. Although Dora had dated other men before Juan, her husband remained the first and only one with whom she'd had sex.

During courtship, Juan had been attentive and solicitous of Dora's needs, but—beginning about a year after their marriage—he'd changed into an ultrapossessive *macho* husband in the grand tradition. Recently Dora had discovered he was also having an affair with an

Angla nurse at the hospital where he practiced. Not unexpectedly, her husband's philandering in tandem with his domineering manner made her self-doubts, feelings of rejection, and low self-esteem coalesce into constant sadness and feelings of unworthiness. But when she confessed her troubles to her mother and aunt, both of them told her that "that's how Latin men are," and shared stories about their own husbands' infidelities. Latinos looked for easy sex on the street, her mother told her, but always returned home to their wives. "Yes," Mamá continued, "That is the trial of *la mujer latina*." So Dora submissively suffered in silence.

NEW LAND, OLD ATTITUDES: THE VIRGINITY MANDATE

Although sexual attitudes are diverse among Hispanic women, there is a common thread linking most of them. This sexual mind-set is shared by Latina immigrants as well as the daughters of immigrants born and raised in Miami, Los Angeles, New York, and the rural areas of the Southwest. Indeed, of all the cultural conflicts with which Latina immigrants must grapple, those involving traditional sexual attitudes and behaviors are possibly the most deeply entrenched and the hardest to resolve.

In this chapter, we'll show through client case studies and the latest research that being sexual *no es malo*. Not only is it not a sin, in a loving and responsible context it's one of life's great blessings. We'll help you see that the *marianista* principle of sexual self-denial can prevent you from becoming a complete person. We'll also give you exercises and quizzes to help you reconnect to your natural *sensualidad* and outgrow traditional Latino/a sexual biases which no longer apply to you.

Let's consider Dora as an example of the ingrown sexual inhibitions with which even acculturated Latinas are burdened. Although she is second-generation, Dora continued to follow the *marianista* principles of sexual behavior. She couldn't specifically remember learning that to be *una buena mujer*, you had to be a virgin until marriage. But she'd learned it anyway. That's why her husband was the first man she'd ever slept with—and not until her wedding night.

For the American woman, losing or maintaining her virginity is a personal and individual choice, not a family affair. But for the Latina, virginity is *un asunto de honor*, a matter of honor. Indeed, it becomes a critical family issue because of the overwhelming importance attributed both to *macho* honor and *marianista* sexual purity in Latino society. In fact, the Cuban psychologist Oliva Espin believes that the virginity mandate continues to be a cultural expectation for countless Latinas living in the United States. Virginity is inextricably linked to *familismo*, which is the glue that holds Hispanic cultural expectations together.

Certainly there are countless Latinas who do have sex before marriage. Nevertheless, our clients have maintained that virginity is still viewed as the dearest of all treasures and the greatest evidence of a woman's love for a man. Not surprisingly then, we often detect a sadness and guilt in our clients after sexual initiation, at the loss of something precious, even when those feelings are accompanied by the excitement of discovering a new world of intimacy.

The following questions will help you sort out memories and feelings regarding the question of virginity and the cultural and social mores associated with sexuality:

- Where would you place yourself on the continuum of sexual behavior, going from traditional to liberated?
- Do you consider yourself to be sexually inhibited?
- Do you believe a woman should be a virgin until marriage?
- Do you think it's right for a woman to have sex with her fiancé?
- How do your mother and other close female relatives react to "liberated" sexual beliefs and behavior?

- Do you feel that Latina women in general are sexually repressed?
- How did you learn what constitutes appropriate sexual behavior for women?

Sexuality and Self-Esteem

We can see in Dora's case that her feelings of sexual incompetence, awakened by her husband's playing around, badly impacted on her self-esteem. She's not unique. For many women, sexuality constitutes the last frontier of self-love and self-acceptance. Many Latinas are able to describe themselves as competent *profesionales* and loving and worthy *madres y esposas*, yet express severe self-doubt when the subject is sex.

If you don't like yourself, you might shy away from sexual involvement because intimacy allows another person to get too close and see "the real you," who is unworthy and undesirable. Even if you're generally self-confident, you might have sexual relationships but hold back because pleasure makes you feel guilty or undeserving. Perhaps, because your self-esteem is low, you repeatedly become involved in unsatisfactory and exploitative affairs. Or, unsure of your own worth, you may feel driven to constantly prove your physical attractiveness and sexual wiles. Too many Latinas who believe they don't deserve to be treated with *respeto* and appreciation tend to be attracted to abusive or unsatisfying partners—and end up feeling worse about themselves.

There is nothing more important to sexual intimacy than your sense of self-worth, which often gets translated into your feelings about your body, your physical appearance, your personality and sexual competence. According to anthropologist J. U. Ogbu, competence is equated with mastering culturally significant tasks. Frequently, he writes, failure to achieve competence results in life crisis, poor health, depression, and troubled relationships with others. But, the Latina must ask, if mastering a task requires knowledge and skills, how does one learn to be sexually competent?

After all, in Latin America, men are often taken to prostitutes to learn sexual skills, while women are utterly forbidden sexual practice and subsequently acquire no skills at all. That's culturally intentional, since according to *machismo*, a man is 100 percent responsible for teaching his woman what to do in bed. Indeed, the strong element of repression running through Hispanic tradition helps women ignore their own erotic impulses before and after marriage.

Given these traditional sexual restrictions, it's no wonder that some Hispanic women feel sexually incompetent—not because they aren't capable of becoming sexual beings, but because of outdated inhibitions fostered by cultural beliefs. It is important here, as elsewhere, to remember that you are not to blame yourself for your problems with sex. When you feel tempted to, remind yourself that Latinas, in the fashion of true *marianista* martyrs, habitually blame themselves for everything.

Once you move beyond blaming yourself, you can begin developing how to express your sexual identity. Our job in this chapter is to guide you through the maze of conflicting cultural commands so you can claim your sexuality at last.

A Family Secret

One of the things that Dora discovered in therapy was that she knew very little about sex before she married Juan and had always felt unsure in that area. As a good *marianista*, she blamed herself for Juan's taking an American mistress, because according to her, gringas are more liberal in their attitudes and behaviors toward sex. "If you grew up in my family," she said in one of her sessions, "you learned that sex didn't exist. Many times I wondered how I got here and of course assumed I'd been born with all my clothes on. How naive could I have been?"

In traditional Hispanic households, sex is a taboo subject which is simply not discussed. Even in therapy, it takes a long time before Latin women can bring themselves to mention sex. To make matters worse, the sexual messages transmitted in Latino/a households tend to be confusing and skewed, intermixed with issues of duty, honor, security, self-worth, and control but never with pleasure or satisfaction.

These messages from the past are so strong and intimidating that they continue to impact on your life in the present. In fact, unless you come to grips with them, they can adversely affect you for the rest of your life. Are you aware of your family's sexual messages? Can you remember how you first learned them?

Dora was helped immensely by the following exercise devised by psychologist Gina Ogden, which gave her insight into the sexual messages she received from her family. You might also find it helpful, especially if you write down your answers. Since sex is a subject many Latino/a parents feel uncomfortable discussing with their children, you might have to put a lot of thought into this exercise before you gain a good understanding of the sexual attitudes of your family and yourself:

1. What were your family's attitudes toward sex when you were growing up? (Make sure to list any differences between the messages sent by your mother, father, aunts, and other members of your extended family.)
2. What is your earliest memory regarding sex?
3. What messages did you receive about sex as an adolescent?
4. What kind of positive sexuality did you see modeled between your parents or other adults in the household—for example, tenderness, playfulness, passion, hugs, dancing?
5. How would you describe your present attitude toward sex?
6. If you have a partner, is your relationship in any way like the sexual relationship between your parents?
7. If you have children, do you find yourself transmitting the same sexual messages you received from your family?
8. If you could sum up your family's sexual attitudes in a word or phrase, what would it be?

Here are some actual examples from other Latinas like yourself:

- Your virginity is your most precious possession.
- Men are out for only one thing—S-E-X.
- Sex is dangerous.
- Sex is dirty.
- Sex is not pleasurable.
- Sex is sacrifice.

Integrating North American Values

There's no doubt that, whether or not a Latina considers herself "liberated," the process of acculturation impacts on her sexual attitudes and those of her family. We know, for instance, that as part of the immigration process, people tend to create myths regarding the culture of the new country, often as protective measures against what is seen as new and challenging, not to say threatening. So it is that many immigrating Latino/as regard the U.S. attitude toward sex and sex roles as shockingly free. To many Hispanics, then, an American female is *una mujer liviana*, a loose woman.

Clearly, the reality of the situation is that not all members of a societal group think or behave in exactly the same manner. Some American women are "liberated," while others have more "traditional" sexual attitudes. It's really a question of relativism. What's important here, though, is what you think about Angla sexuality.

Do you feel that Latinas are more sexually conservative than their North American sisters? Is it possible you have developed this idea of liberated American women in order to be like them? Is it equally possible you have developed this idea in order to criticize it? Is American sexual liberation just too threatening to you?

Take the case of the Garcias, a Cuban family who have lived in New Jersey for the last twenty years and were referred to therapy by the guidance counselor at the high school attended by their sixteen-year-old daughter, Maria.

Very serious conflicts developed when Maria refused to let her mother, aunt, or older sister chaperone her on dates. She also defied her father's curfews and dressed, according to Mr. Garcia, *muy provocativamente*. He went on to express his rage at Maria's becoming too "Americanized," at her open defiance of his authority and her compromising the family honor, as well as at his wife for being *una mala madre*. Mr. Garcia furiously condemned the poor woman for raising such a rebellious daughter, who could easily become *una prostituta como las de La Habana*.

Maria, of course, just wanted to be like all her American friends and classmates and couldn't understand what the hysteria at home was all about. She pointed out that her parents were the only ones in the community who expected their children to comply with "old rules." She also claimed that her twenty-four-year-old sister, Blanca, to whom her mother and father constantly compared her, was responsible for all the trouble. Blanca hadn't resisted being chaperoned because she was a prude, Maria insisted. Blanca was destined to be *una solterona*, an old maid, like her Aunt Fila.

To provide ammunition for his case, Mr. Garcia dragged along to subsequent sessions his mother, Maria's *abuela*, and his "old maid" sister Fila. That's when conflicts ecalated. *La abuela* blamed her daughter-in-law for not teaching Maria to be *una mujer decente*, and embarrassing her son by having his authority undermined by a sixteen-year-old girl. But she didn't stop there. She continued lecturing the group about the dangers of Americanization and the need to maintain *las normas morales*, the moral standards, of traditional Cuban society.

Surprisingly, it was Tía Fila who jumped to Maria's defense, confronting her mother with the fact that they were not in Havana and Maria would never be able to show her face at school again if she consented to be chaperoned. She felt her niece needed to know how to "protect" herself, and that by not explaining sexual behavior to her, they could be creating a problem that was genuinely serious. Suffice it to say it took many sessions before individual family members could actually listen to each other's opinions and find a middle ground.

We'll revisit the Garcias later in another context, but the point to be noted here is that the women of the family were at different, clearly delineated points on the transcultural continuum—as evidenced by their attitudes toward sexual behavior, with the more conservative family member, *la abuela*, invoking the myth of the wanton gringa as the direst of warnings.

These next questions will help you explore your own sexual attitudes in relation to the acculturation continuum. Here again, make sure to write your answers down.

Where on the acculturation continuum would you place your sexual attitudes and behavior?

- Do you think women should be passive in expressing their sexuality?
- Do you feel you do not have to behave sexually according to the orthodox *marianista* mandate?
- Do you feel free to talk about sexual issues with men, co-workers, and your parents?
- How do you feel about using contraceptives to prevent pregnancy?
- If you have children, do you wish them to behave sexually in the traditional Latin manner?
- Do you feel comfortable initiating sex with your partner?

After you've reviewed your answers, try to determine as honestly as you can whether you're still holding on to *marianista* sexual beliefs, or whether you have more liberal views, or feel that you belong in the middle of the acculturation continuum. We'll now go into more detail about the ingredients of the *marianista* sexual mandate, to help you clarify your own feelings, which may very well be mixed. Central among them is the Mother–Whore dichotomy.

Las Madres y las Putas

It is indisputable that each culture has its own unique way of defining human sexuality. In Latin countries, as you know, female sexuality is expressed in two, either/or forms. The first is procreation, regarded as the heart of femininity. Every woman who strives to be *una buena mujer* must first become *una madre*. Motherhood is the only acceptable role for a woman in traditional Hispanic society.

The second expression of female sexuality among Latinos is eroticism, which is considered utterly negative. According to Marcela Lagarde, the Mexican anthropologist, a woman automatically becomes *una mala mujer* if she opts for this second sexual expression by becoming a prostitute, a mistress, a single mother, a divorcée, a seductress, a flirt, a "hot number," or *una mujer sola*, a woman alone. Needless to say, all women have the capacity to fit into any of these categories if they allow their sexual feelings free expression. But once they do, they face inner guilt and societal rejection. This combination cannot fail to produce low self-esteem.

The dogma of *marianismo* not only mandates what *una latina buena* should be, but also parallels the absolutism of *machismo*'s definition of *un buen hombre*. Thus *marianismo* regards the ideal woman as submissive, subservient, self-sacrificing, self-renouncing, sexually pure, and erotically repressed. This emphasis on self-sacrifice and renunciation, combined with the importance placed on *la virginidad*, fertility, and the inability to feel and express eroticism, becomes characteristic of sexual development in many Latinas—far different from what North American girls are taught.

For the Hispanic woman to enjoy sexual pleasure, even in marriage, is wrong because it indicates a lack of virtue. To shun sexual pleasure and to regard lovemaking as solely the obligation a wife owes her husband, and as a necessary means to have children, is the single proof of virtue. As Evelyn Stevens writes in her seminal article on *marianismo*, "Good women do not enjoy coitus and endure it when the duties of matrimony require it."

NECESSARY EVILS

Stevens's perceptive observation applies to the case of Alicia, a thirty-four-year-old widow and mother of two from a well-to-do Guatemalan family. She was referred to therapy by her physician, who could find no organic cause for her headaches, gastritis, back pain, and insomnia. A devout Catholic, Alicia actually expressed pride in her lack of sexual pleasure or desire.

Before the death two years earlier of her older, playboy husband, Alicia had stoically tolerated the disrespect and disinterest that defined her partner's attitude toward her. For the sake of her children, who meant the world to her, she had complied with her husband's sexual demands, but hated every moment of it. In therapy, Alicia quickly admitted to feelings of guilt, incompetence, and worthlessness. One day she told her therapist, "Without disrespect, the Virgen María knew how to do things. She knew how to give birth without having to sleep with San Jose. Wasn't she lucky!"

In truth, when she spoke those words, Alicia was really expressing her longing for an understanding and sweet man who would be sensitive to her needs and desires, sexually and emotionally. Slowly, as she came to term with her desires, she began to deal more honestly with her curiosity about sex and displayed an interest in marrying again if she found the right man. In time, she met that man. But it was then that her innate association of sexual pleasure with moral guilt really kicked in.

We'll follow up on how well Alicia fared in her quest for the freedom to be sexual. Now we just want to reiterate that she is not unique. Learning to disassociate sin and sexual pleasure isn't easy for many Latinas. Dora once asked during therapy if *las mujeres malas*, like prostitutes, experience enjoyment during the sex act. Here's yet another Hispanic sexual myth that acculturating women must contend with. A scientific study of Mexican women by Marcela Lagarde proves that although we might assume a *puta*'s life is one erotic thrill after another, just the opposite is true. Prostitutes, in fact, do not derive pleasure from what are essentially economic transactions. Lovemaking is their job, and the aim of it—not unlike the job of the *marianista* wife/mother—is to give pleasure to others, not to themselves.

However, because of the persistence of this myth, many Latinas feel *como mujeres malas*, like prostitutes, when they experience erotic satisfaction. Although both *mujeres buenas y malas* engage in sexual relations, only those who repress pleasure and give birth earn the honor of being called *las madres*—just like the Virgin Mary. On the other hand, the *puta*, or *mujer mala*, represents the intrinsic *maldad*, the wickedness, of erotic sexuality. While the so-called wicked ones might pay society's price, the others—*las madres*—pay silently with their self-esteem.

Being-for-Others

Maritza, a twenty-nine-year-old immigrant from El Salvador, comes to mind here. Maritza has lived in Boston since she was three. She is married to forty-two-year-old Javier, has three children, and works as an elementary school teacher. Maritza loves being a mother. No sacrifice is too great for her to make if it ensures that her children will be healthy and happy. In relation to her maternal role, Maritza's self-esteem is justifiably high. When the subject turns to her marriage, though, things change. Maritza admits she experiences no pleasure from having sex with her husband but feels it is *un servicio que le hace a él*, her conjugal duty.

Maritza is a perfect example of how the mythical maternal instinct subordinates eroticism. Marcela Lagarde argues that a traditional Latina is supposed to exist only as *ser-para-los-otros*, in other words, as being-for-others, because her body and soul are consecrated to her family. That is why for orthodox *marianistas*, being *la madre*, the eternal mother, rather than being *la esposa*, the dutiful wife, is the core of existence.

Think of it. You can only exist in relation to others, which is a total negation of the self. Consequently, your self-esteem is enhanced whenever you give of yourself. But when you give *to* yourself, you feel

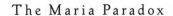

guilty, selfish, even sinful, and your self-regard diminishes even further. It isn't surprising that many Latinas with whom we work have difficulty enjoying lovemaking, because in allowing themselves to feel pleasure, they are violating the *marianista* mandate of self-denial.

We Latinas often forget that our bodies are the main vehicle in which our needs and frustrations find expression. Drs. Lee Robins and Darrel Regier have pointed out that many physiological disorders can develop due to deep-seated emotional problems which are termed somatic. Somatization pertains when people seek help for a physical complaint, like migraines, for which there is no organic cause. In other words, our bodies are able to translate psychological difficulties into physical symptoms which are less threatening to our sense of self—for instance, a backache is easier to deal with than the marital problems which may actually be provoking it.

It's pertinent to mention that J. I. Escobar and J. E. Mezzich, renowned Latin-American psychiatrists practicing in the United States, have conducted research which indicates that Latinas both here and in their native countries suffer from somatic disorders at a substantially higher rate than North American women. We believe that this high incidence of emotionally connected complaints might well be the result of *marianista* martyrdom, of self-denial and self-sacrificing behavior. More directly related to unmet desires and persistent anxieties are Latinas' complaints in health and mental health settings, such as those involving hysterectomy, menopause, abortion, pregnancy, and birth control. Hispanic women must begin questioning traditional sex mores. In order to be healthy physically and emotionally, we need to recognize our own needs and first give pleasure to ourselves, in order to be able to give it to others.

SEXUAL REPROGRAMMING

So you've acknowledged your own needs and desires. What do you do next? We repeat, you must maintain a commitment to self-compassion without self-judgment. Remember, Latinas' sexual behavior is not a product of biology but rather of cultural conditioning. That having been said, how then do you change this historical "programming" that regulates your sexual responses?

For one thing, do some soul-searching to find out if the *marianista* sexual mandate really meets your needs as you acculturate. If you're not happy with your sexual life, it's time to take some calculated risks. One of them is accepting the fact that you are a sexual being, like everybody else in the world, with a right to experience and express perfectly normal erotic feelings without feeling guilty and sad. It is crucial to constantly remind yourself that you have nothing to feel ashamed about.

Try this exercise. Find a quiet moment to sit down, close your eyes, relax your muscles, and visualize a blackboard in your mind. Imagine that on the blackboard is written the family messages you have absorbed. "A woman should be pure, virgin, passive, self-sacrificing, and—in order to be *una mujer buena*—should deny her sexual being." Once you see it written on the blackboard, read the specific sexual attitudes of individual family members written on the blackboard. Next, envision an eraser in your hand. See yourself erasing all the writing from the blackboard. One by one, the messages vanish.

Tell yourself that since these messages don't exist, they no longer matter. Now picture yourself writing on the blackboard. What you write will be this affirmation: "I am fine. I am good. I am not *mala* because I have sexual feelings. I am *una mujer buena* who experiences erotic feelings. It is okay to feel them."

Feel free to do the visualization exercise and repeat the affirmation as often as you want. Both techniques are especially useful when you're in the grip of anxiety, guilt, or self-doubt. If you find that you're putting yourself down, these exercises can genuinely help you banish the blues.

When you realize that the restrictions of *marianismo* are undermining your self-esteem and holding you back from happiness, you can begin modifying the traditional commands in your inner conversations with yourself. Here again, a good way to do this is to create a mantra.

This is one that Caroline, a client of ours, wrote in response to the *marianista* rule that *una mujer buena* should not allow herself to feel sexual pleasure: "Denying myself sexual pleasure was an old expectation in my old country. I am not happy following it now. I want to feel sexual pleasure. God gave me my body and He allows me to enjoy His creation. I am *una buena mujer*. I am *una buena mujer*. I am a new *marianista*."

Hot Violet/Shrinking Tomato

Old habits die hard. Recently, we witnessed the following exchange between Lucia and Ana, two Latina executives in the health care field who hadn't seen each other for a while. Lucia, a recent divorcée, announced she was dating an American man. "You look wonderful!" Ana exclaimed. "You changed your hair, and it's really becoming! There's nothing like having a man in your life."

Ana's message that Lucia appeared physically more attractive because she had a boyfriend reflects the basic Hispanic relationship between a woman and her body: being-for-others. We think you'll agree that in Latino culture, girls learn very early to embellish their bodies and make themselves pleasing to be desirable to men. Most Latinas do their hair, their nails, perfume and dress themselves for men, not for themselves. What this means is that women follow these rules in order to be loved. Ask yourself these questions to determine how much you depend on men for the way you look:

- How often do I wear a certain dress because he likes it?
- How often do I dress in a certain way because it excites him?
- Do I keep my hair long because he thinks long hair is sexy?
- Do I use a specific brand of perfume because it pleases me—or pleases him?
- Is the color I wear most my favorite—or his?

- Do I steer away from certain styles because he doesn't like to see me in them?

If you answered yes to at least three of these questions, your physical appearance is being determined not by you but by the man in your life. If he wants you to look "sexy," it's his definition, not yours. If he wants you to look "like a lady," it's his concept of class, not yours. You are both a shrinking tomato and a hot violet. As such, your reliance on your man to determine your look has to have a detrimental effect on your self-image. You become less a person and more an extension of him.

- What would happen if you were more assertive and determined to wear what you like?
- How would you feel if you took control of your own looks?
- How would your husband/partner react?
- If you're dating someone, are you worried he won't be attracted to you unless you dress a certain way?
- Are you afraid he'll reject you if you don't look the way he wants?

The way you feel about your body is closely related to how you feel about yourself, and we have seen very few Latinas suffering from low self-esteem who don't also have a problem with their body image. Keep in mind that both positive and negative feelings about your body reflect cultural, even more than personal, standards.

This is how some Latinas describe their physical selves. Lourdes complains, "My stomach is too flabby"; Isabel, "My breasts sag"; Josie, "If I could only lose fifteen pounds . . ." while Mercy feels, "*Soy muy planchada,* and Latinos love buttocks!"

The list is endless, but suffice it to say Latinas have trouble knowing and loving their bodies because, in a profoundly affecting way, their bodies don't belong to them. Of course, this holds true for women of any ethnic background, but we've found it applies more strongly to Latinas. They love what they think men find attractive and hate and fear those aspects of themselves which men could find undesirable. Paradoxically, according to the *marianista* mandate, women should publicly dress *con pudor*, with modesty, so as not to excite men and become *mujeres malas*. Yet they must style themselves to attract a man's eye. Here again, the shrinking tomato both clashes and coexists with the hot violet.

If you have a love/hate relationship with your body, you need to make friends with it. Try this exercise:

When you are alone and won't be disturbed, take off all your clothes, including jewelry, and stand in front of a full-length mirror. Use a hand mirror or a second full-length mirror so you can see your back. How do you feel about confronting your naked self? Is it scary? Many Hispanic women feel that way because it's difficult to look at themselves without the camouflage of clothes. Many look only at their face and hair and ignore the rest of their body.

Try to view yourself without judgment. Whatever you do, don't put yourself down—or concentrate only on the parts you think aren't perfect. Once you have some idea of how you look, let go of the need to chastise yourself for what you think are the "ugly" parts of yourself. Now repeat the following affirmation many times: "I am fine. I look fine. I like me just the way I am. It's okay. My body is okay."

A hint: Once you admit you like your body, you will begin to think of new ways to take care of it, get to know it better—and look terrific at the same time. Exercise is key here. Consider joining a gym or a workout class. If you've always wanted to take tap dancing or karate, why not do it? If you've always longed for a massage, go get one. The bonus here is that working with your body will make you hyperaware of its sensual and sensory aspects. In North America, there's nothing sexier than a well-toned, graceful form. Tending lovingly to your body is key to personal freedom and enhanced self-worth.

The New *Marianista* vs. the Traditional *Macho*

You may be wondering how to deal with your Latino partners, especially those men who continue to follow traditional sexual beliefs. It is important to recognize, unfortunately, that a Latino's self-esteem is greatly enhanced by behavior demonstrating extraordinary erotic potency. In immigrating Hispanic men, this myth of grandiose sexual power may mask insecurity and shaky self-esteem. In any case, according to M. Lagarde, studies indicate that Latinos are about as potent and sexually active as males of other ethnic groups—no more, no less. Yet the myth persists. Sadly, traditional Latino culture sentences men and women to equal unhappiness—men because of the obligatory exaggeration of potency, and women because of the repression of sexuality.

Some of our clients have experienced sexual awakening and been able to establish a dialogue with their Latino partner in which they could express their needs and desires. In many cases, we're happy to report, these men have even become more responsive to their mate's request for gratification.

We have also worked with women whose partners were rigidly bound to the tenets of *machismo*. In some of these cases, the Latinas were able to become assertive enough to advocate for their right to experience sexual pleasure as well as provide it, and eventually to succeed. Others had to make some tough decisions regarding continuing the relationship. Each woman must of course evaluate her unique situation, the strength of the relationship, and the flexibility of her partner, as well as her own desires. We don't claim any of these choices will be easy, but we want to leave you with the belief that, according to the mandate of the new *marianista*, you have the power to make your own decisions about your life, your sexual gratification, and as we will now discuss, your life or death.

Un Asunto de Vida o Muerte

If you love yourself, you will choose "safe" sexual situations and also take precautions to make lovemaking as risk-free as possible *en la época del SIDA*, in the age of AIDS. It is essential that you understand the issues of AIDS and HIV—the virus that causes it—its transmission and how to protect yourself. We would feel we were not fulfilling our duty as health care professionals if we did not discuss this subject with you.

For Latinas, the AIDS epidemic brings into focus conflicts created by traditional sex roles and sexual behaviors, which—according to research findings of psychologists Adeline Nyamathi and Rose Vasquez, based on statistics provided by the Centers for Disease Control—put us in a higher-risk category. Twenty-three percent of all women in the United States who have been diagnosed with AIDS are Hispanic. Of children with AIDS, 24 percent are Latin, the majority born to HIV-infected mothers. And the number of AIDS cases among Latinas has been increasing more rapidly than among other ethnic groups.

At the beginning of the epidemic, women generally felt safe because AIDS was associated with male homosexuality. This has contributed to many Latinas' inability to see themselves as possible victims. We have worked with Hispanic women who are still in denial about their vulnerability to this horrible illness because they identify it with gay men, general promiscuity, anal intercourse, and drug abuse. Unfortunately, the facts tell us it's not that simple.

Many Hispanic women unknowingly engage in unsafe sex with partners who might be HIV-positive for various reasons, from "sleeping around" to sharing needles with IV drug users. The traditional *macho* and *marianista* sexual mores discussed in this chapter are contributing factors to putting so many women at risk. Here are some of them:

1. *Machismo* gives sexual rights and decision making to the man.

2. The expected double standard of Latino men leads to frequent infidelity.
3. Bisexuality is never explicitly manifested.
4. *Marianismo* demands submissive behavior of women.

Latinas tend to demonstrate real difficulty in discussing safe sex because of the aforementioned reasons. They are afraid of hurting their partners' feelings if they question their integrity or masculinity. Certainly Hispanic men don't make it easy for women, since they continue to insist they "know best," will do what pleases them, and won't wear condoms.

The best rule to follow when having sex with a Hispanic man is to assume he will not protect you. Not even the law is on your side, because a physician cannot break confidentiality even if he knows your partner is infected. So who will protect you? Nobody will—except yourself. It's your life, after all. *Morir por amor,* dying for love, is very romantic, but it's also very stupid. If any societal factor can force you to break the *marianista* mold of total sexual submission, it is AIDS. Your life is in danger. You must always take your own precautions—a diaphragm with spermicidal foam to cover the vaginal wall, or a female condom—and find the courage to say no to sex if you can do so without fear of violence from your partner.

Diana found that courage. She is a twenty-nine-year-old unmarried Peruvian-American who has been living in the States since she was three. Through her job as an accountant at a multinational firm, Diana met a man she really liked—Jesus, a thirty-six-year-old computer programmer from Colombia. After they'd been dating for about two months, they joined a group of co-workers for a long ski weekend in Vermont. In therapy, Diana admitted she was looking forward to becoming intimate with Jesus but expressed concern regarding safe sex.

Although sexually active, Diana didn't believe in taking foolish chances. She was convinced that Jesus had been intimately involved with other women before they met, although she didn't believe he was seeing anybody else at the moment. Still, the prospect of asking him to wear a condom made her anxious, since she was certain he would respond to the suggestion, like any *macho*, by becoming angry and upset. Therapy gave her the chance to rehearse how she would handle the matter.

"Jesus," she began her scenario, "I really care about you and desire you, but we must be careful. I don't want to get sick, and I don't want you to. Who knows if the women you dated before me were sick and didn't tell you?"

"No problem," Diana imagined Jesus responding. "I'm a very strong man, and no woman is going to give me a disease."

Armed with very little hope but with a package of condoms containing nonoxynol-9 on the tip—since the therapist had told her that type offered the greatest protection against disease—Diana set off for Vermont.

In therapy the following week, she related what had happened. Jesus's first response to her suggesting he use the condoms she had brought along was, "How could you ask that of me? I really care for you, Diana. I'd never do anything to hurt you!"

However, he admitted he'd never been tested for AIDS, although he'd slept with his share of women. As Diana had anticipated, he told her he felt confident he wasn't ill, and that he was strong. When she argued that taking precautions would benefit him, too, since he didn't know the details of her sexual history, he got upset but ultimately admitted it was old-fashioned of him to assume she was a virgin. Diana jokingly told him, "You know, we're not in Bogota!" In fact, before she met Jesus she had been considering marrying an old lover, but decided against it because while the fellow was sufficiently acculturated not to expect his future wife to be chaste, he was *macho* enough to be emotionally abusive to her.

So that issue was settled, but immediately Jesus presented Diana with another objection—that the condom would desensitize him and diminish his pleasure. "Yes, I guess that's possible," she responded, "but think of how much longer you'll be able to last!"

What really brought Jesus to agree with Diana was that she said next, "Jesus, I believe you do care about me and the relationship. My father always said that Latino men were created to protect us women. So do your duty as *un macho* and protect me!"

For Diana, the weekend was a triumph on several levels. She had a truly romantic time on her terms, her self-esteem was enhanced, and she enjoyed the satisfaction of having accomplished the seemingly impossible—getting a traditional Latino to put her needs before his own.

However, if you feel that refusing your partner unprotected sex could enrage him and expose you to rape or abuse, be safe rather than sorry. There is now available to you the female condom we mentioned. It's called Reality and is a soft, loose-fitting plastic pouch that lines the vagina. This presents you and other women with a new alternative method for taking control of your health and your life.

Be sure to use a spermicidal foam that covers the inside of the vaginal wall, as well as the female condom. You can also protect yourself by making sure the male condoms you and your partner use contain nonoxynol-9 on the tip. Be sure you have some of them with you at all times.

As a further precaution, if possible, both you and your partner should go for an AIDS test before ever having sex, then use condom protection for six months, then go for retesting. At that point, your decision about whether or not to continue to use the protection is up to you and your partner and is based on mutual trust.

Don't be afraid to question your partner's integrity. If you're interested in a man, try to find out if he has been tested before you have sex with him. When that's not possible, make absolutely certain you use protection. Should the relationship continue, persuade your partner, as Diana persuaded Jesus, that you should both be tested.

In addition to changing your behavior in a sexual relationship, you must take the following precautions:

Prepare ahead of time for blood transfusions you or loved ones might require sometime in the future. Think of donating your own blood in advance. Share with family members and friends information about blood type compatibility, after making sure you all are tested for HIV. This is a precaution you and all Latinas should follow closely because it could save your life and the lives of those you care most about.

Be alert during injections, blood tests, and dental work. In this age of AIDS, we must all ensure that medical and dental procedures are conducted by health care workers wearing gloves and using sterilized equipment. Make sure that any needle or syringe used comes in a sealed package and is opened in front of you.

Never forget, you have the right to live and therefore have the inner strength to say *basta!* Make yourself proud of your strength by taking command of your life and making sure the sex you desire is safe!

THE PATH TO SEXUAL EMPOWERMENT

We appreciate that it's difficult for many Latinas to express their *sensualidad* sexually, but we—and the women in this chapter—know it can be done. Dora, the woman with the flagrantly unfaithful husband, for instance, devoted herself to therapy sessions, exercises, and consciousness-raising literature in the areas of both self-esteem and sexuality. To her delight, the more her belief in herself grew, the more sensual feelings she allowed herself. In time, she realized her husband would probably have gotten involved with another woman even if he'd been married to Sharon Stone, because of his own insecurities. After all, Juan needed the confirmation of many affairs to feel truly *macho.* He'd had that belief instilled in him by his father and grandfather just as Dora had learned about chastity from her mother and grandmother. Realizing this was a breakthrough for Dora because it made her aware that the self-esteem problems were her husband's as well as her own. Once that became clear, she could confront Juan and begin exploring the possibilities of dialogue with him.

However, her husband's infidelities presented another, more serious problem. Although he was a physician as well as a man who slept around, Juan never used a condom when they were making love.

Dora's decision to protect herself against AIDS and other sexually transmitted diseases forced her to challenge *marianista* tradition and convince him to take precautions. When she first made her sentiments clear, Juan was stunned that she had the courage to make such a demand, but he eventually complied.

These improvements notwithstanding, Dora continued to be unhappy in her marriage and Juan continued to have affairs. By the time a few years elapsed, she asked herself, "Why do I need to put up with a situation in which my own husband doesn't have respect for me?" Her work in therapy had bolstered her self-esteem enough so that she no longer needed to replicate the silent suffering and submissiveness of her mother and grandmother. Luckily, she acknowledged, times had changed; she had a career and a salary on which she could support herself. She didn't have to have a man to survive. "Thank God," she mused, "that I have options. My mother and grandmother didn't. They were trapped."

Dora's sexual empowerment was a major element in her decision to divorce Juan, since she now felt better prepared for a more satisfying relationship with another man should he come along. To be sure, Dora's mother and aunt initially expressed shock and disappointment when she broke the news of her decision to them, yet later her mother was able to tell her, "*Mi hijita*, you are doing the right thing. I wish that when I was your age, I could have done it too."

Remember Alicia, the widow torn by sexual self-doubt, who had just met a new man when we last encountered her? Bruce, an American college professor, had lived in Guatemala for five years when he was in the Peace Corps, and understood *marianismo* and *machismo* all too well. Alicia recounted to us the story of her first dinner date with him. After they'd been seated, he asked her what she'd like to drink and eat—a radical change from the behavior of her late husband, Emilio, who used to order for both of them without bothering to consult her. And that was only the first of many surprises which made Alicia "feel like a person." Bruce involved her in other decisions, such as where they

would eat or what movie they would see. He also was frank about discussing what were clearly her feelings of self-doubt.

At first, Alicia viewed Bruce mainly as a supportive and understanding companion, who would often make comments like, "I know that's the way you were taught to think and feel about yourself, but here in the United States you have options regarding your likes and dislikes." He was enormously helpful in Alicia's starting to perceive herself as an adult capable of making choices. Only after she felt comfortable with him and sure of herself in general did Alicia realize she was sexually attracted to him, but the feelings scared her because they were so new. In therapy, she was encouraged to fantasize about what it would be like to go to bed with her new beau, and no matter how guilty she felt, to do visualization exercises as well as repeat this affirmation, "I am entitled to have sexual feelings. I am good. I am a good woman," when she felt guilt overwhelming her.

When Alicia first had intercourse with Bruce, the old feelings of sinfulness and unworthiness crowded out her sexual pleasure, but she felt free to express that to her lover, who was supportive and understanding. He helped her to verbalize what would give her pleasure as well as to get to know her body and feel good about it. Bruce never forced himself on her and was patient, gentle, and loving. It was only a matter of time before Alicia was able to confess to her therapist, "If I'd only known what I was missing!"

Maritza, the excellent wife and mother who felt she was frigid, also overcame her fears. In therapy, she learned she had to love herself and shift her focus from *ser-para-los-otros* to *ser-para-sí-misma*, because only then could she fully express her love for her family. She also remembered how strictly she had been brought up, how deeply devout her family had been, and that sensuality was rarely displayed in the home. She had to learn things many other women grew up knowing.

How did she do that? She used behavior modification exercises, visualizations, and affirmations, and began to explore her body. Slowly, she began to feel and want to express her *sensualidad*. Next, she decided to share her worries and concerns about sex with her husband,

Javier. Javier was surprisingly responsive and encouraging, and in order to make things easier for her, consented to accompany her to therapy. A sensitive and gentle man, Javier was more interested in Maritza's happiness than in protecting his *machismo*. In time, with his full support, Maritza experienced what it was like to feel "sexy" and still be *una buena mujer*. Toward the end of her treatment, she turned to Javier during a session and told him, "We've got to raise our daughters differently than I was raised. I never want them to feel the sexual frustration and confusion I've felt all my life until now! I want them to know that when the time comes and the right man appears, they can have a wonderful physical relationship which will enrich their marriage—as my awakening of *sensualidad* has done for you and me."

La Latina Liberada

While a great number of Latinas do not feel comfortable with their sexuality, we've seen in this chapter that many of us are identifying it as an issue we need to deal with in order to lead more fulfilling lives. Of course, no two women's conflicts are identical, and we all resolve them in different ways.

For instance, Dora's resolution was divorce, while Alicia was able to work on her sexual repression and find a man compatible with her needs. Maritza, who thought she was frigid when she was really just scared, made the connection between sexual confidence and self-esteem and learned that when she improved the former, the latter likewise profited. Diana learned to take action and assert herself in protecting her right to health.

Indeed, these and other Latinas have summoned the courage to walk away from the *marianista* suppression of the sexual self that was causing them needless unhappiness, to learn to relate to and love their bodies, and to expand their sensualism to include sex as an expression of love. They are all *nuevas marianistas*, who have rewritten the traditional motto "Good women are able to bear great suffering" to read, "Good women are able to feel great pleasure."

7

"Do Not Be Unhappy with Your Man, No Matter What He Does to You":

Noble Martyr vs.
Nueva Marianista

Bertilia, a thirty-four-year-old Mexican-American computer programmer married to Beltran, a thirty-nine-year-old Salvadorean waiter, knocked on the therapist's door for the first time looking pale and quite distressed. Exceedingly apologetic, she emphatically expressed how sorry she was that she hadn't waited for the therapist to return her call but had simply shown up at the office. She was clearly grateful that the therapist could fit her in because, as she put it, *"Tenía que verla de inmediato"*—I had to see you right away. She then proceeded to recount an experience that had genuinely terrified her.

Her husband, Beltran, had become very upset when he saw

Bertilia's laughing and chatting with male colleagues during an office party. He accused her of disrespecting him because he was not as educated as her co-workers and didn't speak English as well as they or she did. First he called her *orgullosísima*, arrogant and conceited, then accused her of being unfaithful to him with a certain man in the office. This was only the beginning of a litany of baseless accusations, including calling Bertilia *manoseada*, slut. When she denied his false charges and cried, "Estás loco," he lost all control, and began slapping and choking her.

After this behavior became chronic and she discovered in addition that Beltran was having their phone tapped, Bertilia moved herself and her two daughters to her mother's house. Immediately, Beltran appeared with flowers, regrets, and tearful promises that it wouldn't happen again. Although Bertilia had severe doubts about returning to Beltran, her mother and brothers advised her that she should think seriously about it. After all, they told her, he was simply reacting to what he perceived as a threat to his manhood. Also, they reminded her, she had recently discovered she was pregnant again. Her children, they concluded, should be her top priority.

Feeling misunderstood and alone, Bertilia acquiesced and moved back with Beltran—who soon required that she report her whereabouts to him at all times. He insisted on driving her to work and picking her up, and demanded she call her friends and tell them how terribly she'd misjudged her truly wonderful husband. In addition, Beltran would explode in anger at unexpected moments. When they were watching the Simpson trial, for instance, he abruptly began ranting that Bertilia was *una puta infiel* and continued haranguing her all night. While Beltran needed constant reassurance, it didn't even make a difference in his behavior. Bertilia felt as if she was losing her mind.

During one of their fights, Bertilia announced to Beltran that she didn't need him to support her. After all, she spoke good English and was a college graduate. Unfortunately, he never forgot that remark and held it up to her time and again, demanding that she quit her job. Furthermore, if she wasn't feeling amorous when Beltran wanted sex, he accused her of no longer being interested in him because she was see-ing other men.

A few days before she appeared at the therapist's door, Bertilia had been on her way to pick up Beltran but got stuck in a traffic jam and showed up an hour late. Her husband *estaba tan molesto*, he was so beside himself, that he immediately began choking her and slamming her head against the car window without even asking her why she was late. Bertilia ended up in the emergency room so embarrassed that she told the doctors she had been in an accident with the car. The truth is, she was terrified to go home, but of course, like so many battered women, she did. Bertilia was lucky; her church brought a counselor to speak to the congregation about domestic violence. After the presen-tation, Bertilia mustered the courage to speak to the presenter about her situation with Beltran.

Bertilia told the counselor a diluted version of what was happen-ing to her. "Oh, Beltran is, you know . . . so *macho*, he's just very pos-sessive," Bertilia said at first. Airing problems to people outside the family, after all, is anathema to *la marianista*. So is the very thought of criticizing your man. "What do you mean when you say 'possessive'?" the counselor insisted. Slowly at first, Bertilia began to open up about what was really going on between her and Beltran. It was lucky for her that the counselor had good experience in this field. What Bertilia said is what many women say and think initially. The counselor helped Bertilia to see that there is no reason in the world for anyone to be abused like that, and instilled in her the importance of seeing someone professionally.

The Numbers Speak for Themselves

This is a chapter we wish we didn't have to write, but violence toward women is too critical and widespread a subject not to be discussed, as the following statistics from New York State Domestic Violence Fact Sheets make abundantly clear.

Each year approximately three to four million American women are abused by their spouse or partner (E. Stark et al., 1981).

It is more likely that a woman in the United States will be attacked, hurt, sexually abused, or killed by her partner than by any other person (A. Browne and R. Williams, 1987).

Ninety-five percent of the victims of domestic violence are women (Bureau of Justice Statistics, *Report to the Nation on Crime and Justice: The Data*. Washington, D.C.: Office of Justice Programs, U.S. Department of Justice, October 1983).

The literature on domestic violence suggests that wife beating results in more injuries that require medical treatment than sexual assaults, automobile accidents, and robbery combined (E. Stark and A. Flitcraft, 1987).

Each year, more than a million women seek medical assistance for injuries caused by abuse (E. Stark and A. Flitcraft, 1987).

The Federal Bureau of Investigation reports that 30 percent of female homicide victims are killed by their partners—in contrast to only 6 percent of male victims (FBI, *Crime in the United States*, 1986).

Findings from an in-depth study of all U.S. homicide cases between 1980 and 1984 report that more than half (52 percent) of female victims were killed by their partners (A. Browne and R. Williams, 1987).

Abused women constitute 20 percent of injured females in hospital emergency rooms (E. Stark et al., 1979).

It is estimated that violence will occur at least once in 66 percent of all marriages (M. Roy, ed., 1982).

Women are three times more likely to be a victim of violent crime by a family member than are men (P. A. Klaus, 1984).

During an average of six months after an incident of domestic violence, approximately 32 percent of abused women become a victim again (P. A. Langan and C. A. Innes, 1986).

Spousal abuse occurs frequently during pregnancy. Twenty-one percent of pregnant women in one study were found to have been abused. These women had twice the number of miscarriages than women who had not been battered (E. Stark et al., 1981).

The statistics listed above are most probably underestimations of the magnitude of domestic violence. It should also be noted that social stress and isolation are powerful motivators for violence—and that the underrepresentation of partner violence almost certainly exists nationally among the poor and non-English-speaking population (A. Weidman, 1986). In fact, the consensus among researchers throughout the nation is that the actual figures of partner violence cases is probably double the two million cases reported in the United States annually.

Using the figures above, it is possible that one out of four women in the United States have been victims of partner violence. If you or someone close to you has experienced physical abuse at the hands of a husband or boyfriend, know that you are not alone. Know too that countless others with your problem have resolved it. Many, many women we have treated bear witness to those positive and healing solutions. You may also feel the abuse issue doesn't pertain to you because your experience may presently involve only verbal abuse. But keep in mind that verbal abuse is far too frequently the prelude to physical battering.

Just as in any other area we cover, we reiterate that spousal abuse is not experienced solely by Hispanic women. Spousal violence knows no bounds of nationality, race, or class. But there are special, deep-seated facets to the problem which can be exacerbated by *marianismo*, and thus are most relevant to Latinas. And those are what we will deal with here.

In the course of this chapter we will continue describing how your *marianista* beliefs can keep you a prisoner of abuse—and an unknowing contributor to it—as well as provide the means by which you can turn traditional cultural beliefs to your advantage and make your home a peaceful place. Through case stories we will provide guidelines for you to get what you want from your man without incurring his wrath. We emphasize that you must seek help when these strategies do not work.

Now answer the following questions, being as honest with yourself as you possibly can, because candor is absolutely key. Denial is never a good thing, but when the issue is domestic abuse, it can literally be a fatal mistake.

- In your life, do you feel you might be buying into the belief that *las mujeres primero deben ser damas*, women must always be ladies, and as a result letting your man insult you in public in order not to make a scene in front of friends or others?
- Are you afraid of your partner's wrath?
- Do you fear that your family will try to convince you he is a good provider and worth putting up with?
- Do you think the only way out of an abusive marriage is becoming a divorcée or a separated woman—in other words, an outcast in traditional Latin society?
- Should you stay with a bully and take the abuse for the sake of your children?
- Are you plagued by the dread that you won't be able to make it on your own?

After you've written down your responses, reread them, and you'll have a clear idea of what your domestic situation really is, as well as how *marianismo* is contributing to your problems. For many Latinas, immigration and abuse go hand in hand.

 ## THE IMMIGRATION PROVOCATION

The immigration process in general is a difficult one. The many pressures accompanying acculturation greatly enhance anybody's regular level of tension, as you may well know. When you add in other stress factors such as unemployment, poverty, drug and alcohol abuse, inability to communicate in English, and a general lack of education and job skills, it is clear that many emigrating Latinas stand a strong chance of finding themselves at risk in the home. Economic constraints, role expectations, and a desire to maintain the traditional values of *marianismo* and *machismo* augment the level of stress in families, and contribute to potential violence.

Social scientists indicate that immigrant families experience conflict along the lines of gender and age. Within the context of age difference, which is here defined as different generations, parents can experience a great deal of conflict with their children in terms of different values, dating patterns, and in the general level of acculturation, since children adapt more rapidly than adults. As far as gender goes, we have seen in our practice how a woman too often blames herself or is blamed by her mate for his personal frustrations with the new culture. Calling upon his belief package of *machismo*, the man may avoid dealing with his own diminished sense of self-worth by translating it into his woman's failure to live up to *marianismo*. In psychoanalytic literature, this process is called displacement.

Displacement is an unconscious activity by which an individual transfers the emotions produced by a specific person or event onto a completely different object or situation. Instead of focusing on difficulties you are having with your own sense of self, you blame others for your unhappiness or for things that cause you frustration. In the case of a couple, for example, the man may blame and attack his partner because his boss harshly criticized him in front of his co-workers. Sometimes in such combative occurrences a man may also resort to transference, which you will recall means "enacting" unresolved conflicts from childhood in a totally inappropriate situation. Remember Ana, the Costa Rican woman from Chapter 3 whose troubled relationship with her overbearing mother made her supersensitive to a bossy woman at work? She was carrying around a lot of heavy emotional baggage without even knowing it.

Likewise, an abusive Latino's baggage often includes problems, insecurities, and needs to defend his self-worth that originated in his early relationships, such as the one with his mother. Frequently, these insecurities are inflamed by a failed earlier marriage, by the immigration process, or by inability to find a job. In simple terms, it's as if the man puts his woman in the place of the childhood figures who pained him by being overcritical, unnurturing, unloving, or who were themselves abusive. When this man is unaware that he is transferring, he will persevere in repeating the old patterns. Inevitably, the recipient of his outbursts cannot understand why she is being punished.

Unfortunately, this chronic displacement of male frustration on a woman cannot fail to lower her self-esteem, which in turn makes her more vulnerable to abuse and less likely to defend herself. As a good *marianista*, she is colluding with her abuser and taking literal responsibility for all suffering.

When Your Man's Pride Is Threatened

As we've said, the problem of domestic violence is not confined to Latinas, but immigration can make people more conservative and obedient to the old ways and attitudes. Perhaps this is due to linguistic and/or legal-status issues or to an unconscious attempt to hold on to a familiar identity. Whatever the reason, your mate's expectations of you can be excessive at a time when you're saddled with a whole new set of responsibilities that require managing a larger set of tasks and chores without additional help. When you cannot meet his demands—or choose not to—the conflict could reach a boiling point.

Conflicts between male and female acculturation are all too frequently expressed through the man's anger. He might feel, *"No me quiere atender,"* that his woman no longer wants to take care of him, or has become *muy independiente*, too independent, or simply that a woman's place is *en la cocina*, in the kitchen. If you no longer agree, his *macho* pride may suffer and arguments can break out because he feels you are not giving him the respect due him according to the old rules.

A very traditional *macho* expects you to do most or all of the household chores even though you work outside the home. When your family income hasn't yet reached the level you enjoyed in the Old Country or that is required to support your family in North America, you might not be able to afford to go to a movie or out to dinner. If you're just making ends meet, you probably can't afford a babysitter, and as we've said, even if you can Latino tradition frowns on outside help with children. Such stressful changes in family life undoubtedly serve to make things more tense at home.

To make matters worse, the acculturation process is not necessarily experienced identically by men and women. In fact, the social scientist A. Ginorio has found that women acculturate at a slower rate than men—except in the area of role expectations, which, simply put, means the things men are supposed to do and women are supposed to do. The traditional woman may feel that it is her duty to do the household chores alone, and to attend to her husband in every way, but often she does not like doing these things. She accepts her mate's decisions and orders as her "duty," but again she doesn't usually like doing so. A traditional *macho*, for example, may not even consider it correct to consult his wife about immigrating. He simply expects her to go along with his desires and not complain or disagree about it. And if his decision doesn't bring him the satisfaction he's expecting, he may very well take his disappointment out on his spouse.

This was how it was with Larissa and her husband, Leandro, a couple in their mid-thirties who had moved back to the Dominican Republic after living in New York for fifteen years. Although they had both come as adolescents to New York, where they met, married, and had two children, Leandro couldn't adjust to the city and complained that his job as a furniture store manager wasn't fulfilling him. When the bank where Larissa worked offered her a transfer to their Santo Domingo branch, Leandro insisted she jump at the chance—although she was perfectly happy in New York and didn't look forward to the move. However, behaving like a good *marianista*, she felt she had no choice but to follow Leandro to a place where he might be happier.

Ironically, the move to Santo Domingo turned out marvelously for Larissa. Through work, she quickly made new friends with whom she played canasta on Tuesday evenings and tennis on Thursdays. She had a loving family with whom to spend holidays, and a wonderful support system of old acquaintances with whom she was thrilled to be reunited. Her life was enviable, and she appreciated every minute of it. Leandro, unfortunately, felt otherwise, and within a couple of years began suggesting *que un cambio le vendría muy bien,* that another change would do him a world of good.

That was when he admitted he'd been in contact with his brother Ernesto, who ran a successful chain of meat markets in New York and was looking for a partner—especially someone he could completely trust, like his brother. Larissa was shocked when she realized that her husband's new business venture was a done deal and that his brother had already gone ahead and found an apartment for their family near a school in Queens, New York. Unable to believe what she was hearing, Larissa blurted out her objections to Leandro and in return was told that her place was by his side. In fact, when Larissa continued to voice her objections to relocating, Leandro reminded her, "You can find another job and other friends a lot easier than another husband!" Deeply hurt and depressed, Larissa again consented to follow her husband as any good *marianista* would.

Then things went from bad to worse. Claiming his brother needed him right away, Leandro immediately departed for New York and left Larissa to see to the details of once more uprooting herself and the children. By the time they arrived in their new home, she discovered that both brothers had furnished the apartment from top to bottom without bothering to consult with her. Larissa felt as if she'd come to Leandro's home, not her own. And that was only the beginning, since Leandro insisted that Larissa stay at home rather than going to work, because their children, a girl of ten and a boy of twelve, needed her supervision. He felt that New York was a very dangerous city, and that Larissa's place was at home tending to the children and him.

Being a resourceful person, Larissa set about making friends and getting involved in activities she enjoyed. Yet, to her surprise, Leandro was far from approving of her adaptability. She couldn't understand why her husband suddenly became intensely possessive when he hadn't been that way at all in Santo Domingo. It was about this time that she began to develop a spectrum of physical complaints, ranging from asthma to stomach problems, and was chronically weepy, angry, irritable, and terribly lonely. She came to therapy, in her words, to "sort out her head." "My world has ended," she wept. "I don't know Leandro anymore because he's changed so much, he's a different person. He's absolutely *odioso!*"

Leandro's hatefulness and hostility were expressed in psychologically abusing his wife by calling her names such as *gorda, basura,* and *engreída*—fat, garbage, and stuck-up—and by offending her when she criticized his behavior or the furnishings he had selected for their home. He would simply announce that he was the one who made the money and was working hard for his family's sake, and boasted about his intellectual superiority. "*¿Cómo puedes ser tan desagradecida?*"— How can you be such an ingrate?—he would roar. Bereft of a job she'd loved and an ambience in which she had been happy, faced with the abrupt transformation of what she'd always considered a good marriage into an abusive one, Larissa found herself in the middle of an unbearable situation.

Dr. Jekyll y Señor Hyde

The process of acculturation does not necessarily have to be unhealthy. In fact, there are many individuals who suffer little disruption when they go through it. Unfortunately, others have a much rougher time. Leandro's radical personality shift is a good illustration of the manner in which an unhealthy acculturation process may affect an individual. When a man like Leandro doesn't allow himself to experience the changes in role expectations which are integral to acculturation—either by choice or because he is psychologically unable to—he reverts even farther into *machismo*. Cuban psychologist Oliva Espin exemplifies this reaction when she points out how families in their defensive efforts to acculturate tend to idealize the home culture to the point of caricature. This idealization is a reaction against a sense of identity loss, and may not always be parallel between couples. Consequently the potential for domestic conflict grows by leaps and bounds.

Espin describes the stages of adaptation and acculturation as a continuum: (1) initial joy and relief, followed by (2) disillusionment, and then (3) acceptance of reality—which signifies acknowledging both the positive and negative aspects of the new culture. But if, especially in terms of gender-based role expectations, the man is mired separately in the second stage, the home becomes a potential battleground—as Larissa so painfully discovered. The more traditional the family roles, the more difficulties an acculturating Latina can expect from her spouse—and the more resistance to the change acculturation requires she can anticipate.

Keeping Up Appearances

We've repeatedly pointed out that as you acculturate, you may feel confused when your traditional values conflict with your new reality and altered life circumstances, especially in situations involving women's subordination to men—so when you first hear the word "violence," you may not associate it with your life. You may actually deny it. That is the reason why we asked you to take the quiz early in the chapter—to counteract your possible denial.

It is imperative that you learn to define what constitutes abuse. Perhaps your man insults you by calling you *estúpida* in front of his family, your family, or friends. He might belittle you and may call you incompetent, find fault with everything you do, insist you do not see friends, expect you to give him all your money, and worst of all, abuse you physically—either by pushing you or by actually hurting you. You should stop him at the very beginning of what feels to you like abuse. Too often many women cover for their men because *marianismo* insists *en mantener las apariencias*, on keeping up appearances, at all costs.

It's difficult to think of a culture which puts more weight on *mantener las apariencias* than the Hispanic. Professor Juan Bosch, in his book *Composición Social Dominicana*, refers to many eighteenth-

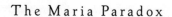

century colonial landowners who were ruined by their excesses in dress in an effort to appear as affluent as the aristocracy. As he recounts the history of the Indies, Bosch also refers to women who emigrated from Spain and their experience with poverty in the Dominican Republic when sugar cane production declined. Those who stayed despite this increasing need began going to church at daybreak to avoid being seen in shabby attire when they couldn't borrow a dress from a friend. Even worse, many went without food to buy clothes—all for the sake of keeping up appearances. And this is true all over Latin America.

Take *quinceañeras*, the traditional Hispanic party given in celebration of a daughter's fifteenth birthday. Families who cannot really afford to have a lavish celebration often go into crushing debt because *pertenecer*, fitting in, is all-important to them. These beliefs have survived for centuries, and their ramifications are so deeply embedded in the culture that they extend into many other areas of our lives. Be assured that where domestic abuse is concerned, keeping up appearances can be a foolish and literally fatal mistake. You can also be certain that you'll have a healthier relationship with your partner if you convince him his behavior is embarrassing you and making you feel ashamed. Of course, the best-case scenario is always to prevent the abuse in the first place.

If you are a victim of repeated haranguings from your mate, realize it is in your power not to let them escalate—in fact, not to be a victim at all. The answer is to feel sure enough of yourself not to allow yourself to be badly treated, no matter if tradition is telling you it's your duty to take whatever a man hands out.

STOP THE ABUSE BEFORE IT STARTS!

When despite your best efforts your man won't stop abusing you and/or the abuse escalates, it's wise to seek professional help. However, if things are still at the stage where they can be contained, we can help you change things for the better.

Let's first examine some of the behaviors to which you may be subjected that signal the first stirrings of domestic violence:

- Your partner feels you are deliberately trying to make him angry when in fact *solamente estás bromeando*, you're just kidding around.
- Your partner actively discourages you from being friendly with the neighbors or visiting your relatives. He gets so angry he smashes dishes or objects in the home.
- He drinks heavily and/or uses drugs and becomes angry and belligerent when doing so.
- He accuses you, without cause, of flirting and making him feel humiliated.
- He is excessively jealous, doesn't approve of your clothes, and demands you dress the way he wants you to.
- He forbids you to call him at work or, worse still, show up there.
- He roughhouses you for such minimal transgressions as misplacing his papers, losing things, or disagreeing with him.
- He angrily blames you for the children's misbehavior and/or feels you frustrate him by not being as agreeable to his ideas as he would like.
- He ridicules you by calling you epithets such as "dumb" or "stupid"—alone or in front of his friends, or yours.
- He speaks of women in general as *putas*, as weak, or generally as bad.
- He screams at you instead of talking when he is angry at you for any reason.
- He blames you for things that go wrong over which you have no control, such as when the dinner does not agree with him or a man looks at you in a sexy manner.

If you can see your own personal experience mirrored in any of the above examples and you tolerate the behavior, you may well qualify as *una mártir noble*, a noble martyr, and if you do, you most probably are—whether you know it or not—trying to be *una buena marianista*. In order to change and enhance your self-worth, you're going to have to be very firm with yourself.

Write down what you consider your strengths.

Ask your friends what they honestly think of you and how they would describe you to someone else.

Make it a point to review your list of assets several times a day.

By so doing, you are taking action to stop being a victim, and begin the journey to empowerment by stopping the abuse. Whatever steps you take, don't let your shame at being a victim keep you one. And don't assume you can't succeed. We have treated many, many Latinas who made the transition from noble martyrdom to full recovery and personal empowerment. They did so by stepping back from their situation, refusing to let their *marianismo* cloud their vision, and examining it objectively. When they did so, they realized the necessity for taking immediate action.

You Don't Have to Take It Anymore

Undoubtedly, the first step toward changing a potentially dangerous situation is to recognize that you do not have to put up with *lo inaguantable*, the unbearable, for the sake of your children. In fact, keep in mind that doing that could only perpetuate the dilemma by influencing your daughters to accept this behavior in the future, and your sons to become perpetrators of abuse. Your children will feel entitled to be taken care of and obeyed in a manner that is no longer realistic. Even worse, frankly, you could lose your life.

You must always be aware that when you rationalize a hostile spousal atmosphere by putting off change until things get better—until he stops drinking or gets a better job or your mother-in-law leaves— you're probably kidding yourself. Excusing the abuser is simply not going to help him or yourself. Abuse that is not *arrancado de sepa*, nipped in the bud, will only escalate. And don't even try to tell yourself, "He never hurts me physically. He only loses his temper and calls me names." Calling you names is attacking you by infantilizing, humiliating, and disrespecting you. You should never allow it, never. In fact, *"Jamás"* should become your motto. That's what Petra had to learn.

Petra is a thirty-six-year-old Cuban-born pharmacist, who no longer practices her profession because she finds taking care of her husband and two children a full-time job. Her husband, Joaquin, owns a chain of clothing stores and since his English is not fluent, Petra serves as his buyer. She also handles all the accounting and public relations as well as attending all of her children's school functions. In addition, Petra makes sure Joaquin's clothes are impeccable, even polishes his shoes, coordinates the care of her lavish home with her domestic help while still doing her own grocery shopping, and keeps herself elegantly groomed and in the height of fashion.

When Petra came to therapy, she was extremely vague about her problems. All she could say for sure was that Joaquin couldn't understand why—since she had two beautiful sons and every luxury money could buy—she was unhappy. However, as therapy progressed, Petra admitted that Joaquin was *muy áspero,* too rough. He would scream at her publicly if she forgot to do something or if, in his estimation, she made a mistake. Since he had to feel he was always in command, Petra began lying to him if she'd slipped up on some chore. She was constantly on the verge of tears, but when she asked for Joaquin's help, he replied he was busy or, worst of all, told her she was crazy.

This horrendous verbal abuse lasted for five years—until one night at the movies, Petra said something that annoyed Joaquin and right then and there he slapped her. After that, confused about exactly what she'd done to provoke her husband to physical violence in public, she—like a good *marianista*—tried even harder to please him so the abuse would stop. It didn't. That was when Petra began having headaches, experienced frequent dizziness, and developed stomach problems. As she would later come to see in therapy, she was somatizing—or, as we've mentioned earlier, experiencing her emotional distress as physical illness.

When Petra came for treatment, she did so *a escondidas*, behind her husband's back. Initially, she wasn't even aware she was depressed, but merely blamed herself for not being happy and for failing at being the homemaker her husband wanted her to be. Soon, however, she was confessing that since that night at the movies, Joaquin had escalated from screams and excessive demands to chronic slapping and pushing. At least, through treatment, she was able to realize she was the victim of abuse. But that was only the beginning of her empowerment. The next step was getting Joaquin to stop.

Petra's first action was to tell her husband she was in therapy, at which point he called the therapist directly to threaten her. He claimed that his wife had changed for the worse since she'd begun treatment and insisted the therapist cease treating her. Now Petra was faced with a terrible dilemma—whether to accede to her husband's demands and continue to be miserable, or to continue with therapy and risk his wrath.

THE ABUSE CONTINUUM

We can see from Petra's experience with Joaquin that abuse builds in stages toward a continuum. The story of Maira also illustrates this dreadful truth all too well.

Maira, a forty-five-year-old Ecuadorean-American, worked as a cleaning woman in a large Manhattan office building. Despite her long, grueling days, Maira's husband, a mechanic named Miguel, expected her to cook him a full dinner when she got home. If she went to bed first, he would come into the bedroom and turn on the light, not caring if he woke her up. Miguel insisted on driving an expensive car "to keep up appearances," even if it cost most of her meager salary. When Maira bought clothes, he reprimanded her for being *una gastadora*, a spendthrift, although he spent lavishly on himself. Miguel constantly called her *estúpida y tonta*, stupid and clumsy, often in public. When Maira protested, Miguel became more verbally abusive. Maira was afraid that he would lose control and hurt her physically. Eventually, a concerned client connected to a community clinic persuaded her to go to therapy.

Marianista to the core, Maira soon revealed she felt her husband's behavior was her fault. Why? Because her cultural conditioning told her it had to be, and her husband constantly confirmed it. Because she felt she had to be the guilty party, she was too ashamed to discuss it with her relatives and friends for fear of being regarded as a marital failure. "*En mi familia no existen divorcios*—there are no divorces in my family," she told her therapist, "It's against my religion and in my country—*una desgracia!*"

In treatment, Maira was able to begin to identify the symptoms of her low self-esteem, which were tied to the insults she constantly heard her husband leveling at her. In true *marianista* fashion, she believed she was worthless and could not survive without her husband's support. She also felt ashamed, because although she could admit her marriage was troubled, she regarded it as her fault. Tearfully, she went on to express her misery with pitiable eloquence. "I have no one I can trust," she sobbed. "In my country, it was different. We were poor, but we had dignity. Here, I feel nobody cares, nobody appreciates me for who I am. I came to the United States to have a better life, but I feel like a total failure!"

Maira went on to acknowledge that her husband was also feeling like a failure in this "land of opportunity," but the fact that she couldn't make him feel better made her feel even worse about herself. Slowly, the therapist led her to see that she was expecting much too much from herself and that the self-loathing that is the product of perfectionism had actually become a habit, as well as an integral component of her self-image. By announcing her failure to the world, so to speak, she was actually seeking validation of it—and unknowingly encouraging her husband to transfer his own negative sense of self onto her.

You may or may not identify with Maira. As we have said, there are many different gradations of abuse, and no two situations are alike. Therefore, you need to ask yourself if you fall into a category of domestic violence that might have potential solutions, even though they're difficult ones. Or you may be in a relationship that demands you terminate it, whatever it takes. If you want to save the relationship, be prepared to fight for your right to live abuse-free. There are no failure-proof guidelines to give as to when a relationship is worth saving. The best advice we can give you is to see a professional expert in the subject and follow his or her professional advice. A rule of thumb is that continuing physical abuse that escalates in intensity is a dangerous thing and the best thing to do is to get out of the relationship.

Learning to Be Good to Yourself and Finding Support

The Maira who came to therapy was a true *marianista*, a victim both of her husband and of her cultural values. However, the Maira who completed therapy had learned she was allowing, even encouraging her victimization. That was the beginning of her empowerment, which involved getting an education so she could equip herself to share in the rewards North America had to offer her. "I have to go learn something," she confidently told her therapist, "not only because it will make me feel better about myself but also because it will help me have a better life, which I deserve!" Eventually, she learned English, obtained a GED (high school equivalency diploma), and became a licensed real estate agent.

We're happy to report that over time, Miguel became more understanding and helpful, and their relationship really did improve. Maira learned to stop feeling guilty about Miguel's shortcomings. She also learned to communicate to him that he was being hurtful by calling her names. She reported that she was surprised that once he knew she was serious, he began to be much more supportive and no longer felt the need to be abusive.

It is important to note here that Maira's depression began to lift only after she mastered the ABCs of being good to herself. She monitored her own reactions closely and made sure she fought against her natural tendency to label herself in a negative manner. She also realized that she could be a good mate and a good human being without being a subservient and opinionless woman or trying to be everything to everyone.

A crucial aspect of all this is that regardless of your decision, you need support. All too frequently, abused women follow a pattern of isolation—the worst move they can make if they are to end their suffering. And for this reason, many abusers forbid their spouses to have friends or other contacts that could influence their lives. If this is the case for you, you need to seek therapy or some form of counseling for support.

In Maira's case, she became part of a group of Hispanic women she met through her English-language classes. They all shared a common problem or interest, and met once a month to trade recipes and stories, and provide support for each other. In a later chapter, we'll explain how you can form a group like this, which is called *una tertulia*. Maira's *tertulia* was an invaluable source of support as she became sufficiently empowered to face her husband and tell him how upsetting his behavior was to her. Her *comadres* had encouraged her to ask him to come to therapy, and to her shock, he did. Both the therapist and Maira were surprised by how verbal, insightful, and positive he was about the process. Proudly he exclaimed, "This isn't as difficult as I imagined!"

If you feel your partner is a good candidate for therapy, all you have to do is get him to the first session. From then on, it is the therapist's job to engage him and to help you both. As an important part of her empowerment, Maira came to see that she could use such traditional concepts as *familismo* in a new and positive way by implementing negotiation strategies that appealed to her man's *macho* sense of responsibility.

Yes, you can ask your man to be a good *macho* to you. While it's true, as Evelyn Stevens writes, that the doctrine of *marianismo* mandates that if women can endure all suffering, they must endure all suffering inflicted by men, we feel you can turn this dictum to your advantage. Appeal to your man. Ask for his help. If you must, convey

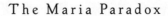

to him that you're really not strong enough or capable of enduring all suffering. But certainly get across the point that suffering is not what you deserve. For instance, ask for his help with the shopping; say that the packages are too heavy for you. Tell your mate you need him to help you sleep a little longer, because otherwise you will be too tired to last all day and be a good wife to him. Ask him to take you dancing because you derive pleasure from doing things with him.

Larissa played to Leandro's sense of *macho*. She did this in conversations that were sensitive and helpful to the relationship. (See details under the heading "*Las Nuevas Marianistas*," page 174.) When she asked Leandro, "Would I want to be with anyone else, other than you?" she really meant this: "It is not fair that you are the one who works so hard, by yourself. It also is not right that you have to bear the responsibility of making all the decisions by yourself. You are a wonderful partner and you are taking very good care of your family, but you are a human being, and trying to do everything by yourself is tiring and debilitating emotionally. I love you and want to care for you, so I need to participate."

Negotiating Change with Your Partner

We also are aware that no relationship is hostility-free. But your aim should be to nip it in the bud before argument becomes abuse. Following is a list of angry taunts your partner may hurl at you, and how to deal with them nonviolently:

- You never do anything right, you stupid bitch!
- Where the hell are my socks? I told you to put them in the drawer!
- I give up on you! You're always screwing up—just like your mother!
- These children are wild animals, and it's all your fault!
- This dinner stinks! You can't do anything! You can't even boil water! You're completely useless!

- I refuse to allow your mother or your family into this house!
- Your friend Marta is a troublemaker and a loose woman. I forbid you to see her!

If you have personal scenarios to add to this list, please do. How do you defuse these emotional time bombs? While there is of course no single solution, it must be said that the key lies in negotiating changes with your partner. However, if your mate tends to be violent, skip these exercises and seek professional help as soon as possible. If he is not, many of the above examples can be resolved by dialogue. The most important condition to bring to the table is your feeling entitled to be respected.

Wait until your partner has settled down to approach him. That may be postponing the discussion till later that night, the next day, or even on the weekend. When you honestly feel his anger has dissipated, tell him you'd like to talk with him. You might begin by saying, "It really hurts me when you . . ." Now you repeat to him what he ordered or forbade you to do or whatever he said to humiliate you.

He may respond, "Hey, you're too sensitive! You get your feelings hurt over nothing!"

Then you can tell him, "Yes, I am sensitive, and it would mean a lot to me if you could remember that I am."

In other words, don't be embarrassed that you feel offended. You're just reacting with feelings to which you are entitled. And never lose sight of your entitlement.

Or he could respond by saying, "I was only joking," to which you should answer gently, "But jokes like that aren't funny to me because they hurt my feelings." You must stay centered on your feelings.

Be willing to hear what your mate has to say if he begins to open up, since you have the power to hurt his feelings, too, and may unwittingly have contributed to the outburst. Remember, once you get a man to talk voluntarily about his feelings, you're ahead of the game! If it turns out that you did step on his toes, make it a point to avoid taking the provocative action in the future. Don't invite your mother over on a Sunday afternoon and expect him to entertain her instead of watching baseball, soccer, or football. Give him a little private time when he comes home from work to cool off from the day before bothering him with problems or letting the kids run wild. Explain to him that you've had a rough day at work yourself and are feeling a little jangled.

Sometimes we can't avoid doing things that annoy others, especially our mates. In fact, couples almost always possess individual habits which drive the other person crazy. But those things which can be fixed should be fixed.

Look at what possible behaviors you perform that are annoying to your mate. Do you do them out of anger? If so, what is it that's making you angry enough to retaliate? Tackle that anger directly. For instance, tell your partner, "I have to tell you I really felt humiliated when your mother took it upon herself to rearrange the living room curtains. It hurt me that you sided with her and never pointed out that it's my living room."

In summary, you must look into yourself and see whether you can realistically improve the situation. This is far different from blaming yourself or feeling you're solely responsible for changing things or making everything okay. In fact, it's working together as a couple. If you feel you must do things by yourself in a relationship, you should ask yourself, "Should I be doing this alone? Really alone? Do I want to be doing it alone?"

Maybe you don't, but if you're being forced to by your partner's intransigencies, you must consider taking more radical action and seeking help outside the home.

LAS NUEVAS MARIANISTAS

Traditional *marianismo* says that women are spiritually superior to men and capable of enduring all suffering. But you have come to a new country, to a new culture, and you most likely feel that you deserve to be your own person. Once again, we urge you to become *una nueva marianista*—who believes women are spiritually superior to men and capable of enduring the pain of change. In the context of domestic abuse, this means that you and only you have the responsibility of doing something to straighten out your dysfunctional relationship.

Petra, who had quit her job as a pharmacist to be the buyer for her husband's clothing stores and to raise their children, realized her responsibility to herself. She vowed to continue treatment despite her husband Joaquin's violent objections. At first, she had to pretend she was no longer seeing the therapist, which of course made her feel bad because she hated to have to lie. However, when she realized it was their future that was at stake, she was able to put her action in perspective. Eventually, she felt strong enough to tell Joaquin the truth and insist she was not going to stop since she felt therapy was making her less anxious and edgy. Without rancor or accusation but with assertiveness, she tried to convince him to see things her way. She knew there was a good chance he wouldn't be able to understand, but she felt her major responsibility was to do the best she could for herself.

Petra acquired empowerment by gaining control over her life. To do this, it was necessary to reconnect with her early feelings of helplessness and give them closure. Only then could she ask for respect and expect to get it. But she couldn't get it from Joaquin, no matter how hard she tried. Now she realized that the woman who had found his overbearing *machismo* attractive no longer existed. The new Petra wanted very different things from a man than Joaquin could give her, such as support. For Petra, divorce was finally the only option. It took great personal courage for her to admit there was no point in continuing a dead-end relationship and moving on. We are happy to report that she has now met a gentle, caring man and is having a happy and peaceful relationship with him.

Larissa, the Dominican who found her husband turned into a *macho* man in New York, also took upon herself the responsibility to make things better for herself. She began to feel empowered when she understood she was entitled to feel angry at her husband, Leandro, who had left her out of so momentous a decision as moving to another country. She also came to realize that although he claimed to be happy with the move, Leandro was having his own problems readjusting to North American life. Finally, Larissa's decision was to talk to her husband in very clear, very self-assured terms, over a candlelit dinner of his favorite foods, complete with music he loved and a bottle of champagne. She made sure she gave him time to relax after he got home—since his brother wasn't the easiest person in the world to work with—and wore a dress he especially liked on her.

In this setting *apropiado para un rey*, truly fit for a king, Leandro was lulled into realizing that before the recent move the strength of their marriage had always been in partnership and comradeship and that he needed Larissa by his side now more than ever. She explained calmly but powerfully how hurt she had been to be excluded from so many decisions, and what was necessary to end the tug-of-war that their relationship had become. She told him how much she missed the way things used to be between them and wanted them to be warm and loving again. She convinced him how much easier things would be at work if he had her support at home. That was the beginning of Larissa's very successful campaign to get back the man she had fallen in love with. It took time, but gradually things improved enough so that when she told him she wanted to get a job, he gave her his blessing. Larissa took good care of herself by devising a nonthreatening way in which dialogue could be initiated with Leandro.

None of this would have happened if Larissa hadn't first validated her feelings of wanting to be respected and consulted, which freed her to ask that her needs for companionship be met. Knowing what you deserve is intimately tied to your level of self-esteem. It helps you to be clear about what you are willing to accept, and what you have the right to demand, from significant others in your life.

As you can see from the experiences of Petra and Larissa, there are different paths out of the darkness of abuse, but there are also iron-clad rules for dealing with it. One is overcoming *marianismo* and realizing that your man has no right to hit you or insult you regardless. It means that when you are in need of therapy support or resolution of a crisis, he should not have the right to call you crazy. You're not crazy. It means you're undergoing a life crisis and must seek help. Another iron-clad rule is to know in which situations of domestic violence to look for outside support and not try to change things alone. That support might come from caring friends, from a group organized around the problems of abuse, or from psychotherapy.

But remember that change begins with your accepting the fact that you are being abused and that this is happening because you are allowing it. You must tell yourself over and over that abuse is unacceptable; there is no way to rationalize it as being okay. You must assess your individual situation and then start planning your escape strategy. You must also expect progress to come in small steps. As with any permanent change, such as weight loss, you must be patient. But, we repeat, be patient only with changes that do not involve the actual abuse. Do not wait for things to get better on their own accord. They won't.

We realize you may feel trapped in a dysfunctional relationship. It's certainly a reality that women stay in bad situations due to economic factors. In fact, many women tell us they remain in abusive environments for the sake of the children or because they don't want to go on welfare. And for some of you, your undocumented status may make it impossible for you to seek public assistance. We know that shelters are not ideal places, but we want you to be aware that sometimes as a temporary measure they may be your only readily available resource. The point is, do not try to resolve abusive situations by yourself.

In closing, let's return to the story of Bertilia, whom we saw in an emergency room pretending she'd been in a car crash after her husband, Beltran, abused her. After taking the advice of the counselor who made a presentation in her church, Bertilia began therapy. She was helped to confront the very real risks she was facing. She was also advised of the resources available to her in case she felt endangered. The main thing was to provide her with relevant information on the seriousness of her problem and how it could escalate. She was helped to sort out resources, including seeking an order of protection if necessary. Finally, she herself admitted that nothing on earth justified a man's abusing a woman or vice versa.

Bertilia was clear about wanting to try to work things out with Beltran. After careful examinations and explorations, the therapist felt this wish should be respected and agreed to see them in couples therapy. Luckily, Beltran was truly interested in getting help, was quite remorseful, and admitted that *un hombre de verdad*, a real man, doesn't hit a woman. Although he was working seven days a week, which of course was only making his disposition worse, he agreed to take time off to attend their sessions.

Both Bertilia and Beltran were also helped to see that they were having a communication problem, since they only talked to each other when they were angry, shouting and accusing without really looking for solutions or seeking to meet each other's needs. Now, in a reasonable climate, Bertilia could convey to Beltran that she was upset because he wasn't there for her as he'd been in their country, and he could confess he felt Bertilia was ashamed of him because he wasn't urbane or sophisticated like the men in her office.

Gradually, Beltran was able to share his frustrations at being regarded so differently in North America than he had been in El Salvador. When he felt humiliated and exhausted, he now realized, he took it out on Bertilia. Bertilia also became aware that when their fights were really bad, she was making things worse by calling him names such as *maleducado e inepto*. Once the air was cleared and communication reconnected, they could again become each other's ally. In fact, possibly for the first time, they became good friends as well as husband and wife. That was five years ago. Every Christmas since, the therapist feels a special satisfaction when she receives their card.

Respecting Yourself Means Protecting Yourself

Please remember that this chapter is intended to make you conscious that domestic violence is a gravely serious problem—as you can see from the statistics we've presented. Granted, many abusers benefit from psychotherapy or counseling, but there are some situations that may not get better. Like the women in this chapter, you must be aware of the abuse, not blame yourself, and know how to seek help. You owe it to yourself and your family.

8

"Do Not
Ask for Help":

*Superwoman Mother vs.
Healthy Human Being*

It was Christmas week, and Violeta, a thirty-three-year-old Dominican-American banker, married to Jorge, a thirty-eight-year-old accountant, was busily preparing for her family's holiday. She had baked cookies with her six- and eight-year-old daughters, decorated the house, made *los pasteles* and ordered *el pernil*—that succulent pork roast without which no Christmas Eve feast is complete. Eighteen people from both sides of the family would be coming to dinner.

She had planned the children's annual trip into Manhattan to see the Christmas pageant at Radio City Music Hall and the Christmas tree at Rockefeller Center. Violeta was happy to be able to check off on her gift list the name of every niece, nephew, third cousin, aunt once removed, and family friend. Since it was her turn to host the meeting of the tenants' association of the co-op, she arranged to hold it after the children in the building had finished their night of caroling—an event Violeta was also in charge of. She even managed to pick up a new dress for her husband's firm's Christmas party—which of course was going to be held the same afternoon as the bank's. All this while working her full professional schedule at the bank.

Violeta was actually doing quite well at this remarkable juggling act when disaster struck. Her sister-in-law Charo, Jorge's brother's wife, called to say she and her brood couldn't come to the dinner. For some very complicated reason, Charo reported, her parents had been forced to change their flight from Santo Domingo and were arriving for their holiday visit at nine p.m. Christmas Eve instead of the day before. Of course, they had to be met at the airport. Since the absence of the Charo contingent would put a serious dent in the holiday *familismo*, Violeta immediately resolved instead to reschedule the dinner one night earlier, which was a Saturday. At least she didn't have to go to work that day. But it still created a crisis because the new date was the day she had promised to take her kids and niece and nephew to Radio City. Canceling that would put a serious dent in her *marianismo*, since she would be disappointing her own children as well as her niece and nephew. What was she to do? There had to be an answer. There was!

"*El pernil* needs to roast for hours and hours anyway," reasoned Violeta. "So I'll put it in a slow oven before we leave, and by the time we get back from the city it will be done. Plus I can precook the rice and reheat it when we're all ready to eat. And there are a couple of other things I can do in the morning. It'll be fine!"

Unfortunately, by the time the fateful day came Violeta was so exhausted from having to attend the back-to-back Christmas parties in addition to dealing with the holiday whirlwind that she overslept. That meant she had to do all the work in half the time. But she did it. She cooked the rice, put *el pernil* in the oven, and set off for Radio City with the kids.

All the children enjoyed the Christmas show enormously, and their joy gave Violeta pleasure even though she arrived home a mere half hour before the guests were due. At least, she told herself, *el pernil* was ready. Except for one thing. She'd forgotten to turn on the oven, and what she found was a very raw *pernil*. Although that would have felled a lesser mortal, Violeta would not admit defeat. She jumped in the car, dashed over to a Spanish rotisserie five minutes away, and managed to grab the last piping-hot *pernil* in the shop.

It will come as no surprise that Violeta's relatives marveled at her fantastic organizational skills and at how beautiful and perfect every aspect of the dinner was. A wonderful time was had by all—except the hostess. In fact, when Jorge stood up and proposed a toast to his wife, *una mujer excepcional*, Violeta burst into tears and ran into the kitchen. When Jorge followed her and tried to put his arm around her and ask her what was wrong, she shrugged it off and began crying harder.

"Did I do something?" he asked. Sobbing, Violeta surveyed the mountains of dirty dishes still to be washed and all the leftovers still to be wrapped and blurted out, "Do something? You did nothing! Nothing at all!"

That was the episode that sent Violeta to therapy. "Poor Jorge," she told the therapist. "He was so shocked. I feel terribly guilty about criticizing him for not helping me. And I guess I shouldn't have taken him to task over things which are my responsibility." When asked what her responsibilities consisted of, Violeta launched into a recounting of her pre-Christmas schedule which was exhausting merely to listen to. Although the therapist observed it would have been hectic for a full-time homemaker, Violeta disagreed and claimed all her problems arose because she couldn't take time off from the bank. Did she have to work? the therapist asked. Well, Violeta replied, it was nice to have the extra income, but no, Jorge made a very good living. Did she want to work? Did she enjoy her job? Violeta responded positively to both questions.

"So," the therapist summarized, "perhaps your problem is less about the bank than about trying to be a full-time homemaker and a full-time working woman at once without much help. You should con-gratulate yourself for making it this far under such killer stress!"

EVERYTHING TO EVERYBODY

It's amazing but until the therapist pointed it out to her, Violeta wasn't aware that she was trying to please her husband in exactly the way that her mother had tried to please her father. But the old ways just weren't working in a North American context. The price she was paying was depression and severe anxiety. She was weepy, had trouble sleeping, constantly criticized herself and others at work and at home, was irrita-ble, and felt utterly trapped. Although she considered herself liberated for wanting "to have it all" like any Angla, Violeta was actually being done in by her *marianismo*.

While it's true that many other traditional societies have rigidly prescribed gender roles (and thus this book will be helpful to them, too), we are approaching the subject as Latina clinicians working with Latino/a clients. Our intention is to help you gain a greater awareness and understanding of the all-important role the dark side of *marianismo* plays in shaping the way you relate to your family and to yourself. As a woman with a job outside the home, you may unconsciously be trying, like Violeta, to be everything to everyone. That means you're living according to the *marianista* precept that women can endure all suffer-ing—which, in this context, means assuming an almost insurmount-able burden of both work- and home-related stress.

In the course of this chapter, we're going to study how former *doñas perfectas* like Violeta—and like Josefa, the overburdened "mom" in the mom-and-pop grocery store you met in Chapter 4—come to re-alize that they cannot be *mujeres superdotadas* and lead a fulfilling life in North America. We'll show you how the clash between *marianista* perfectionism and the desire to have it all exacerbates the collision be-tween Old World expectations and New World goals—causing depres-sion and overwhelming feelings of inadequacy in both realms. Lastly, we'll give you evidence that it's possible to readjust your expectations and reorder your priorities so you'll be a considerably less stressed-out wife, mother, and career woman who's proud of herself and thoroughly enjoying life in the United States. But first let's look at some specific *marianista* beliefs that can affect your self-esteem as a working wife and mother.

BELIEF 1. A good wife and mother must always provide her husband and children with a good meal which she prepares herself.

BELIEF 2. A good mother does not argue with her husband in front of the children.

BELIEF 3. A good wife must put up with her husband's relatives, no matter how offensive or inconsiderate they are.

BELIEF 4. A good wife must have an impeccable home and preferably must keep it that way herself.

BELIEF 5. A good Latina must obey traditions *al pie de la letra,* to the letter of the law.

BELIEF 6. A good mother must take care of her children herself or with the help only of very trustworthy relatives.

Measuring Your Own *Perfeccionismo*

To identify your own counterproductive strivings you might start by doing a mental exercise, which should point out how acting on the belief that you can withstand all stress can be very destructive for you and your family. This exercise was very helpful to Violeta.

Begin by asking yourself what you're doing that indicates you're being unnecessarily stoic. Are you doing things for others that you recognize cause you too much stress, since realistically you don't have the time to do them—and that others can do for themselves? Or is your behavior in any manner similar to Violeta's?

Do you feel guilty if you don't do the tasks that you set yourself to do in one day? In one week? In one month?

Do you feel that no one but yourself—including both family members and professional domestic help—is capable of adequately cleaning the house or diapering the baby?

Do you feel that your mate and/or children are unwilling to assume—or are incapable of assuming and adequately performing—household responsibilities at all?

Does your mate do annoying things like constantly forget to buy milk, even if he drains the last container himself, requiring you to make an emergency trip to the store before breakfast so the kids will have milk for their cereal? Do you rationalize the trip to the store as preferable to engaging him in a domestic dispute?

When your husband or mate is unwilling or unable to help you with the chores and with the children—and is unwilling or financially unable to hire all the professional household help you need—are you able to communicate your total exhaustion in a clear and direct manner?

Is it difficult to ask for help, because you feel guilty and unconsciously believe if you're not doing all the chores, you're inadequate?

Can you entertain the thought that catering to your family in traditional *marianista* fashion is spoiling them and creating unrealistic expectations on their part which enhance your feelings of conflict?

Do you find yourself accepting extra work at your job out of guilt over coming in late as a result of your familial responsibilities?

Do you feel guilty or angry that you're the only one who has to take time off from your job because of duties related to the children's school?

Do you end up taking the children to school picnics, parties, and so on, and then feel like a "failure" because you don't have time to do what it takes to move up in your career?

Do you feel resentful—or at least ambivalent—when you can't attend professional conferences or other work-related events because your children need you at home on weekends?

Do you feel you don't have time to keep up with the news and with literature related to your work—yet resent your husband for feeling free to watch TV, read, or work out while you knock yourself out preparing dinner and helping the kids with their homework?

Are you doing things you hate but feel you must? Are you forced to do them because although you've asked the family many times to help you, they still don't listen? List these chores, then contemplate whether or not you're communicating your needs and frustrations clearly.

It's very important to examine how you communicate your needs, because many *marianistas* miscommunicate cries for help, or accept all the responsibility and then blame their mate or husband for not helping.

Now, before we get started on reducing your stress and subsequently enhancing all aspects of your many-faceted life, we want to remind you there are no absolutes in any culture. Not every working Latina wife and mother experiences the same amount of *marianismo*-inspired *perfeccionismo*. And for countless women of all ethnic persuasions who want both a family and a career outside the home, stress and conflict are unavoidable. However, given the ironclad social codes of *marianismo* and *machismo*, Latinas may experience more ostracism by their spouses—as well as colleagues—when they try to mix home and career. With all this in mind, let's briefly revisit the process of socialization, which we introduced in Chapter 3.

No Exit

You'll remember that socialization is what and how we were taught as children and what and how we, in turn, will go on to teach our own children. Generally, the socialization of women and men in Latin America operates according to specific, clearly defined gender conventions. Simply put, that means that men do certain things and women do others. You don't need to be told, for instance, that boys aren't expected to help with domestic chores while girls are required to.

So, from birth, the Hispanic woman is instilled with the belief that her top priority is to ensure the total well-being of her children, spouse, and other family members with whom she maintains close contact. Failing to perform this predetermined role responsibly can impact deeply on her own sense of adequacy.

We have come to believe that always putting your family's needs before your own is often unhealthy and unrealistic, and is magnified by the dark side of *machismo*. Also, we acknowledge that children's needs do have priority, but only in certain spheres and only up to a certain point in their lives. For example, there is no reason to have to cook for your teenaged son and daughter when they're old enough to help with meal preparation—particularly when you simply don't have the time to do it all by yourself.

Thirdly, we have observed that for many Latinas, fulfilling household chores and taking care of their families at a level perceived to be similar or superior to their mother's and grandmother's performance can actually enhance their sense of self-worth. However, when immigration and acculturation are factored into the equation, everything gets more complicated, and *marianismo* begins to reveal its dark side by imposing a series of shoulds and musts which, when not met, make many of us feel inadequate and *malas*.

As the psychologist Lillian Comas-Diaz has observed, the family, regardless of ethnicity, is historically charged with the task of preserving cultural values and beliefs. But as she further states, for nonimmigrant families in a heterogeneous setting, there is little outside pressure to change these traditions. On the other hand, immigrating Latino/a family members, especially women, often find themselves attempting to maintain the old values at the same time they are adapting to new ones. This is the double self we've described in Chapter 2 extended to a group.

The Hispanic woman in the United States still bears the familial responsibility of keeping tradition alive. She also quite often must function with a level of support diminished from the one she would enjoy in her own country. And regardless of the support she receives or whether she is rich or poor, she still feels the pressure of perpetuating aspects of the culture. As we have said, the pressures increase when she finds herself trying to incorporate aspects of two cultures that may clash. This is the dilemma that, if not understood, leads directly to feelings of inadequacy, which in turn lead to lower self-esteem.

As therapists, we see case after case of Latina professional women who require themselves to be superefficient, only to feel like failures for not being able to fulfill such unrealistic expectations as trying to be just like or better than their mothers. They may come from a factory, clerical job, or law firm, but still feel they must keep the house spotless and their children perfectly groomed. They also feel they must prepare three-course meals from scratch, night after night regardless of how tired they are.

When the women of another time were responsible for the household, be it a ranch or hacienda, they had help. In fact, homemaking even had a management component, similar to a corporation's. But when families were forced to emigrate to cities for economic reasons, the division of labor held firm—except that women were also forced to work outside the home. This meant that in addition to their "day jobs," these women had to return to the household and fulfill the traditional roles. Unfortunately, this tradition of being "everything to everyone," with its accompanying burden of guilt, continues to drive many women within the Hispanic culture to this day.

If women don't fulfill both roles, they suffer the chronic pain of guilt, self-contempt, or inadequacy. If they do, they end up transferring their impossible expectations onto their loved ones, allowing them to believe the status quo is acceptable. But at what price? When you are driven by a double self trying to live in the modern and traditional worlds simultaneously, emotional and physical exhaustion ensues. But, to *una doña perfecta*, emotional overload, even physical collapse, is preferable to that gnawing *marianista* guilt of not having fulfilled the caretaker role.

The *Marianista* Within

Psychologist Monica McGoldrick and colleagues tell us in their book entitled *Ethnicity and Family Therapy* that there is increasing evidence that ethnic values and identifications are retained for many generations after immigration. That means that although you may not consciously be aware of it, the traditions your mother taught you may still determine what you do. It's as if your mother were inside you, lecturing you on being a good *marianista*. Granted, women of other cultures readily identify with their mothers, but since they don't have *marianismo* to contend with, they don't as naturally become *una mártir de la casa*—a household martyr.

Melania, a thirty-seven-year-old Ecuadorean-born womenswear buyer at a major Manhattan department store, comes to mind. Melania is married to Oscar, a Latino management executive who couldn't care less about what he puts on his back. For years Melania not only selected what suit Oscar would wear each day but also polished his shoes and performed other, needlessly menial tasks that she felt were necessary for his grooming. She also waited on her two teenaged sons hand and foot, to the extent of ironing their baggy jeans and their T-shirts.

When she first came to therapy, Melania couldn't see any way out of these predetermined duties. After all, as she put it, *"Esto es lo que hace una buena esposa"*—This is what a good wife does. Unfortunately, being a good wife wasn't helping to relieve her chronic depression and sense of personal worthlessness. And why should it have? Acting like a slave has never been a good prescription for enhancing self-esteem. Melania was further troubled that her responsibilities to her family limited her ability to attend out-of-town designer shows, which in turn was keeping her from getting a promotion. Of course, it never occurred

to her to question whose expectations she was actually trying to satisfy—her family's or her own.

If you feel that, like Melania, you're behaving according to traditions that don't pertain anymore, are you so ashamed and guilty that you're keeping your feelings secret? Why do you feel ashamed when rationally you know you can't possibly be everything to everyone?

Why? Because you feel ashamed to be trapped between your own cultural expectations and your guilt. That has to be the case, because objectively it makes absolutely no sense to try to go to a job, whip up elaborate dinners for your family and friends, plan your children's birthday parties complete with piñatas, drive *la cría completa,* the whole brood, to school, lessons, and practice, and still feel like a human being. Here again, having it all is not only a Latina problem, but many Hispanic women endure it with a unique and passionate intensity.

An acculturating Latina should be aware that her mother, no matter how nurturing and loving, may simply not serve as a good role model for a woman who wishes to have both a family and a profession. Similarly, her father's expectations of what a wife and mother should be ought not to be the way she judges her husband's expectations. Quite simply, many of the clients with whom we have worked discuss mothers who were not professional people themselves and who continue to view being a mother and housewife as the most important aspect of their daughters' lives. And although they would not object or consciously discourage their daughters from acquiring an education, they still view the domestic role as paramount. These clients feel trapped between the past and present, between two incompatible philosophies, no matter how highly competent they appear to the world.

THE MOTHER TRAP

In our practice, we encounter so many Hispanic women who, intelligent and sensible as they may be, continue to invent incredible rationalizations to adhere to *marianismo* by modeling themselves after their mothers. Violeta, it turned out, was actually discouraging Jorge from sharing the chores by deciding he would be so bad at them he would actually end up making more work for her. It's true that he didn't wrap the trash as neatly as Violeta did before he threw it out, but after all, who could? The fact is Violeta considered tasks adequately done only if they measured up to her perfectionistic standards. She used the same excuse when the subject of domestic help arose, by claiming that no outsider could possibly be as good a housekeeper as she was. But Violeta was kidding herself. The real reason she didn't accept help is that embedded in her unconscious was the belief that she not only had to be good at everything, but bore sole responsibility for her house and family. It didn't initially occur to her that the welfare of the house and kids was Jorge's responsibility, too.

Through therapy, Violeta came to see she simply never felt good about herself, although she had ample reason to. Instead of satisfaction, all she felt was guilt—because in every area of her home life, from child rearing to cooking, she felt she wasn't measuring up to her level of expectations. Violeta's predicament was similar to that of many other women in this book: They wished to incorporate the mothering they had, and sometimes the mothering they wished they'd had, within their present modern lives. They often idealized their childhood experiences and subsequently emulated what they perceived to be their mothers' and their grandmothers' interactions with their fathers or other family members. In many cases, these often inaccurate family memories came to dominate their lives.

In our therapy sessions with non-Latinas, we of course find problems related to unrealistic competition and identification with the mother, but it seems clear to us that there is an added dimension to this rivalry in the *marianismo*-driven Hispanic context: trying to surpass your mother and grandmother together not only in the domestic realm but in the professional as well. Once you do break the mold, there is a virtual certainty you'll have to deal with your own mother's and your mother-in-law's guilt-producing accusations that you're not *una buena madre*.

What you've got to keep in mind is that to do it your mother's way is a no-win situation. Leading some version of the life you want while still practicing orthodox *marianismo* will surely make you feel like a failure, because you simply won't be able to find enough hours in the day. Adding to the confusion is that in North America, to put yourself last and sacrifice your own career dreams for homemaking will make you feel even worse. Despite—or because of—that, too many Latinas actually collude in their own misery, sometimes wallowing in the insecurity of not being an efficient housekeeper, wife, daughter, and/or professional. This collusion is actually the outcome of the conflict between wanting to surpass your mother and dreading to do so.

We want to remind you here that the guilt of superwomen like Violeta and Melania wreaks particularly painful havoc on their self-esteem because they forget it is culturally inherited. But we know from our experience with clients like Marta, whose story you're about to read, that you can move beyond your guilt if you work hard enough at it.

The Energizer Bunny Makeover

MARTA BEFORE
Marta, a thirty-two-year-old Argentinian-American restaurant hostess, is married to Antonio, a Spanish-born contractor, and has three children, a very demanding job, and a husband who enjoys large meals prepared from scratch, like the ones his mother used to make for him in Spain. She describes her nonstop days of attempting to fulfill constant demands in terms that bring to mind the Energizer Bunny—who just keeps going and going and going.

Now Marta loves rare and beautiful things and enjoys having them around her. There are, for instance, the exotic orchids she grows in the enclosed porch of their house and the spectacular collection of tropical birds the children delight in. Caring for these precious possessions she naturally trusts only to herself. So Marta's day begins at dawn, when she tends to the orchids, cleans the birds' cages and changes their food and water, then marinates the meat for dinner, wakes up the family, prepares breakfast—a different choice for each person—dresses the kids, does the laundry, straightens the house, dresses herself, and manages to drive the five miles to the restaurant where she works, all by ten in the morning.

The restaurant, a very nice one in which customers must be seated by the hostess, is located near a couple of industrial parks, and does a phenomenal lunch business. So Marta's on her feet from noon, when lunch is first served, to three, when the restaurant closes to the public until five. After hours of having to be pleasant to all the patrons, as well as taking dinner reservations, after three Marta must go over the receipts and get things ready for the evening hostess. When she's lucky and none of the evening staff call in sick, she can usually leave by four. So she picks up the kids, gives them an afternoon snack, calls to check on her mother-in-law's health, puts the roast in a slow oven, then drives the kids from borough to borough for late-afternoon activities and appointments. Later, she drives them home again, begins dinner, greets Antonio, gets the meal on the table, talks to her best friend, Melania, with the cellular phone tucked in her shoulder while doing the dishes, and helps the children with their homework. After that, she tries to watch TV with Antonio but starts to fall asleep, wakes up, makes him the popcorn he likes with his after-dinner beer, puts off washing her hair, which means she'll have to get up even earlier in the morning, climbs the stairs, takes off her makeup and brushes her teeth, and falls into bed. If you, like Marta, wish to do all of this, fine, but do you have to? Should you be trying to do all these things at once? Should you, too, just keep going and going and going?

Marta's plight may strike us as comical, but it becomes less amusing when it is viewed as the driving force behind an enormous amount of anger directed at herself. "What is wrong with me?" she asks her therapist. *"Tengo tanto, pero me siento tan infeliz"*—I have so much, and yet I feel so unhappy. Marta doesn't yet realize that she is desperately trying to keep up with the standards she imagined were set by her mother and grandmothers, whose full-time job was only one aspect of

Marta's. She refuses to hire someone to help with the housework because she claims it's easier to do chores herself rather than waste time trying to teach someone else to do things precisely her way. And remember, she does all this without the help and support her mother took for granted.

Marta spends hours in therapy sessions weeping inconsolably, overwhelmed and exhausted, but has no idea how to even begin changing things, because she sees any change as a failure. Don't, we implore you, do a Marta on yourself. It's not the answer, and it won't do anything except exhaust you and further diminish your self-worth.

MARTA AFTER

Marta's therapist helped her face the fact that she was trying to quiet self-doubt acquired from her own hypercritical mother by being *más marianista que una santa*. The therapist also helped her to understand that she was transferring her own expectations onto her husband. Marta felt that Antonio expected as his due a lavish, home-cooked meal every night. Actually he didn't, although of course he enjoyed it. You see, the pressure wasn't coming from him but from Marta.

When asked if she directly asks her husband for assistance, Marta admits, "No, Antonio should know what I need." "How should he know?" inquires the therapist, "through telepathy?" Laughing nervously, Marta asks, "Are you really suggesting I should tell him over and over what I want? He'll just get angry and call me a nag! Besides, I have told him before and he doesn't do anything!" Soon Marta is facing the fact that she tends to have these discussions with her husband when she herself is furious, which is the worst state in which to initiate a productive discussion.

Making demands in anger actually causes you to be less assertive because it limits your ability to communicate your needs and desires clearly and rationally. Asking for what you're entitled to can only make you angry when you don't receive it. A far better way to get what you want is gathering the family together and telling them without hysteria how you feel. Don't hold back. Let them know exactly how overwhelmed you are. Involve them in thinking up ways to help you, assigning tasks, and selecting one person to act as a monitor to make sure the duties are done.

The wonderful thing that awaited Marta once she learned these lessons was that her family listened to her. Appreciating that there was nothing wrong with only being human, she began to be a more contented person. When she brought up the subject of a housekeeper with Antonio and the kids, they were shocked but gave the new arrangement a try. Marta assured the kids they could interview applicants, and they played a major role in deciding who was hired. Marta also learned in therapy that it was unlikely that Antonio would ever turn into Mr. Mom. Eventually, she accepted the best he could do as sufficient and praised him when he did a good job rather than just criticizing him when he was less than perfect. This was Marta's healthy choice—becoming both realistic and flexible.

The secret of her remarkable transformation was putting *marianista perfeccionismo* behind her, convincing herself that she deserved the help, nurturance, and support of her family—and learning to ask for it in a nonthreatening, nonaccusatory, I-am-a-victim manner.

GETTING REALISTIC: THE MAGIC OF PRIORITIZING

We recognize that we Hispanics have an especially dynamic relationship with our family members. There is no doubt that *familismo* is one of our culture's great strengths. It defines the extraordinary importance of the intimate bonds between ourselves and those closest to us. *Familismo* often motivates us to go on with our lives when we feel despondent, whatever the reason. Even the most "liberated" among us put our families' needs very high on our list of shoulds and musts. So the last thing we would recommend is sacrificing the joys of family for career.

The first thing we would suggest is learning to start prioritizing, and asking—or if necessary, demanding—the participation of your mate and children in implementing change. The ability to do so is key to your empowerment. It's amazing, but when we've asked Latina colleagues what they felt they could drop from their list of responsibilities, they invariably say, "Nothing." Respected professionals they may be, but *marianismo* continues to drive them to stretch their days into night. For the most part, the diligence with which they do all the things they have to do is literally heroic.

Stop and think of things you do which you can identify as left over from the Old Country, which don't realistically have a place in your new life.

Ask yourself if you're doing these things simply because not to do them makes you feel guilty, rather than because they are really necessary.

Write down those beliefs that are impairing your sense of well-being, then meet with friends and consult about what they do with their families. See if you can teach each other how to change certain aspects of your life that you find problematical.

Meeting with her friend Marta helped Melania, the department store buyer, to get things on the right track. During her nightly call with Marta, she mentioned for the first time how truly stressed she was feeling, and since her friend had been sounding a lot happier lately, she asked her advice. Marta suggested they meet for dinner at a restaurant (not her employer's), where they could talk freely. Melania was hesitant to agree, since she didn't know who would fix dinner for her family. Nevertheless, she decided to meet Marta.

Telling her family she was meeting her friend for dinner and having the kids say, "Cool!" and her husband, Oscar, say, "Fine, we'll call out for pizza," was really the beginning of Melania's new life. Through therapy and through discussions with Marta and other friends, she saw for the first time how possessive she was—just like her mother. She also came to see that she selected her husband's clothes less because it was her duty than because he tended to mismatch his shoes and ties. She was protecting Oscar and almost literally mothering him, because his mother had dressed him all his life. Melania was not only competing with her own *perfeccionismo* and with her mother but also with her mother-in-law—although her husband had made it very clear how much he'd always hated his mother's selecting his clothes. She was also made aware that by slaving over her husband and kids, she was setting a traditional example of *marianismo* and *machismo* which was better left unlearned by her *niños*.

At first, when Melania let Oscar dress himself, he was angry and upset because he'd come to associate his wife's doing these chores with her loving him. However, he calmed considerably when Melania explained that she was giving him a chance to take care of himself, and that she was going to show her love in other ways—such as being more affectionate and available for conversations. In time, he asked her for advice on what to wear, and she lovingly gave it, astonished that he was developing just a hint of a fashion sense of his own.

Next, she explained to her boys that she had been too doting a mother, that it wasn't good for their sense of self-worth, and that she would show them, too, her love in better ways than stifling their independence. The kids were relieved to finally admit that they actually felt smothered by Melania's attentiveness.

Melania only began to change when she realized she was misusing *marianismo* to show love to those around her. If you are doing the same thing, you need to develop new models of affection that benefit yourself and those you care for.

As was the case with Marta, Melania was thrilled to discover that her family actually listened to her when she discussed her demands with them. Even better, she could see that her world did not fall apart when she began to ensure that her own needs were met. In fact, her family couldn't have been more pleased because with less to do, she was not as stressed and a hundred times more pleasant and easier to be with. Before therapy, Melania considered herself a modern woman, when in fact she was modeling herself on traditional stereotypes. Now she can bask in the elation of being *una buena madre* nineties style. And her family can bask in the pride they feel when Melania, now a head buyer, flies off to Paris for a week to attend the fashion shows.

Something for Everyone

The message is simple but deep: Don't try to be good at everything you do, and don't try to do everything in order to be good.

We know from professional and personal experience that truly believing this mantra and adopting it into your belief system may not be easy, but it is possible. As a start, go back to the *perfeccionismo* quiz beginning on page 184 of this chapter. Repeat the exercise again and see whether you can now resolve some of your home/office cultural collisions. Whatever you find, you must bear in mind for the future that resolving your conflict requires detaching your feelings of adequacy from the compulsion to do everything simultaneously and flawlessly. Only then can you begin to prioritize and use your time judiciously.

We say judiciously because if you attempt to fill every second of every day with tasks, you may end up a workaholic—unhappy, angry, exhausted—and find that most people, including your family and yourself, dislike you.

Trust your feelings. If you happen to be home on a weekday afternoon and you feel like watching *La Novela de Moda* or *General Hospital*, do it. Do it no matter what assignments are pending. The show's only an hour. Or don't book a business lunch one day; go shopping and buy yourself something that makes you feel like a million dollars.

Make a fixed schedule. Pretend your office/home workday ends at a certain hour. Make it a rule that after that hour, you will take a bubble bath, watch TV, listen to music, or do your exercises. Inform the kids that you can only help them with their homework until then because you need your quiet time to be there for them.

If it's possible, and through the miracle of faxes and modems it may be, try to arrange to work at home one day a week, especially when your kids are small. You might also consider starting a small business alone or with friends that you can operate from home.

Sometimes your job will force you to work overtime. If it's only seasonal, get together with your family and plan strategies that will get you all through it. If the overtime is not seasonal, try your best to limit it.

Make it a rule to take Sundays off to have fun with your family, your mate, your friends, or yourself. We can assure you that taking quality time reduces stress substantially and consequently enhances self-esteem.

Declare at this moment that you are beginning your new life and organizing your priorities. That means objectively deciding what is essential and doing it first. But remember, you can't have it all; nobody can. At different times, you may have to delay something to ensure others are cared for. Perhaps you'll have to table your dream of going back to school to get your master's until your babies are in school. Reassure yourself that it's not a question of never, but rather of later. While you're home with the kids, try to keep up with the literature in the field you'll soon be returning to study. And when you do return to school and you have to study for exams, work out survival strategies with your husband and kids as a family, so it'll become a team effort.

If your mate or kids want to have friends over when you're preparing for a big presentation or have to work overtime, make it clear to them that for a finite number of weeks, you won't be available to entertain. Assure them that once this work period is over, you'll make it up to them.

By the way, if the children are too young to grasp the abstract concept of time, cross off each day on the calendar so that they'll be able to calculate how long they have to wait. This is also a good idea because it teaches a lesson in delaying gratification, which is essential to living an emotionally healthy life.

Let's pay a visit to Violeta, Melania, and Marta to see how they're doing since they stopped being superwomen *marianistas* and started being healthy human beings.

Now that she has a housekeeper, Marta realizes Juanita is worth twice her salary. In addition to being wonderful with the kids, an excellent cook, and terrific with household tasks as well as very obliging, Juanita is Latin-American and makes sure the kids speak Spanish for at least part of the day—something Marta and Antonio are very pleased about. The children now go to school by bus and Juanita waits for them at the bus stop. Marta still gets dinner on the table but when she comes home, Juanita has preparations started.

Likewise, Marta supervises breakfast but appreciates that the children, who are seven, nine, and eleven, can get their own cereal and milk, and fruits, or toast some bread in the toaster. She's also taught them to set their own alarm clocks so she can afford to get up a little later, do her hair, and still have time with the birds and orchids before the family descends on her.

Juanita arrives just about the time breakfast is done so she can clean up and allow Marta time to get dressed for work. Now that she's been made assistant manager of the restaurant, she wants to look especially nice and welcomes the extra time she gets to spend on her appearance. Without having to worry about picking up the kids at the end of the workday, she's truly enjoying the new job, although it requires her staying a couple of hours later in the afternoon.

Now, when she arrives home, she can take off her shoes and relax before Juanita arrives with the kids. By the time they get back and Juanita prepares to leave for the day, Antonio comes home and gives Marta a big hug. Dinner is now a wonderful occasion, where everybody discusses their day and laughs and jokes. Marta's also made preparing the meal a family event, where everybody, including Antonio, sits around the kitchen and helps out. The three kids have even formed a team to do the dishes and clean up under Marta's supervision.

After dinner, both Marta and Antonio help the kids with their homework, then send them upstairs to watch TV and get ready for bed. The grown-ups now have some quiet time to talk things over and watch TV together. Marta still makes the popcorn, but now they both enjoy it. What she hadn't counted on is that her stopping being a superwoman has done wonders for her marriage. When her family gave her trouble about hiring a housekeeper, Antonio staunchly defended her and told them to back off. His wife, he told them, was living in the world of today, and he applauded her for it. Once she stopped trying to be everybody's mother, including Antonio's, Marta realized, he began to see her as a desirable woman. One night, in fact, when they were watching TV, he put his arm around her, gave her a kiss, and told her, "You know, you're even more beautiful now than the day we were married!"

As for Melania, she is due again to leave in two days for her Paris buying trip, and she's working out a survival plan for her husband and boys while she's away. Oscar's agreed to readjust his office hours for the five days in order to take the boys to school and pick them up. In fact, he's glad to do it. The kids can make their own breakfasts, and they buy lunch at school. So the days aren't going to be a problem.

Melania's arranged with her friend Marta and with her in-laws to have Oscar and the boys over for dinner once during the week and once over the weekend. She's suggested to Oscar that he take the boys to a baseball game one night. The boys have a sleep-over date for another night, which is the night Oscar plays cards with his *amigos*. That leaves one night free for her men to totally trash the house. She's due back on a Saturday, so she's having the cleaning person she now uses every two weeks come on Friday and clean up what she knows will be a huge mess.

She'll check in from Paris every day to make sure things are going all right, as she always does when she's away. In fact, during her last trip, she called home and was quite upset because Oscar and the boys sounded like they were having such a good time. "Oscar," she asked in a rare resurgence of *marianismo*, "don't you need me?" "No, Melania," he replied. "I don't need you. I want you."

You'd never know from looking at Violeta that it's Christmas Eve. She's not tense, not frantic, not exhausted. How could this be? Well, abandoning her superwoman *marianismo* and learning to prioritize made her realize for the first time that she had options. One of the options was not being sentenced to Christmas.

The first thing she did was call Charo, the sister-in-law to whom she was closest and whom she regarded as *una amiga* as much as a rela-

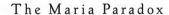

The Maria Paradox

tive. "Listen," she told her, "I am only blaming myself here, but this Christmas thing I always insist on doing alone is just getting to be ridiculous. I don't want to end the dinner by weeping the way I did last year. So I was wondering, is there any way we can sort of spread the responsibility around?" "Thank God," Charo laughed. "I never thought I'd ever hear you say those words! You bet we can share. I'd love to."

They decided that the Christmas Eve dinner should rotate from year to year among them and the other daughters-in-law, who were enthusiastic when the idea was presented to them. In addition, whoever held the dinner would make the main course but everybody else would bring a dish or dessert, to be agreed upon in a meeting beforehand. It was also agreed that all the nieces and nephews would go into the city as a group to see the Christmas show and the tree, but that the responsibility for taking them would also rotate. Clearly, whoever was hosting the dinner would not also be shepherding the kids. The sisters-in-law also arranged to help each other with the last-minute preparations, and to ask their husbands and kids to see to the cleaning up. None of the kids or men involved objected. In fact, they felt participating would make Christmas Eve more of a family event.

Violeta herself got smart and started giving gifts that didn't require hours and hours of shopping—whether they were gift certificates, articles from catalogues, or items she saw on a home-shopping television show. Instead of wrapping the presents, she bought beautiful gift bags, wrapped each gift in decorative tissue paper, and put it in the bag, saving herself an immense amount of wrapping time. She also suggested to the other members of the co-op board that they not try to schedule meetings so close to the holidays. Needless to say, everyone was thrilled. She also proposed that the supervision of the caroling group be rotated among the parents of the kids who participated.

This year, she spent several lunch hours looking for just the right dress for Jorge's office party. She chose a tailored but very form-fitting black dress with a short skirt and a rather low neck. She even made time to get her hair done the day of her back-to-back office celebrations. Everybody, in her office and Jorge's, seemed to be seeing her differently and in a very flattering way. Jorge noticed it too, and it made him proud. He even asked her to wear her new dress to Christmas Eve, which was being held at Charo's: "I want the family to see that I have the most stunning and sexy woman of all!"

So here is Violeta on Christmas Eve, laughing, contented, surrounded by the people she loves. And as the adults raise their glasses in a toast to the holiday, instead of bursting into tears, Violeta heartily wishes everybody Merry Christmas—and means it.

Your New Home in the World

Traditional *marianismo* says that your home is your world. North American culture tells you that often, out of economic need or the desire for personal satisfaction, that is not the case. Your home is part of your world. It is crucial to the well-being of those you love, including yourself, that you steer a course between these two views and avoid collision. We are telling you that if you do so, you can forge a happy blend of two exciting cultures and continue to get the best from both.

In closing we want to repeat that the most important gift you can give yourself and your family is permission to love yourself without guilt. And loving yourself means knowing when to adapt, when you are reaching your performance capacity, and when to ask for help. Then you can arm yourself with an all-new definition of love of self—

Latina
On the
Verge of
Empowerment!

9

"Do Not Discuss Personal Problems Outside the Home":

Struggling Alone vs.
Finding Support

Gloria, a twenty-three-year-old Dominican, was terrified. Suddenly everything frightened her, although she had no specific reason to be afraid. In fact, she had every reason to feel secure—including an attractive, successful, and supportive husband and an adorable baby daughter. True, her husband's job as a dentist both in private practice and at several local clinics kept him away from home many evenings, but there was no doubt that he spent his time working hard to support his family, not fooling around.

Still, the more time she spent alone with her daughter, the more Gloria was gripped by the terror that *algo horrible*, something awful, was going to happen to her *niña*, and that whatever it was, it was going to be Gloria's fault. Since she was driven by *marianismo*'s impossibly high standards for motherhood, competency was nothing more for her than an illusory dream in the first place.

Gloria's mother still lived in the Dominican Republic, and the young woman had few relatives in North America and hadn't yet made many friends, since she and her husband had only recently moved to New York from Houston, where Alejandro had completed dental school. Gloria had worked as a dental assistant even before she met her husband, and enjoyed it. However, once the baby came, she and Alejandro agreed that for the time being she'd stay at home and be a full-time mother.

Alejandro had no idea that Gloria was feeling terrified and inadequate as a mother. In fact, she was particularly careful not to tell him what she was experiencing, because she felt that one of the things about her which he most admired was her self-sufficiency. Naturally *la situación empeoró*, things went from bad to worse, and Gloria was left to suffer alone—trembling, shaky, and exhausted most of the time because she couldn't sleep. Her dread also confused her, contributing to her feelings of inadequacy. By the time evening came and the sunlight faded, Gloria was in a complete panic.

At first, ice cream helped. She needed to consume as much as a quart at a time to feel better, but the weight she put on as a result ended up only adding to her panic and profound sadness. Then she discovered that a glass or two of wine, combined with one of the five-milligram Valium tablets her doctor had prescribed when she'd told him *que se sentía muy nerviosa*, that she was feeling edgy, calmed her enough to feed her thirteen-month-old daughter and get her to bed. It didn't take long before she'd graduated to one vodka and tonic and one Valium.

In the early afternoon, after she put her daughter to bed for her nap, Gloria would have another drink and Valium to make it through the household chores without giving in to the gnawing panic, and if Alejandro wasn't coming home till late, she would again have a drink or two and another Valium between dinner and bedtime to help her get to sleep. *"Qué milagro!"*—What a miracle!—she told herself, that a little vodka and Valium could so effectively keep her relaxed and yet allow her to function. Not only was she calmer but she felt in control. Initially she was very careful in "calming herself" when the baby was awake, and never drank alcohol around her husband unless they were both having wine with dinner.

This pattern of secret drinking combined with Valium persisted for a year. Unfortunately, Gloria's physician enabled her in her downward spiral by prescribing more pills whenever she asked, then raising the strength of the medication to ten milligrams. Since she seemed vastly improved, he didn't bother to probe further. Gloria was successfully hiding her addiction from him as well as from others around her, functioning like a good *marianista* wife and mother, and thought her terrible bouts with anxiety and depression were things of the past. But one evening something happened which would prove Gloria was in serious trouble and desperately needed help.

We don't have to tell you that there are countless Glorias in the Hispanic community—troubled, in need of help, but prevented from getting it by *marianismo*. That you are reading this book indicates you are not one of them, or no longer want to be. In this chapter, we'll present you with the pros and cons of psychotherapy as a way of dealing with problems that may not subside even after you've tried the suggestions in this book. We'll deal with such issues as your fears, your hopes, the kinds of therapy available to you, even what to look for in a therapist and where to find one. Finally, we'll take you outside therapy as we show you how to organize your own support system, drawing on Hispanic tradition in a new and exciting way.

But first, *recuérdate que no es tu culpa si algunos problemas no desaparecen*—keep reminding yourself that it's not your fault if your problems won't just go away. Often, their recurrence may have nothing to do with you as a person. So don't try to fix your painful emotional problems all alone and in secret, as Gloria did. Keep in mind there are problems you're not qualified to solve without professional assistance. We have treated so many Latinas who tried to be everything to everyone, including their own healer. Luckily, they ended up by seeking treatment, but they did so only after prolonged suffering, anxiety, and sorrow.

When does a problem require professional healing? After all, *la vida tiende a ser difícil*, life is hard, and no one's happy all the time. Let's begin to answer this by exploring the subjects of emotional distress.

 ## How Do I Know I Have a Problem?

Most of us have personality traits which can potentially interfere with how we function in certain aspects of our lives—behavior such as:

- constantly being late for appointments
- saying yes to requests you cannot possibly—or do not wish to—do, such as accepting an invitation and then not showing up
- needing to control the people you love
- nagging significant others until they don't want to be near you
- constantly postponing or failing to carry out duties and responsibilities

Problems arise when those behaviors interfere with our interactions with others. We might end up destroying an intimate relationship we treasure, or losing a job we badly need. These traits can also become barriers to our personal well-being by limiting our daily functioning and intensifying our feelings of sadness, nervousness, depression, or anxiety. This is when you need to seek support—be it psychological or spiritual—from professionals, friends, or relatives.

Perhaps there are aspects of your life in which you could use a little help because you're not functioning as well as you'd like. Here is a quiz to help you pinpoint issues that you are having difficulty with:

Close your eyes and review your behavior during the past week, searching for situations which were upsetting to you. Now take a pencil and paper and list your behavior in those situations. For example, you may have had a very difficult week with a relative's illness, and wished you could cancel the dinner engagement you have made, but feel it is not the proper thing to disappoint your friend. Or for the third time your best friend picks on what she considers are your bad habits, disregarding your feelings. You wish you could tell her how you feel, and to stop doing this to you because you find it annoying, but you can't. Sort your own issues during the past week into categories, according to what you consider the urgency of making the change. Look at the ones you want to change the most and ask yourself if you've tried everything in your power to better adjust and simply can't manage it. Remember, we're talking about intense feelings, not being "a little angry" or "a little uneasy." Now:

- Are your feelings related to excessive guilt, perhaps because you feel that saying no to a friend is thinking of yourself first?
- Do you have excessive fears of being rejected? For example, did you feel that your friend would get angry with you for telling her she was annoying you?
- Did you have powerful fears of getting close to others, such as not allowing people to help you because it would make you indebted to them?
- Did you experience feelings relating to your level of assertiveness? Maybe you had difficulty saying no to your friend's suggestion to have Japanese food when you preferred Italian.
- Do you experience paralyzing shyness? Perhaps you were unable to go to a party alone because you felt afraid you

would not have anything to say. Or perhaps you did not talk the entire night, disregarding the fact that you had good and appropriate opinions on the subjects that people were discussing.

• Do you experience an overwhelming fear of being alone? Did you not tell your boyfriend how upset you were with his behavior because you were afraid he would get upset and leave you?

• Was it very difficult for you to make decisions on your own on any major topic?

• Did you constantly feel that other people were more accomplished than you in any task you attempted, making you feel incompetent and useless?

• Did you feel so anxious that, like Gloria, the only way you could relax was through alcohol and/or drugs?

• Were you frequently weepy and irritable without any specific reasons to feel that way?

After completing your list for the week, make another for the month, then a third for the year. When you've done that, list the things you've been unhappy with all your life and are really serious about changing.

Now grade the level of their importance and decide which ones you honestly feel are holding you back in important areas of your life. Once you decide to confront the impact of these disturbing behaviors, you'll be in a much clearer position to evaluate whether or not you have a problem, whether you're *hastiada hasta la muerte*—sick to death—of being maladjusted, and whether you want or need psychotherapy.

As you can now see, pinpointing and defining the problem remains a subjective process. At this stage, it is a process which is up to you. Only you can measure the level of your distress and decide how much unhappiness you can accept before you seek help. However, people close to you may notice that *no eres la misma de antes*, you're not the same as you used to be. Listen to what they are telling you. If what they observe dovetails with what you've been feeling, it will help you acknowledge you have a problem and begin to understand why.

Mental health professionals practicing dynamic psychotherapy—whose orientation is toward obtaining insight into our unconscious—believe that understanding our deepest motivations and then working through this understanding can facilitate permanent changes. This is a theoretically different concept from that held by behavioral psychotherapists, who feel behavior is learned. Thus, they focus on changing problematic behavior without the individual's necessarily having to understand what caused the problem.

Our purpose in *The Maria Paradox* is to highlight the importance of obtaining insight into your unconscious beliefs, particularly as they relate to the cultural teachings of *marianismo*. We are sharing with you the experiences of the many acculturating Latinas we have worked with and helped through this treatment method. It is our hope that you are indeed obtaining insight into how your *marianista* beliefs may have influenced your behavior and perhaps caused you significant grief. Armed with that knowledge, you'll be well on the way to undertaking changes that will make you feel better—for the rest of your life. Next we're going to discuss when and why it's necessary to look for support outside the home.

All You Need Is a Good Rest!

Sometimes, even with the warmest and most dedicated support from family and friends, the relief you feel is only temporary. And sometimes the emotional involvement of the care givers around you can simply be overwhelming. In fact, those close to you can care too much and overempathize, thus becoming incapable of providing you with the objectivity you need. The opposite is also true: Relatives and friends can be hypercritical when they don't agree with what you're doing or saying. They can also, without consciously knowing it, have a vested interest in your staying the way you are. If someone has a fear of losing you and needs you to stay dependent on them, *pueden terminar hacién-dotelo todo en lugar de permitirte a que tú aprendas por tí misma*—they'll end up doing everything for you instead of encouraging you to take care of yourself. Even more important is the fact that friends and relatives, no matter how much they care, don't have professional training. Even if they do, they may not be able to maintain the proper distance required to judge the seriousness of your problems, and thus unintentionally cause you harm by under- or overplaying the nature of your problem.

And remember, as a Latina open to the possibility of getting psychological help, you may be bucking a lot of Hispanic tradition. After all, *marianismo* dictates that since Latinas can endure all suffering, you must be seen as strong and self-sufficient. The only alternatives are being perceived as *loca*, crazy, or *débil y delicada*, weak and vulnerable. So, when you first mention seeking outside help to your loved ones, be prepared to have your expression of interest regarded as frivolous at the very least. We have seen many, many Latinas talk of their fear of being considered *blandita*, a softie or weak, for coming to therapy at all.

Likewise, expect resistance from others in more veiled forms, such as: "There's nothing wrong with you. You're just upset today," "Going to therapy is an expensive luxury. What can a therapist tell you that you can't tell yourself?" or, "All you need is a good rest. Take a vacation." The implications of these statements are all the same—discussing your problems (which will most probably have a strong family component) outside the home will be greeted by denial, or its opposite: you will be stigmatized as being "crazy." During arguments, accusations will be hurled at you in a demeaning way such as, "You're the crazy one! You're the one who has to go to a head doctor."

Jackelyn, a twenty-eight-year-old Ecuadorean-American, experienced such resistance. She emigrated with her family when she was twelve and almost immediately began having problems at school. Basically, she stopped talking entirely in the classroom and was diagnosed with "selective mutism," a condition that afflicts some bilingual children who are confronted with conflicting pressures to favor one language over another. (It affects other children for other reasons as well.) Happily, therapy was tremendously successful for her once her family and teachers understood her problem.

Subsequently, Jackelyn developed into a well-adjusted young woman who became a Wall Street stockbroker. She married Alvaro, a supportive Latin-American attorney of about her own age with whom she had an excellent relationship, which included shared decision making. For obvious reasons, the young woman had tremendous respect for and belief in psychotherapy. So, when Alvaro was offered a junior partnership by a huge Houston law firm and he asked her to sort out her thoughts and feelings about whether she was ready to relocate, Jackelyn wanted to talk things over with her old therapist. Although she felt she had done a good job of acculturating, she knew she still had some *marianista* traits in her that could impact her decision—such as the belief that it is a woman's obligation to follow her husband anywhere and to put his needs before her own.

Once Jackelyn was back in treatment, she told her parents she had resumed therapy to get her thinking straight about the possible move. To her shock, they cautioned her not to tell anyone, especially the family and her in-laws, that she was seeing a therapist. "Why?" she demanded. "The relatives all know I was in treatment with this same woman when I was a child, and they saw how much she helped me!" Her parents replied that was precisely the point. "They shouldn't have known before," her mother insisted. "And they shouldn't know now that you need it again! This is a family matter that belongs in the home!"

We're not saying that this therapy stigma doesn't exist in other ethnic groups, but in Hispanic culture the message that you shouldn't share intimate secrets with a stranger gets conveyed loud and clear. We want to stress here that it's crucial for you to learn to recognize cultural prohibitions for what they are and not take them literally. If your family is providing enlightened support, God bless them. If they're trying to cajole you into staying *marianista*, the best thing to do is turn a deaf ear. We'll be discussing in the next chapter methods of coping with others' anxiety as you change. Suffice it to say here that for you, *la nueva marianista*, suffering alone is neither noble nor smart.

We want to help you get rid of the myth that deems you weak if you seek professional help. We want you to acknowledge that there are situations that require it, including when cultural collision is contributing to your problems. In fact, trying to solve chronic emotional problems by yourself is like treating a broken leg by taking an aspirin and waiting for the bone to knit. We're assuming that by now you sufficiently appreciate the powerful role *marianismo* plays in your life not to let it prevent you from conquering emotional pain severe enough to call for therapy.

Warning Signs

The problems presented throughout this book suggest predicaments which frequently merited and were resolved by therapy. In addition, there are a number of emotional conditions which demand the immediate intervention of a competent professional. We'll briefly list them, using guidelines presented in *DSM IV*, the *Diagnostic and Statistical Manual of Mental Disorders, Fourth Edition*—which classifies the major mental disorders in a standardized manner using codes and categories, and is a primary reference tool of mental health providers. Although both men and women suffer from all forms of emotional distress, we'll concentrate primarily on depression and anxiety, as they are diagnosed most prevalently in women.

Debilitating depression: You may be having a major depressive episode if you feel particularly sad (young children and adolescents may appear irritable as opposed to sad), have lost interest in daily chores and other aspects of your life, and are unable to perform nearly all your customary activities for at least two weeks. In addition, you must have at least four of the following symptoms:

1. Changes in appetite and/or weight
2. Changes in sleep patterns
3. Changes in psychomotor activities, such as insufficient energy to walk, get out of bed, get to work on time, even bathe or dress
4. Difficulties with concentration and decision making
5. Feelings of worthlessness and/or guilt
6. Recurrent thoughts of death or suicide, including having a plan or having made a suicide attempt

The symptoms must be present nearly every day of the two weeks, and you must feel bad enough so that your mood impairs your social and occupational performance. Without being fully aware of it, Gloria was having many of these symptoms, as well as terrible anxiety. However, by medicating herself with depressive substances like alcohol and tranquilizers instead of mood elevators like Prozac administered under the eye of a competent and caring physician, she was only tackling half of the problem—and in fact, compounding it by requiring increasingly larger dosages of the "downers" to keep the sorrow and panic at bay.

It's relevant to state here that studies report depression is more common in women than in men, whether or not they're Hispanics. However, psychologist Glorisa Canino, who studied depression in Puerto Ricans, feels that Puerto Rican men may be less vulnerable to depression than Puerto Rican women because of differing social expectations and the fact that traditional female roles such as homemaking have been assigned such low societal value. Following a study conducted by S. Rosenfield during the early eighties, we would like to add that the pressures of *marianismo*, including the need to repress justifiable anger, are a further contributing factor to Latinas' susceptibility to depression. In fact, Rosenfield believes that the frequency of depression among Hispanic women is possibly due to the lack of acceptance and lack of tolerance by others of their expression of anger.

Finally, we want you to be aware that in addition to the symptoms already described, social scientists such as Melba Vasquez, Glorisa Canino and her colleagues, and others tell us that Hispanics can experience depression through ongoing somatic complaints such as headaches, shakiness, aches and pains, skin problems, allergies, and stomach problems. So, if you feel you fit the "depressive" profile, it is important you get professional help as soon as possible.

Other serious disorders include the following.

Excessive fears that can culminate in anxiety attacks: Gloria is a prime example of someone suffering from an anxiety disorder, as well as depression. In fact, her anxiety attacks—whose symptoms included palpitations, sweating, excessive and often irrational fears, dizziness, nausea, chest pains, and difficulty breathing—were what led her to substance abuse.

Post-traumatic stress response: Occurring in the wake of a personal tragedy such as the death of a loved one, a serious accident, rape, physical or sexual abuse, this condition is characterized by intense fear, helplessness, and horror—often in a delayed manner and frequently involving substance abuse in an attempt to ease anxiety and reduce sadness.

Compulsive, chronic substance abuse: This includes excessive drinking, drug use, overeating, or refusing food completely in anorexia or bulimia—often accompanied by denial. Here again, Gloria comes to mind. What began with ice cream, a "comfort food," soon became a glass of wine, a "comfort substance," which before long escalated into the chronic need for hard-core alcohol and tranquilizers. Gloria, of course, never realized that combining any amount of tranquilizing medication with alcohol radically enhances their individual potency and can be dangerous.

Other problem areas in which psychotherapy has proven effective include but are not limited to:

- Difficulty in trusting and getting close to others
- Sexual dysfunction
- Marriage and family discord

- Coping with a developmentally disabled child
- Coping with an older relative with Alzheimer's

We repeat that while therapy doesn't offer miracles, it offers hope for a happier, more self-full life to many, many people. But first they have to make the decision to get help. And for many Latinas, like Gloria, that's very difficult.

Is Therapy for Me?

Throughout this book we have shown there are steps you can take to help you work out problems, especially those with a strong cultural component, on your own. We have also encouraged you to continue availing yourself of culturally relevant support systems—which could involve friends, family, religion—that provide you with comfort. However, we want you to remember that there are life situations in which you or a loved one can be made to feel permanently happier with professional psychotherapeutic help. So, bearing in mind that everyone feels sad, anxious, angry, and useless once in a while, we begin our discussion of whether or not you should seek professional help with the reminder that if any of the feelings listed above persist for more than a few weeks and grow increasingly more intense, you may want to start thinking about treatment.

Who Should Seek Professional Help?

People seek professional help when they're confronting problems of living. Some begin treatment to get more out of life or because they are curious about the psychotherapeutic process. Others seek reassurance that they're not "crazy" or simply to please a significant other. However, the majority of clients who come to us do it because of interpersonal problems most often related to marriage, family, and other significant relationships such as boyfriends or co-workers, or to the lack of significant relationships. Not all problems you may experience require professional intervention. Actually, many can be resolved with the support of your mate, your sister or brother, another relative, or a good friend. Sometimes all we need to know is that a nonjudgmental, noncritical person is there for us and that we personally are coping as best we can.

We've observed that women and men who have successfully steered a course through difficult personal times tend to describe having had a vision that nothing, good or bad, lasts forever. The belief that things will pass, an absence of personal blame, and an understanding that bad things do indeed happen to good people seem to be the most effective tools for weathering life's storms. When people cannot see the light at the end of the tunnel, when their pain is unbearable and seemingly endless, therapy is in order. If you have tried the exercises in this book and, although you're clearer on just what the problem is and even what may be causing it, you still feel despondent, you should consider that you may need to see a therapist. How do you go about deciding what would be the best type for you? You might ask yourself:

- Should I go for individual treatment, for couples, family, or group therapy?
- What type of theoretical background would work best for me, and how do I find out what the various types are?
- Should I see a Latino/a therapist?
- Where do I find one?
- Does gender matter?

First, let's define psychotherapy. It could be defined as a procedure which assists individuals to make changes in their personalities and in their behaviors that cause emotional discomfort to themselves and to others they may interact with. The same definition could apply to self-help books. But there is a crucial difference. When you're undergoing individual psychotherapy, you develop a special relationship with a professional who can help you look at your life options and will support you in understanding them. Sometimes the need for individual therapy shifts—for example, when you're having specific problems with your mate and feel the relationship is worth saving, you might want to seek couples therapy with an experienced counselor. Likewise, if you're finding it difficult to parent a child and it's affecting the entire household, you might choose family therapy. But here again, it is the therapist's experience and sensitivity which should determine your final choice.

How Do I Know What Works?

That said, we must also add that your significant others may not be the only ones who question the validity of psychotherapy. You may have doubts yourself. Questioning its effectiveness is nothing new. In fact, there have been many studies that report conflicting results on the usefulness of therapy. It appears that questioning the validity of psychotherapy stems at least in part from an exclusion in the design of these studies of psychotherapy's four basic components, which are, according to psychiatrist Fuller Torrey:

1. A common worldview shared by the patient and the therapist, so that the healer can fully grasp the client's cultural values
2. The personal qualities of the therapist, which include warmth, compassion, and understanding
3. Client expectations. As we've already noted, don't expect miracles from therapy, because it can only help you change behaviors and traits that you want to change despite the pain, risk, and fear entailed. Therapy helps people resolve emotional problems, but not without the client's self-awareness. Furthermore, therapy can only help *you* change, not your significant others.
4. An emerging sense of mastery, which means the patient is able to make the hoped-for changes and thus to develop a sense of well-being

Otto Ehrenberg and Miriam Ehrenberg, who are psychologists and therapists, suggest that not all types of therapy are beneficial to all people in every case, but that some psychotherapies are beneficial to some people some of the time. More important, Lester Luborsky and his colleagues conducted an extensive study at the University of Pennsylvania on the effects of psychotherapy. They concluded that the success of the treatment depends on the formation of a positive alliance with the therapist. Therefore, don't burden yourself trying to grasp all the qualities implied in the different specializations between various types of therapies and therapists. You should concern yourself only with choosing an approach that makes sense to you, and choosing a competent and compassionate therapist who will be able to help you. Later in this chapter, we'll be giving you guidelines to consider when choosing a psychotherapist. Now, though, let's get back to Gloria, whose anxiety over her little daughter's welfare was literally driving her to drink.

When Push Comes to Shove

Although Gloria successfully hid her addiction from her husband, Alejandro, by chewing gum or using breath spray and never drank too much when he was around, her condition was getting worse, although she didn't know it. Then came the evening Alejandro was working late at the dental clinic and Gloria was feeling particularly blue, despite her one drink and two Valiums. So she made herself another vodka and tonic and decided just this once to take another pill. After all, her daughter always slept through the night, and Alejandro would be home in a couple of hours to check on the child.

Suddenly, Gloria began to feel *acalorada y con la cabeza un poco tonta*, warm and a little light-headed, so she opened the window of their sixth-floor apartment to get some fresh air before settling down in front of the television. "I just fell asleep without realizing it," she confessed later to her next-door neighbor and *amiga*, Alicia, a thirty-five-year-old Puerto Rican registered nurse with whom she had a lot in common, "and I'll never understand what made me wake up when I did. It must have been God. Because I was instantly alert and my eyes automatically flew to the window, and there was my beautiful *niña*, who had managed to climb out of her crib and toddle into the living room, and was halfway out the window!"

This brush with tragedy, which confirmed Gloria's worst fears about herself as a mother, upset her so much that she confided in Alicia, who had successfully conquered her own problems centering on prescription drugs and alcohol. Alicia suggested she attend an AA meeting with her, but Gloria insisted she wasn't an alcoholic, she just needed a little vodka to calm her nerves because she was jumpy all the time. Gloria didn't know that her need to sedate herself in order to function was a symptom of an addictive disorder, but Alicia did and urged her to see a therapist. That's when Gloria really got upset. "I can't do that!" she sobbed. "My husband will think I'm crazy and divorce me!"

The truth of it was that Gloria, who already felt bad about herself, saw therapy as the ultimate *marianista* proof of failure. To her traditional Hispanic mind-set, if you couldn't get better by yourself, you simply weren't trying hard enough. And if your mothering skills were so impaired that you needed professional help, you weren't fit to be your husband's wife. Gloria also believed that psychiatrists dealt only with crazy people and that most therapists were Anglos, who didn't understand Hispanics. Besides, personal problems belonged inside the closed doors of the home. Since taking them out into the world constituted a betrayal of the rules of *familismo*, seeing a therapist would make her feel like an unworthy person. However, for the first time, she saw that maybe she didn't have a choice. She could go on as she had been, driven by *marianismo* deeper into addiction and despair—or she could seek professional assistance.

Gloria's first step toward solving her problems was conquering her fears about the so-called stigma of being in therapy. In this case, she was fortunate to have her friend Alicia, who could put many of her fears to rest and aid her in answering her questions. Most people do find a therapist with the help of someone else—a friend, co-worker, relative, or pastor. Some people check their health insurance plan for a list of providers. Others look through the Yellow Pages and get referrals from organizations that either train mental health professionals or license them to make sure they follow a specific code of ethics.

You should be aware that a psychotherapist's code of ethics ensures full client protection. What that means is that the therapist keeps the information you share with her or him strictly confidential—just as a priest does in confession. For example, if you're seeing a mental health provider behind your mate's or parents' back out of necessity, your provider will not disclose anything about your seeing her or him, or about what you've said, without your permission. (The two exceptions to this rule are if the client has abused a minor and, in some states, if the client is planning a murder.) Another important aspect of the ethics code followed by all competent therapists is that if they feel the patient isn't showing improvement after a reasonable period of time, they must refer them to another provider.

THE THREE COMPONENTS OF PSYCHOTHERAPY FOR LATINAS

We've already given you the major components of psychotherapy in general. Now we want to describe the major components of psychotherapy for Latinas, which, as described by Melba Vasquez, a Latina psychologist, are gender, ethnicity, and socioeconomic class. We will emphasize the therapeutic importance of considering *marianismo*, since it seems to cause variations in behavior and development which require special understanding on the part of the therapist. This applies even if an acculturating Latina is convinced that the North American worldview is the one truth she wants to embrace. She may even fool herself into thinking she's already discarded traditional Hispanic beliefs. However, cultural concepts about the cause and treatment of illnesses are deeply ingrained, and may continue to surface despite

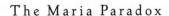

conscious rejection of them. This is particularly true when Hispanic women experience a personal crisis, and to their shock old ideas and values suddenly reappear.

This was the case with Margarita, a thirty-two-year-old graduate student who had been raised in Vermont by working-class Argentinian parents, but moved to New York on scholarship to study for a master's degree in economics. To her horror, Margarita was diagnosed with cancer, but was told by her doctors that it was a nonaggressive type which was treatable and showed a very high permanent remission rate. In time, the malignancy was completely arrested. However, that didn't stop Margarita from developing a serious case of hypochondria. Virtually every time she had a normal headache or a cold, she would rush to a doctor, who would give her a clean bill of health. That relieved her dreadful anxiety briefly, but then she would imagine she was having serious symptoms and consult yet another physician, who would tell her she was fine. Not only were all these medical visits getting expensive, but they weren't relieving her incredible inner pain. At the same time, she was feeling more and more guilty about having left her family and become overly Americanized. That she had a live-in boyfriend made her practically a disgrace to her *abuela*, her mother, and her father.

Now she wondered if her illness had been a punishment for renouncing her Hispanic roots, including her religious practices. She began to feel alien and threatened in her university, her relationship, her adopted city. She found herself spending more and more time at home—the only place she felt safe—and wanting to leave the apartment less and less. It didn't take long before her depression and morbid fears, her phobias, began to take their toll on her relationship with her American lover. But only when she realized she wasn't able to concentrate on her studies and was also missing a lot of classes did she understand she couldn't go on like this—without risking her future.

Finally, Margarita was able to level with herself and admit that her problems were no longer physical, but psychological. She decided to consult a therapist. Since, she reasoned, a lot of her anxiety was culturally related and involved guilt at literally leaving her family and perhaps trying to be more American and less Latin, she felt she wanted to see a Hispanic therapist. And because many of her problems were linked to being a Latina, she decided she would seek help from a Hispanic woman. She wanted a therapist who would help her feel comfortable with her cultural identity, and help her determine which components of her traditional belief package she wanted to keep and which she wanted to discard. So far, she had decided on two of three components of Latina psychotherapy, gender and ethnicity. Now she had to begin her search for the therapist herself, one whom she could afford and who would understand what it was like growing up in a family where money was always a problem. Having made that decision based on socioeconomic considerations, Margarita had now accounted for the three psychotherapeutic components recommended for Latinas by Melba Vasquez.

Looking for Dr. Right

Margarita's first step, after doing some basic research at the library, was to call the general number of a well-known local hospital and ask to be connected to the director of the outpatient mental health clinic. Then she asked for a referral, or recommendation, to a Latina psychotherapist. However, she stressed to the director that she wanted to interview several people before making her final decision. Three different names were supplied to her—coincidentally, a psychiatrist, a psychologist, and a social worker.

First she interviewed the psychiatrist, Dr. Letitia Gomez, a sixty-year-old Cuban-American. Margarita knew from her research that to be a psychiatrist, you have to complete four years of medical school and a one-year internship, become an M.D., and be licensed as a physician as well as board-certified as a psychiatrist. Although she was impressed with Dr. Gomez's credentials, Margarita didn't feel *completamente cómoda*, completely comfortable, with her, but didn't know if

this early in the process she would feel comfortable with anyone. She was honest with the psychiatrist and told her she was seeing two other therapists, and would call her when she'd made her decision.

Now Margarita made a plus and minus list about Dr. Gomez. In her favor was the fact that she was Latina, her training was superb, and she had both great dignity and authority. Since she was a medical doctor, she could also prescribe drugs such as Prozac if she thought they were warranted. When asked if she had a specialty, Dr. Gomez replied that although she had many adult clients, she did a lot of work with children and with parenting problems—not a field of particular relevance to Margarita. Not in her favor was a certain coldness in Dr. Gomez's personality, which made it hard for Margarita to relax because she reminded her of her autocratic grandmother, who was the source of a lot of her familial and cultural guilt. Other minuses were that Dr. Gomez seemed very "upper-class" and that her fee was really steep, more than Margarita could afford and her medical insurance could cover. Dr. Gomez then told her she could be seen at the outpatient clinic, where she worked during the day, and where there was a sliding scale based on the individual client's ability to pay.

Whether or not she ended up being treated by Dr. Gomez, Margarita learned from this first interview what questions to ask:

- Where did you do your residency and training?
- Do you have board certification?
- Do you have training in a psychotherapy institute?
- Are you a member of a psychotherapeutic or psychoanalytic institute?
- Are you a member of the American Psychiatric Association? (This is important because membership protects and promotes adherence to ethics.)

Next, Margarita contacted the clinical psychologist, a very down-to-earth Dominican-American in her forties named Claudia Marquez.

Dr. Marquez explained that she held a Ph.D. instead of an M.D. and that her orientation was psychological, not medical. She was board-certified, having passed the rigorous exam which can only be taken after five years of postdoctoral experience. Margarita discovered that Dr. Marquez also had four years of graduate school training in addition to a year of internship in a hospital seeing patients. When the doctor inquired what had brought her to therapy, Margarita felt freer in talking about her problems. Dr. Marquez reminded her less of her stern grandmother, as Dr. Gomez had, but more of one of her favorite aunts.

The problems were that Margarita's medical plan would cover only part of Dr. Marquez's fee, that her office was a real trek from where Margarita lived and went to school, and that the psychologist could only see her at times of the day which would mean substantially revising her class schedule. Still, Dr. Marquez's upbeat manner and ability to make Margarita relax had left a very positive impression.

Finally, Margarita visited the social worker, Dr. Elena Martin. She could see at once that Dr. Martin was a good person with a warm heart and a happy spirit. A Peruvian-American in her thirties, Dr. Martin began the interview by telling Margarita her schedule was very crowded because she devoted much of her clinical time to working in social service agencies which provided help for the very poor. She explained to Margarita that to become a psychotherapist she had earned a master's degree and doctorate in social work (although it was possible to be a licensed therapist with a master's degree), had graduated from a psychotherapeutic institute, had done extensive work in Jungian psychoanalysis, belonged to the relevant professional associations, and had been seeing patients for ten years.

Not until Margarita began talking about her problems did she realize that Dr. Martin's brand of caring was definitely "tough love." *¡Que no le iba a permitir salirse con la suya!*—she wasn't going to let her get away with anything! Before the end of the interview, Margarita had resorted to the Kleenex box at her side more than once and tried to apologize for getting so upset and not making any sense. Dr. Martin assured her she had nothing to apologize for, because therapy was about feelings and sometimes, often, feelings hurt. "If something hurts," she told Margarita, "you should respond in an appropriate way. After all," she said, "who laughs when they're in pain?" Rather than reminding her of her *abuela*, as Dr. Gomez had, or a favorite aunt, like Dr. Marquez, Dr. Martin reminded Maria of an older sister who lovingly but firmly kept the younger kids in line.

If Margarita so choose, Dr. Martin would see Margarita at a reduction of her usual fee, but made it clear that once Margarita graduated and got a job, the fee would be raised. Margarita's medical plan would still not cover the entire cost of her therapy, but it would help. The problem with beginning treatment was the doctor's busy schedule. She told Margarita she could definitely see her once a week, but not always at the same time or at the same place—which could cause a conflict with Margarita's own academic schedule.

At this point, it's important to add that credentials alone do not make a person the best therapist for you. Here are some questions Margarita asked herself to help make her decision. Perhaps they will help you do the same when you are faced with choosing a professional to work with:

- What are the skills and capabilities the person holds which will best help me?
- What is the person's experience, and how relevant is it to my needs?
- Would I prefer to work with a male or female therapist—and why?
- Would I prefer to work with a Hispanic or a non-Hispanic therapist—and why?

After writing down your answers to these questions and reviewing them, you'll be on the right path to finding a therapist with whom you might well be compatible.

In Therapy, You Have Options

As Margarita can tell you, finding the right kind of help requires a lot of legwork and just as much soul-searching. We want to stress here that no matter how much you've thought about it, you should not settle for the first therapist you see if you don't feel absolutely comfortable with that person. And please don't choose a name right out of the telephone book, because you won't have any idea whom you'll be getting. Always try to get a referral, whether from a friend, a hospital, or a professional association.

Now, since most emotional distress has a strong interpersonal component, how do you decide if your problem would be most effectively dealt with in individual, group, family, or child counseling? You might be surprised to learn that a famous study by Smith, Glass, and Miller in 1980 examined the effectiveness of various forms of treatment and reported that "no school of psychotherapy has a franchise on therapeutic efficiency." What we would suggest is to seek out the recommendations of the therapists you interview. We can't stress enough that what's really important is feeling comfortable with whomever you choose, which means asking yourself:

- Do I feel this person understands me?
- Do I feel this person is really caring?
- Do I feel this person is kind and nonjudgmental?
- Am I frightened by this person?
- Do I sense an impatience in this person?

MARGARITA'S CHOICE
In choosing her therapist, Margarita asked herself these questions and decided that she was a little frightened of the psychiatrist, Dr. Gomez. Not that she didn't respect her or think she was good at her work, but she felt their personalities just didn't mesh well and that Dr. Gomez seemed so aristocratic she might not be able to empathize with Mar-

garita's experiences growing up poor. On the other hand, she had gotten along fabulously with the psychologist, Dr. Marquez, and found her both easy to be with and confidence-inspiring. The problems were scheduling, the location of the therapist's office, and above all, the fee. Margarita was still paying off stiff medical bills from her illness, and she was concerned that putting herself in an even greater financial bind would only add to her anxieties.

Lastly, Margarita considered the social worker, Dr. Martin. She had to admit that she felt comfortable enough with her to let down her guard and weep the first time she'd seen her. Firm but compassionate, Dr. Martin had sensed Margarita's desperation and desire to heal emotionally and hadn't painted a rosy picture of the pain involved in change. That impressed her, as did her instinctual belief that the therapist would be there to support her through the worst of it. Margarita liked the fact that Dr. Martin worked with the poor, and regretted that she couldn't be treated in any of the outpatient clinics at which she worked because of the long waiting list. Still, she felt that Dr. Martin could understand what people who are poor go through. Also, the fee was affordable. Now the only problem that remained was aligning their busy schedules.

After calling Dr. Gomez and Dr. Marquez to inform them she had enjoyed speaking with them but had decided to work with someone else, Margarita contacted Dr. Martin and told her she wanted to work with her. However, she expressed her concern with the scheduling problem. The social worker replied that she felt the scheduling would be difficult only for the next three months. Until then she was sure they could work out something. In fact, Margarita's first appointment was at seven o'clock in the morning—a tribute to the dedication of both therapist and client. Luckily, it was held at a location near New York University, where Margarita lived and studied. Looking back years later, she would judge her choice of Dr. Martin "the best decision I ever made."

GLORIA'S HAPPY ENDING

Remember that when we first met Gloria, the panicked young mother, she didn't even know she had a problem? When we met her again, she was able to admit she needed help, but was too *marianista* to get it. However, with the help of her friend Alicia and the full approval of her husband, who had been aware of her panic attacks but hadn't known how to approach her about them, she began therapy with a Latina psychologist. Who would have thought that this young woman, who was totally resistant to seeking help, would end up telling her therapist, "I'm so happy I picked you!"

You'll be surprised to learn that you've met Gloria's therapist before. In fact, you've met both her and the doctor who referred Gloria to her. First, through a friend of her friend Alicia, she was given the name of Dr. Marquez, the clinical psychologist whom Margarita saw and liked. Gloria also warmed to Dr. Marquez's giving personality, her earthiness, and her familiarity with acculturation-associated problems. Gloria was able to be frank about her fears and depression, which culminated in the blackout episode that had triggered her awareness that she needed help. Since Gloria was fully covered under her husband Alejandro's medical plan, the fee would not be a problem for her.

However, she was unprepared for what Dr. Marquez said to her next. Although she would be more than willing to work with her, the psychologist told Gloria, she wanted her to talk to Dr. Letitia Gomez first. Dr. Gomez, she explained, was a psychiatrist, which meant she was a medical doctor, who could not only prescribe antidepression medication but also monitor how a client was reacting to it on both a medical and a psychological level. Dr. Marquez suggested that such medication might help Gloria cope with her anxieties, and thus diminish her need to medicate herself with alcohol and tranquilizers. Also, Dr. Gomez was an expert in dealing with parenting problems—issues which were very key to Gloria's situation. Although Dr. Marquez didn't say much about Dr. Gomez's personality, she told Gloria she thought she would get along well with her. What the therapist was thinking was that since she sensed part of Gloria's problem was missing

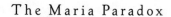

her mother and grandmother, a therapist of Dr. Gomez's age and authority might provide much-needed comfort for her.

Dr. Marquez had been quite right about Gloria's feeling comfortable with Dr. Gomez. And once the psychiatrist started her client on antidepressant medication in tandem with therapy, Gloria was indeed able to do without the alcohol and pills. Also, the older woman was able to validate Gloria's quality of care for and nurturance of her daughter. She could also reassure Gloria that her profound feelings of loneliness were justified in situations such as when she tried to make friends with other mothers in the park, and felt alienated by them. After all, her English wasn't as good as theirs, and when she mispronounced a word, it was natural to feel embarrassed. And, she pointed out, it was also only natural for the other mothers, who weren't Latinas, to be puzzled and amused at the little camphor pendant the baby wore around her neck. Gloria's *abuela* had sent it to protect her great-grandchild from colds; a common practice in the section of the Dominican Republic where Gloria came from. In North America, it seemed strange. But that didn't reflect on Gloria's worth as a human being. It was, however, an indication of the hard work and bravery the process of transculturation takes.

Only when Gloria accepted the fact that many of her personal problems were caused by cultural collisions could she stop blaming herself for everything, centering all that personal uncertainty on her mothering skills—a step backwards on the continuum of *marianismo*. That she trusted the therapist's wisdom and experience and felt that when she spoke, she was truly being heard were key to Gloria's healing. Since she felt safe, she could listen to her inner voice and determine the valuable aspects of her culture and feel pride in that identity.

In the course of therapy, Gloria made three major life decisions with Dr. Gomez's help. The first was to improve her English at school. Then she decided to get a job to keep her out of the house, and to stop her obsessing on her daughter. When she was ready, she returned to work as a dental assistant at one of the clinics where Alejandro worked. That meant not only that they had a chance to work together, but also that her *niña* could be placed in the clinic's day care center so mother and daughter could visit during the day. Being employed led to other positive changes. For one thing, she was meeting new people. For another, the additional income paid for child care and made it possible for Alejandro to cut back on his work time and spend more evenings with his family. The third thing Gloria did at Dr. Gomez's suggestion was to join *una tertulia*.

LA TERTULIA:
SUPPORTING EACH OTHER

Do you recall Maira, the battered wife in Chapter 7, who received such wonderful support from a group of Latinas with whom she regularly met? Or Alicia, the grieving widow in Chapter 6 who was invited by Dr. Elena Martin—the same Elena Martin who turned out to be Margarita's therapist—into a group of Hispanic women who met to discuss issues of belief and healing? Both these women were availing themselves of the copious rewards offered by *la tertulia*.

The word *tertulia* is defined by the *Diccionario Manual e Ilustrado de La Lengua Española* as "a group of people who customarily get together to chat or have fun." To that definition we would add the phrase "and to support each other." More and more, Latinas both in Latin and North America are forming these associations of women with a common problem or interest, who meet on a regular basis for dinner or to go to the theater or a museum or on a hike. Since the most important component of *una tertulia* is compatibility, any new members must be accepted by the entire group.

Let's pretend Gloria hadn't joined an existing *tertulia* and wanted to start one herself. First, there must be guaranteed compatibility on some level. All members, as we've just said, must have something in common. There should be a pattern of similarity on a number of issues: age, ethnicity, gender, level of education, occupation, marital status, motherhood, interests (reading, dancing, cooking, baking, knitting, gardening, tennis, hiking, bicycling or other sports, watching soap operas, discussing literature, traveling, religion, and so on). You must decide whether you think you have enough in common to be in the same *tertulia*.

To start her group, Gloria could ask around and even put an ad on the bulletin board of the clinic, or search through the Internet. She could also look through the clinic's phone list, check off Hispanic names in that clinic and the other one where Alejandro worked, and leave a message on the person's E-mail. She had always liked to read but hadn't had the concentration or energy when she was suffering through her depression. Now that she was improving, she had begun to read again. That was an interest she wanted to be able to share. And now that she wasn't housebound, she also realized that she liked to cook, especially to bake, and enjoyed going to restaurants not only as a form of entertainment but because the dishes she ordered gave her ideas she could adapt to her own cooking. Food would also be a subject she'd like to pursue as a group activity.

She could also mention her idea to her friend Alicia, since they were good friends and already had something in common, and suggest that she could canvas her other friends to see if any of them were interested in joining a group. Actually, since Gloria was recommended to a specific *tertulia* by Dr. Gomez, who knew her well and whose opinion on the subject of compatibility she trusted, she didn't have to go through the process described above, but that's how you might want to go about it.

The *tertulia* Gloria joined included eight Latinas of about the same age, some married, some single, but all professionals—and all of whom were working out personal problems which were really cultural conflicts. Being able to talk about the sometimes painful, sometimes hilarious adventures related to handling two worlds—be it through their direct acculturation or their parents'—made everyone in the group feel both supported and a reliable source of support. Once a month on Saturday night, Gloria looked forward to getting dressed up, leaving Alejandro to babysit, going to a really nice restaurant with her *comadres*—or as North Americans would say, her sisters—and having a real *fiesta.*

One of the other women in the group and Gloria became personal friends because of their shared love of reading, working out, and the theater. That woman was Margarita, who had been referred to the group by her therapist, Dr. Martin. Still in perfect health five years after her cancer treatment, she was now an assistant professor of economics at New York University, had broken up with her boyfriend a year earlier, and was on the verge of becoming engaged to a young Argentinian-American investment banker she'd met in graduate school!

We want to remind you that *una tertulia* is not a psychotherapy session. Even when you discuss issues like career and marital difficulties with your *comadres*, you are doing so in an informal manner with good, loyal friends whose support you can count on in difficult times. However, it's nice to have a springboard subject for your meetings, and you might want to use this book as a source of ideas for issues that affect you and the other Latinas in *la tertulia*. You might even want to use the quizzes as a basis for comparison and focus.

Remember that sometimes your meetings will deal *solamente con pasar un buen rato*, only with the fun stuff, and other times one of *las comadres* will be feeling upset, and those emotions and what provoked them will be dealt with by the group. Although this is an association *de apoyo y diversión*, of support and fun, it also serves a more serious social and psychological purpose and thus must be governed by rules and regulations, as well as follow guidelines.

Among the rules to be established in *una tertulia* is to determine what to do if incompatibility develops, which in turn threatens the stability of the group. A member insulting another woman, being rude, belittling someone, or putting pressure on someone like Gloria, who cannot drink, to have a piña colada, are the kinds of disruption that cannot be allowed to persist. Otherwise the gatherings run the risk of becoming hostile debates instead of cheerful sharings. Clearly, the will of the majority should prevail, and if necessary, the offending member could be asked to leave. From the beginning, it must be made clear that harsh criticism and judgmental behavior have no place in *la tertulia*— simply because this is not a therapy group, and there is no one figure who serves as the mediator or the facilitator. Here again, in *la tertulia*, there is a tendency to treat matters lightly so that everyone feels comfortable and free to share.

However, it is altogether possible that through your *tertulia* sessions, you'll become aware for the first time of some issues that are affecting you personally. When this happens, you might want to bring the matter into therapy if you are in treatment, or if you've made a special friend in *la tertulia*, you might discuss it with her. On this score, Gloria was very helpful to Margarita in planning relatively low-tension events for when her family and her future fiancé's family met for the first time. This was an occasion on which it was useful for the group to include both married and unmarried women, since the wives could serve as coaches for the women who were going to be wed. Along those lines, *las comadres* loved to hear their *amiga* Rosario describe the cultural disaster that occurred the first time she introduced her North American boyfriend, now her husband, to her very traditional Dominican family—all two million of them! When everyone's laughter finally subsided, Rosario replied, "I was so mortified! If anybody had suggested that someday I'd be joking about it, I would have told them they needed to see a therapist!"

We feel that to be fully effective, *tertulias* should meet at least once a month, preferably on a weekend, when your time is a little freer. Juggling two sometimes clashing cultural systems can be a very lonely experience, and when you are going through it, regular contact with and support from good friends, many of whom will be your first *comadres* in North America, can really do wonders in sustaining your self-esteem. And not only will you be having lots of fun with people whose company you enjoy, you'll also be actively maintaining Hispanic traditions, which you never want to eliminate from your belief package.

Another member of *la tertulia*, Jackelyn—who had returned to therapy because of her uncertainty about relocating to Texas—was able to explain how, aided by her old therapist and with the full consideration of her husband, Alvaro, she was able both to deal with her parents' traditional objections to therapy and to be frank with Alvaro about her unwillingness to start over again in a new place. He understood and declined the job. Amazingly enough, he held no bitterness but predicted equally good job offers closer to home would come both to him and to her in the future—and he'd been right. They were both doing well and thinking of having a child. The fact that they'd transcended an aspect of _marianismo_ and _machismo_ together had actually brought them closer—and guided them toward a new and rewarding sense of _familismo_.

Support Saves!

We want to leave you with the thought that the only way you should go through the process of change alone is on a one-to-one basis with a therapist. If you decide on therapy and _una tertulia_, you'll be radically enriching your life. It won't take you long to see how much less agonizing working through problems can be when you have support. Besides, having fun is a required component of good mental health. And in _tertulia_, you can put _una nueva marianista_ spin on the Hispanic tradition of _familismo_ by making your friends part of your extended family.

However, whether you choose psychotherapy, _una tertulia_, one of the many twelve-step programs for people with a specific problem like grief or alcohol abuse, the services of a folk healer, or a combination of methods is often less important than the act of seeking help. By putting faith in a healing process, you are likewise putting faith in your own ability to heal—the first step on the journey to empowerment.

10

"Do Not
Change":

───

*Going with the Flow vs.
Making Waves*

Cambiar, changing, is, as you already know, not easy and doesn't happen *del día a la noche*, overnight. It's a tortu-ous process that occurs in incremental stages, regardless of whether the focal area of the change is your body, mind, or spirit. What must be kept in mind is that although you're ready to institute change, you also need to anticipate upsetting the equilibrium of your established relationships. After all, change doesn't happen in a vacuum and rarely in social isolation. What that means is that it's difficult to prepare for change without taking into account not only yourself but also those around you and what their response might be to the "new you."

In this chapter, we'll discuss various aspects of change—relating to *marianismo*, immigration, acculturation—and how to work toward the smoothest possible transitions in brokering these cultural compromises. We'd like to use the Garcia women from Chapter 6 as a paradigm. These women are five Latinas at different stages in the acculturation continuum, with different degrees of adherence to *marianismo* and different levels of self-esteem. Let's review their various positions:

- Mrs. Garcia: A good *marianista* utterly submissive to the will of her husband and mother-in-law, she was accused by them of being *una mala madre* for raising so rebellious a daughter—at least in part because she worked outside the home.
- Maria: A spirited teenager who wanted to behave like her peers, facing traditional Hispanic restrictions at home that made her dream of divorcing her entire family.
- *La abuela*: Mr. Garcia's mother, who was holding on to tradition for dear life by both encouraging and enforcing her son's rigidity.
- Tía Fila: The forty-eight-year-old maiden aunt who sympathized with Maria's dilemma of trying to live in two cultures at the same time, but who, as *la solterona*, wasn't taken seriously.
- Blanca: The Garcias' older daughter, who never openly disobeyed her father and grandmother, thus earning her younger sister's utter disdain.

Through their story, we hope you'll find yourself preparing for the occasionally painful but equally exciting voyage toward discovering *la nueva marianista* in you.

LA NUEVA MARIANISTA

Let's revisit the Garcias in this context. Maria wanted to change, all right. She wanted to change everything, from the ground up—including the fact that her family emigrated from Cuba. She felt it would be easier for her to have been born into a nice, all-American farm family from the heartlands who didn't become hysterical over everything. It's regrettable perhaps but true nonetheless that we don't get to choose our parents, and all of us including Maria have to learn to accept what can't be changed. What you can do, though, is change your attitude about the things you can't change—which, in addition to being an improvement, is a change in and of itself.

It is crucial that you set change goals that are focused, realistic, and doable. "Focused, realistic, and doable . . ." Maria mused during a session of counseling. "Like what?" She was then helped to consider her overwhelming problems more objectively and rationally specify her goals for change. "You know what I really want?" she shared after contemplating all this. "I just want my family to be like . . . more American with me!"

Did Maria's desire seem doable? The therapist thought so. But she also observed that the teenager was shifting the burden of change onto her family without grasping that she was going to have to do some changing herself. We call this an emotional "blind spot," because she refused to acknowledge even to herself that there were positive values to her Cuban heritage, and that by denying these aspects she was contributing to her unhappiness. She was incorporating the negative, discriminatory attitudes of some Americans toward Hispanics and felt ashamed of being a Latina. What she needed to do next was identify her goal for change as reconciling these two clashing aspects of her life. She needed to broker a cultural compromise with herself, with her family, and with her world, and acknowledge that there are wonderful beliefs and behaviors in Hispanic as well as American society. In this way, she would become a new *marianista*—biculturally fluent and proud of both her heritages.

Now that we've given you the parameters for change, sit down with a pencil and paper and respond as honestly as possible to these questions:

- What is happening that's making you feel you can't go on with things the way they have been?
- What is the specific thing you want to change? Is it a way of thinking? A behavior? An attitude? A belief? Is it a set of distressing feelings? Or the way you interact with others?
  - Why do you want to change?
  - What are the Hispanic beliefs and traditions you want to discard from your belief package?
  - Have you considered precisely why you want to discard them?
  - Which ones are you proud of and want very much to keep in the package?
- How painful do you imagine changing will be?
  - How exciting do you imagine changing will be?
  - How do you imagine others will react to the change?
  - Do you expect some part of yourself to resist changing—even though you want to?
  - Do you expect significant others in your life to resist your changing?
  - How can you make your changes permanent?
  - What in your life do you most urgently need to change because it's really causing you pain?

✳ HURTING: FIRST LEG
OF THE VOYAGE TO CHANGE

Often, change begins with the realization that you are distressed and unhappy—in fact, that you're hurting. The high school guidance counselor who referred Maria's family to therapy sensed the teenager's pain and made her aware that something was wrong when suddenly she'd developed a chip on her shoulder and her usually excellent grades were slipping. With the help of a professional who knew what questions to ask, Maria confronted the fact that she was hurting.

Pain, produced by an imbalance in the mind, body, or spirit, is a warning sign that personal needs must be realigned. In point of fact, Maria's testiness and inability to concentrate on her studies were actually distress signals calling attention to her hurting. If she hadn't expressed them, she might never have embarked on the voyage to change. Most people don't change when they're feeling good. Only the intensity of their hurting pushes them to the point where they're willing to risk confronting the deep-seated fears that are holding them captive.

Asking questions of yourself, as the counselor did of Maria, is a useful mechanism which can help you clarify and define your need to heal your hurt and leave the pain behind, but it's important to distinguish between self-examination and self-pity. For instance, it wasn't doing Maria any good to complain, "Why me? Why did I have to be born into a Cuban family? Why won't my mother ever take my side against my father? Why can't I change my name to Meaghan?" because they were leading her nowhere except deeper into a rut.

When the guidance counselor scheduled a meeting with Maria's parents, it was to ascertain if they were picking up their daughter's distress signals, then to ask them to give their explanations for her unhappiness. Mr. Garcia had perceived his daughter's rebelliousness in a totally self-centered way and in place of pain saw defiance against his authority. Mrs. Garcia, however, tentatively shared that she'd been noticing something was wrong with Maria and also felt she was hurting.

That a mother and father should take such radically divergent explanations of their child's behavior led the counselor to suggest they see a family therapist, perhaps a Hispanic, who would be familiar with the family's cultural idiosyncrasies. It will come as no surprise that although Maria and her mother were willing to see a therapist, Mr. Garcia had strong reservations about the whole process. Still, he agreed to it once the counselor pointed out the school's expectations that parents work with their children on issues which were affecting academic performance. When confronted with the fact that he might be viewed as being less than a perfect father—and consequently less than *un macho* in good standing—Mr. Garcia relented.

Mr. Garcia's initial behavior is a good example of the resistance to change that you and other Latinas may encounter in your loved ones, so you must anticipate it and develop strategies to neutralize it. With Mr. Garcia, the counselor used a technique called reframing, which simply means recasting the conflict-producing issue in a new way that will give it undeniable value. With Mr. Garcia, the technique was to turn his fears of appearing inadequate as *un macho* into the expectation that a Hispanic father will do everything possible so his family will thrive. You might be in a similar situation—when the man in your life cannot accept the fact that you want to risk change in order to stop being in pain. If this is the case, try to think of a way to reframe the issue as a positive cultural value which will be acceptable to him.

Confronting yourself can be painful enough without having to ask yourself tough questions while your significant others refuse to validate your hurting. Just remember, on the other side of this hurting lies relief and the hope for a happier life—and that there are healers who will help you work through your fear, frustration, confusion, doubt, sadness, anger, and low self-esteem.

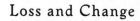

Loss and Change

Maria's school counselor started her on the right path to change by getting her to identify the specific feeling, anger, associated with her hurting. However, we've found that many of our Latina clients get confused about just what the feeling is called. Most often, they settle on *dolor*, the pain and sadness, which is itself generally camouflaged anger. If you are trying to identify the emotion most closely related to your discomfort, we recommend sticking to the basics, such as anger, unhappiness, fear, or guilt.

In this first leg of the voyage to change, we cannot stress enough your accepting that all change—even positive things like starting high school, moving to a new neighborhood, getting married, and certainly emigration—brings loss, and loss is inevitably accompanied by pain. Let's return to the Garcias and examine how the loss that emigration causes, along with the hopes that accompany it, impacted on them. The woman most profoundly affected was—not surprisingly—Maria's grandmother.

La abuela, in addition to experiencing the unavoidable process of change called aging, had never stopped feeling the stress of living in an unfamiliar environment which required mastering strange customs and behaviors as well as learning a new language. She was also gripped by the loss of many lifelong meaningful relationships and the sad realization that she would almost certainly never see her homeland again. Despite all that, she acknowledged that things were better for her and her family in North America than they would be in Cuba. As much as she loved her country, she had chosen to leave it. In the last analysis, that was the crucial choice which made the accompanying pain worthwhile because it resulted in positive change.

As we have seen, Maria and the other Garcia women were hurting because of changes produced by the acculturation process and with it the family conflict created by two warring sets of cultural expectations. Their next crucial step would be defining the problem.

☀ DEFINING THE PROBLEM
SECOND LEG OF THE VOYAGE TO CHANGE

The expression "Beauty is in the eye of the beholder" also translates to defining a problem, since any predicament is open to individual interpretation. We can't think of a better demonstration of this truth than the ongoing Garcia *novela*.

MARIA'S VERSION

Maria perceived the family's problem to be her parents' and grandmother's having been born and raised in Cuba and their insisting that she behave as if she had too. While they felt *que ella tenía mucha libertad,* that she had much too much freedom, she felt like she was in jail. When Alex, this boy she liked, invited her to the junior prom, Maria was on cloud nine—until her father announced he would only give his permission if Mrs. Garcia went with them. That's when her simmering anger exploded into open defiance. Since there was no way she could even broach the subject with Alex without feeling humiliated, she had pretty much decided just to tell him she couldn't go.

What about having Alex over to visit? Maria replied she would be mortified for him to see what her family was like. *La abuela* would corner him with endless stories about Cuba, even though her English wasn't that great. Her father would grill him as if he were a murder suspect. Her mother would force-feed him rice and beans. "Have Alex over? Right," she sneered. "Only if I was trying to dump him!"

By challenging the validity of her family's rituals and customs which meant nothing to her, Maria was definitely making waves. She was suffering through the natural insecurities of adolescence to begin with, and the condemnation leveled at her by her father and grandmother were making her feel even worse about herself. She was tremendously concerned with peer pressure, and to put icing on the cake, Alex was the first boy she'd ever seriously contemplated having as a boyfriend. The natural pain brought on with the process of change in adolescence was enormously intensified by her negativity about her ethnic background and the family's pressures that she conform to the principles of *marianismo*.

LA ABUELA'S VERSION

From the point of view of her *abuela*, Maria was a *marianista*-in-training—like all *niñas y adolescentes* involved in the process of becoming *una mujer buena*. As her grandmother and father saw it, she was openly rebellious and too assertive, and they worried she was much too free about expressing her sexuality. In terms of *marianismo*, she was a heretic. Maria wasn't wrong when she complained that her home was like jail. She was in fact being overprotected to make sure she fell into line with tradition and didn't bring disgrace on the family.

For *la abuela*, it was also of paramount importance that her *nieta*, her youngest granddaughter, integrate the principles of *marianismo* into her thoughts and actions because she would thus be carrying on Cuban traditions. Deep in her heart, the older woman prayed that Maria would calm down and conform, marry a Cuban, and pass on that precious heritage to their children. *La abuela* fervently believed with virtually religious fervor that Cuban cultural values were superior to American ones and must be preserved at all costs.

Consequently, *en su ceguera cultural*, in her cultural blindness, *la abuela* was utterly incapable of realizing that Maria could, by integrating the best of both cultures, have the best of both worlds. She was even more upset than she realized by the fact that Maria's date for the prom was *un americano*—a living, breathing threat to Maria's Cuban identity. Being with an American meant behaving like one, which in turn meant *matar*, killing, those dearly held beliefs and values that had sustained her for the seventy-five years she had been on earth. It didn't matter that *la abuela* lived in the United States. Only her physical self resided in New Jersey. Her *alma y espíritu*, soul and spirit, had never for a moment left Cuba.

MRS. GARCIA'S VERSION

Maria's mother was more understanding of her daughter's desire to be-have like her peers than her husband and mother-in-law, but she was restrained by tradition from expressing her opinion because in so doing she would also be challenging the authority of her husband and mother-in-law. As a good *marianista*, she wasn't going to raise objec-tions. However, she, like her daughter, wasn't happy about herself. She was tired of never being able to express her opinions, of always having to submit but constantly being blamed for everything despite it. That's one of the reasons why she worked as a Spanish teacher in the junior high school of a nearby town. At least there she was listened to and even treated with *respeto*.

But home was a far different story. Her frequent headaches she at-tributed to *los nervios* produced by her aggravation with her mother-in-law, with her husband, and now with her daughter. She felt pulled in two directions while constantly being stepped on. Even Maria didn't show her the respect a daughter should. Mrs. Garcia defined the fam-ily's problem as a combination of her daughter's refusal to conform and her husband's and mother-in-law's rigid and controlling ways of think-ing.

TÍA FILA'S VERSION

As you know, *las tías*, the aunts, play an important role in the Hispanic culture. In fact, you probably have lots of memories and stories about your *tías* from your childhood. Fila's definition of the problem, then, had significance for the family. At forty-eight, Fila had worked as exec-utive secretary to the director of Englewood Community Hospital for ten years and was by far the most acculturated of Maria's elders. She felt it was only natural for a second-generation Latina to have differ-ent, more liberated cultural expectations.

Also, she adored her niece and firmly believed Maria was a very principled young woman who was in no danger of turning into *una putica*, a loose woman, just because she went to the prom with a boy unchaperoned. There was no doubt in Fila's mind that it was possible

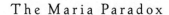

to be more assertive and independent than her mother, sister-in-law, even herself, and still be *una mujer buena*. Unfortunately, Mr. Garcia's *machismo* and pigheadedness didn't allow him to see that.

On the other hand, Fila thought that Maria needed to overcome her negativity about being Cuban. There were many good aspects of that background, which she wanted Maria very much to appreciate— for example, spirituality, the comfort and security *familismo* could provide, *personalismo,* and *respeto* for the elderly. While Maria regarded American values as "totally cool," Fila felt that "totally cool" also connoted actual coldness, a certain materialism, and a general lack of caring about others in the U.S. belief system. All in all, what *la tía* wanted *para su sobrina* was for her to become *una nueva marianista* and integrate the positive elements of both cultures into her life. Personally, Fila expressed regret that she hadn't been younger when she came to America. Still, she said, she was more free-thinking than she ever would have been if she hadn't emigrated.

BLANCA'S VERSION

Now we come to Blanca, Maria's "dishrag" of an older sister, who earned her sibling's scorn by going with the flow instead of making waves. Maria's blanket condemnation of Blanca really wasn't fair because the twenty-four-year-old had managed to integrate American customs in her life without challenging her father. She had even performed the miraculous feat of getting her own apartment in Manhattan without arousing Mr. Garcia's wrath. Doing it, however, had required long-term strategizing.

Blanca's first step on the road to independence had been to enlist her high school teachers' help in convincing her parents to allow her to attend a university in Boston because it was an excellent school and wanted her enough to give her a scholarship. For the first two years at Boston College—a good Jesuit school—Blanca lived in the dorm, then after her junior year moved to an apartment with three Latina classmates whom her parents had met and approved of. When she was preparing to graduate with a degree in marketing, Blanca was recruited by many companies in the New York/New Jersey area, but she only considered offers in Manhattan. It was clear even to her parents that it was silly to commute if she didn't have to, and they were somewhat re-assured when she rented a place with one of her college roommates. While she visited her family every week and talked to them every day, Blanca was able to maintain some distance from them.

Blanca appreciated her little sister's need to be independent and assertive, but she didn't regard doing battle with their father as central to it. An expert at brokering cultural compromise, she had never seen rebelliousness for its own sake as worth the trouble it caused. She re-membered being able to go to her junior prom without her parents as chaperones by having them meet her date beforehand and getting their approval, allowing her father to drive them to the dance, and promising to get home as part of a couples' group. If it had worked for Blanca, why shouldn't it work for Maria? Blanca saw her feisty younger sister as part of the problem because she seemed to be every bit as op-posed to compromise as Mr. Garcia and *la abuela*.

Blanca's story is a fine example of the adaptation mechanisms that can be used in integrating two cultures—a healthy resolution of the tensions implicit in acculturating. Blanca, who never made waves, was quietly crossing the ocean.

The Signals for Distress

We want to stress again here that, as each of the Garcia women defined the family crisis differently in terms of their own life experience, you need to define your problem as you see it while expecting others to see things their way. In defining your problem, you need to separate the traditional values which contribute to your personal growth from those that do not enhance your self-esteem and need to be modified or changed. As we mentioned earlier, an important component of this identification process is the ability to distinguish between distress signals, or symptoms, and the problem which is causing them. Let's use Mrs. Garcia as an example of what we mean.

In simple terms, she was able to articulate the difference between her headaches, the distress signals, and the problem that was causing them, the tension between her and her mother-in-law. Of course, when she had the headaches, taking an aspirin or two relieved the distress signal, but that was only a Band-Aid solution. Clearly, seeking to make the headaches disappear permanently required speaking up to the older woman—even if it meant challenging the *marianista* mandate, but always with the *respeto* that must be paid to the wisdom of the elderly.

However, more often than not, distress signals can reflect more than one problem area at a time and you must take care not to rush to attribute blame to a single factor. In mapping out strategies for change, it will be helpful to know whether you need to target one or several factors. For example, Mrs. Garcia identified that her headaches were produced by the domineering, controlling behavior of *la abuela*. However, it is possible to point to other contributing issues: She didn't think highly enough of herself to question other people's decisions. She felt guilty for wanting to undermine the authority of her husband and mother-in-law. She felt uneasy getting in touch with her desire to challenge the precepts of *marianismo*.

All these factors combined to cause Mrs. Garcia to say virtually nothing at all during the early therapy sessions. Now she was beginning to talk about her own distress signals.

Getting to the Root of the Problem

The next consideration is to realize who is contributing to the problem. Maria, for example, didn't see herself as being part of the problem, only the victim of it. Honestly, though, most interpersonal dilemmas involve you and someone else—although it isn't easy to see ourselves as "perpetrators." We have treated Latinas who seemed to be experts at not facing complicity and at shifting the blame to others. After all, a good *marianista* is a sacrificial victim who is born to suffer! This reminds us of the story of the Latina who got to the bus stop just as the bus was pulling away from the curb. When her psychotherapist asked her why she was late for her appointment, she replied, "The bus left me!"

The reality is that painful as it may be, you must face the truth that you are in part responsible for the situations that cause you pain. "Owning" your part in the problem is terribly important because the strategy for change has to include everybody involved, including yourself.

There is an exercise to help you focus on selecting an issue in life that you want to change. You may use the exercise to deal with any relationship in your life that you feel needs work. Get your pencil and paper ready, sit in a quiet room where you won't be disturbed, and think of a current relationship that makes you feel unhappy enough to want to modify it. First, consider what's problematical about it.

1. Write down a relationship issue that troubles you.
Example:
I do not participate enough in important decision making.
2. Decide whether the issue is a distress signal or the cause of the problem.
3. If you decided the latter, write down what you think is the cause.
Examples:
   A. There are problems in my relationship with my partner.
   B. In my country, the man is expected to make the major decisions.
   C. I don't feel capable of making important decisions for myself.
4. Write down what you perceive to be your partner's personal and cultural expectations regarding you and decision making.

Examples:

    A. He doesn't see my not participating in decision making as a problem.

    B. He feels I am not interested in making decisions.

    C. He feels men are better suited to decision making.

5. Write down what you perceive to be your contribution to the problem.

6. Write down your perception of how other people contribute to the problem.

7. Look back at your answers to 3. and make a list of acceptable changes for each problem you identified.

8. What actions are you willing to take to correct your part of the problem?

9. What actions do you want your partner to take to correct his part of the problem?

If you answered all the questions in an honest manner, you have just charted a personal map of your voyage to change. Now that you have a clear idea of what you and your partner need to change in order to improve and resolve the problem, your journey is off to a good start!

RESISTANCE: A LULL ON THE VOYAGE TO CHANGE

Hopefully, by now you have been able to finally pinpoint your problem and you have a solid fix on what needs to be done to improve your relationship. In fact, you're feeling so proud you can even say to yourself, "I can feel the first stirrings of *una nueva marianista* in me!" And you're right to feel optimistic about your ability to generate change.

However, after a solid start, there are things between you and your partner that are still not moving forward. In fact, you feel as if you're spinning your wheels. Let's say you and your husband are driving back from church with the kids when he mentions out of the blue that he's on the verge of renting a summer house in the mountains. The kids would love spending the weekends there, he announces without ever having asked them if they would, and it would also be a great place for the whole family to vacation. In addition to being shocked because this is the first time the subject has come up, you're disappointed because you were going to talk to your husband about renting a house by the ocean.

You deeply resent the fact that the man you married didn't even bother to ask you what kind of vacation you preferred, but only thought of himself and the children. Of course, a hard-core *marianista* would automatically go along with his plans because that's her role in life. But now you can't help but feel that it's every bit as important for you to enjoy the summer as it is for the other family members, no matter how much you love them. This time, you've got to tell your husband how you feel.

In order to make sure you're doing the right thing by wanting more say in the decision making, you decide to consult with your *tío*, your favorite uncle, a very wise man whom you've always trusted. But when you do talk to him, you're crushed because he simply doesn't see the problem the way you do and insists you must concur with your husband's decision. Then you begin to backtrack into *marianismo*, flagellating yourself with accusations that you're causing trouble by wanting too much, by demanding to help make major decisions when your husband always does such a good job of it. And you begin to feel selfish.

Now you waver back and forth and decide to wait just a little longer until you find the perfect moment to approach your husband. "Oh," you tell yourself, "I'll talk to him *mañana*." But *mañana* follows *mañana*, and the right time never seems to come. We will tell you the outcome of this situation later.

What you must understand when it seems that the change process has stalled is that any plans, especially ones for change, rarely run smoothly. The unexpected happens. Outside forces impact the direction and speed of your efforts. It's even possible that without being aware of it, you're either boycotting or slowing down the process. Don't lose heart! You've simply encountered a lull on the voyage to change, called resistance. So what can you do to make the wind rise once more? Again, let's look to the Garcias.

After a few therapy sessions, Mrs. Garcia found herself acknowledging that what her husband considered some of Maria's most outrageous demands, such as wearing miniskirts, were age-appropriate for a modern teenager. She could sympathize with her daughter's fears of being ridiculed if she took her *abuela* along on a movie date. Soon she was able to admit some things about her own position in the family. She acknowledged that it annoyed her tremendously when her husband didn't allow her to participate in family decision making. For the first time, she understood that being left out didn't reflect her personal inadequacy, but rather very traditional Hispanic traditions—*marianista* mandates which were neither helpful nor practical. That led her to see that as Maria had to integrate two cultural styles, she herself had to do double duty as the mother of a Cuban-American daughter.

The Turtle Trap

However, Mrs. Garcia's root problem went deeper than how to deal with her younger daughter—although it was camouflaged in her fears of what people would think if she didn't go along with her husband and mother-in-law regarding Maria. As with many other Latinas, the root of her problem was that she was terrified of asserting herself, because she felt that doing so could lead to abandonment, rejection, and isolation from her family, friends, and community. This menace to her sense of belonging became a powerful form of resistance which paralyzed her. Mrs. Garcia was caught in what Dr. William J. Knaus calls *la trampa de la tortuga*, or the turtle trap, because capitulating to the fear of change is like a turtle's pulling its head back in its shell when threatened. For human beings, though, it's only *una curita*, a Band-Aid solution, to avoid confronting deep-seated fear. It was not until Mrs.

Garcia could acknowledge that her fears were the root of the problem that she began to focus on her own needs.

Most people do encounter fear on the voyage to change, so be careful not to fall into *la trampa de la tortuga*. But if you do, keep in mind, as Mrs. Garcia did, that it's merely a delay, not the end of the journey. To her delight, she discovered that Maria, Blanca, Tía Fila, the school counselor, and the therapist actually became more approving as she became more assertive. Buoyed by their support, she began to feel more confident about standing up to her husband and mother-in-law. Little by little, the turtle was poking its head out of its shell.

The Self-Pity Ploy

Another lull on the voyage to change is helplessness. Granted, we live in a world of overwhelming uncertainties and insecurities, where unexpected events impact on our lives more powerfully than at any other time in history. In such an era, many Latinas may feel doubly paralyzed when faced with what they perceive to be drastic change. While some will overcome their immobility and take the first steps to modify, adapt, or change, others will feel too frail and vulnerable, throw up their hands, and claim they can't do anything about their lives.

In the early stages of therapy Mrs. Garcia was a good example of a Hispanic woman suffering from a severe case of helplessness, hopelessness, and self-pity—because she felt she'd handed control of her life over to her husband and mother-in-law. When she was helped to review her past, she found many instances where she had indeed made significant choices—including giving her relatives the power over her.

When she was in Cuba, Mrs. Garcia had studied to be a teacher despite her father's opinion that women should stay home and tend to their own children, not other people's. She had never for a second regretted that decision. Yet although she was twenty-six when she and her family emigrated, she had never taught because Mr. Garcia preferred for her to stay at home. However, her career choice came in handy when they arrived in New Jersey. While Mr. Garcia was back in

school getting another law degree in order to practice in North America, she learned English, went to school to get her teaching credentials, and got her teaching job in the public school system.

She also felt that her decision in agreeing to marry Mr. Garcia in the first place had been a good one, which she didn't regret. Despite his rigidity, she felt he was a good man who wanted to do the best for all his loved ones. Their present problems notwithstanding, she announced she wouldn't trade him for any other man.

Recalling these past decisions made Mrs. Garcia acknowledge that she was capable of acting on her own behalf and that since her helplessness was learned, it could be unlearned. Only then did the wind rise for her with such force that she sailed immediately on to a breakthrough.

That breakthrough came when Mrs. Garcia was able to announce in a session that she trusted Maria's judgment and didn't feel she needed to be chaperoned at the prom. Both *la abuela* and Mr. Garcia were stunned. "*¿Y qué te ha entrado a tí?*"—What has gotten into you?—he demanded, to which his wife replied, "*Nada, que soy una buena mujer y madre*"—Nothing. I'm a good woman and mother, and I'm simply thinking of my daughter and considering her feelings. Tía Fila and Blanca immediately rallied to Mrs. Garcia's defense and agreed Maria should be allowed to go to the prom without her parents in attendance. Maria herself announced that she was "blown away."

The Martyr Maneuver

Now we revisit Tía Fila, who had her own form of resistance to overcome. In Chapter 8 we gave you many examples of Latinas who get upset because they can't be everything to everyone. Their thinking, which goes along the lines of, "I am the best or I am nothing," guarantees their striving for goals they cannot possibly reach. Therefore, it's only natural for them to feel paralyzed when faced with the prospect of change.

During a general discussion about Latinas and assertiveness, Tía

Fila revealed her own lull in her transcultural voyage. She confessed that although she had been executive secretary to the hospital director for a decade and was always praised by him and her co-workers, she couldn't summon the courage to ask her boss for a well-deserved raise. Like the women in Chapter 3, she had from childhood been discouraged from showing assertiveness because it was considered unfeminine to do so. In true perfectionist fashion, she'd managed to twist her inability to express her desire to be rewarded for excellence into the feeling that somehow she wasn't doing a good job, which made it impossible for her to talk to her boss with any conviction. Fila admitted this was far from the first time in her life that perfectionism had been a major stumbling block for her. She was such a *perfeccionista*, she admitted, that she'd never married, because she was afraid she wouldn't be *la esposa y madre buena*. *Perfeccionismo* was Fila's personal *mal espíritu*, which had to be exorcised with her family's help.

Blanca was particularly helpful in making suggestions regarding how Fila should approach her boss. She advised her aunt to be assertive and request a private meeting with the director. At the meeting, she should mention how often he complimented her on the job she was doing, and then let him know with *respeto* that she felt excellence should be rewarded not only in words but in actions such as a raise. "Be straight with him," Blanca told her. "Tell him what you're thinking and feeling."

During another session, the family even staged a rehearsal based on Blanca's advice, in which Mr. Garcia offered to play the boss's role and was accepted. Even *la abuela* participated, insisting that *el americano* didn't understand how hard Cuban women worked, and announcing, "Tell him that if he does not appreciate your work, someone else does! Say you already have another offer and are ready to leave. Just see what he says!" With her family cheerleading her on, Fila practiced and practiced and finally got up the nerve not only to confront her superior but to use *la abuela*'s bluff. Tía Fila threw the family a celebratory dinner to share her joy when she received both a raise and a promotion.

The Blame Game

Next in our lulls on the voyage to change comes the blame game—holding someone else responsible for a problem in order to absolve yourself of having to change anything. Maria was a world-class blamer. She blamed her father, her mother, *la abuela,* and Blanca while denying any contribution she could be making to the family's problem. But deep down, the teenager had many self-doubts about who she was. Was she smart? Was she cool? Was she cute? Was she Cuban? Was she American? How could she be Cuban and American at the same time? Like any adolescent, she was unsure of her self-image and in addition felt all the added pressures from her family. Unfortunately, the only way she knew to deal with the overwhelming feelings was to get angry with her family, person by person—with the single exception of Tía Fila.

Before the family conflict could improve, it was necessary for Maria to look at herself, sort out some of her own issues which were adding to the stress, and stop playing the blame game. In doing so she reviewed herself in a positive light. She was a good student and well liked by the faculty and by her classmates. Alex was a very popular boy, and her girlfriends thought his asking Maria to the dance was awesome. At that point, she felt secure enough as an American teen to confront her Hispanic problems. Eventually, Maria was able to see she couldn't and shouldn't want to be completely American or completely Cuban. Her goal in changing would be to integrate aspects of both cultures without feeling conflicted about it.

For example, she didn't ever want to be as submissive to a man as her mother was to her father. One of the things she liked about Alex was that he never tried to order her around. On the other hand, it was occurring to her that there were things about her home life and about Cuban culture that she did like a lot. She loved and admired her Tía Fila and knew she could always count on her when she needed an adult to talk to. Her Tía Fila definitely had *un buen corazón,* a good heart.

She also really liked *el cariño*, the warmth, verve, and gaiety of the Cubans she knew, who, she finally admitted, *no eran fríos y estirados*, were not cold and uptight, like the families of her American friends. Most of all, she adored the passion, extroversion, and love of life her Cuban family showed in the face of all they had lost when they were forced by politics to abandon their homeland.

In one therapy session, she announced that she wanted her family to love and accept her for what she was—a Cuban-American woman. She admitted to her mother that she liked *arroz con frijoles* almost as much as burgers. Maria was even able to confess to her father that she thought *caballerosidad*, the gallantry of Cuban men, was really attractive, because it made her feel special. That was another reason she liked Alex. He treated her practically like a Cuban would. Without actually apologizing, she also wanted her dad to know that she had never meant to be disrespectful but was really upset and wanted to express her feelings to him.

As Maria began verbalizing all these deep feelings, there was a perceptible shift in the formerly intractable Mr. Garcia's attitudes and positions. For the first time, he could see his daughter *no como rebelde*, not as an upstart, but as an affectionate, loving kid trapped between two cultures. "For this sadness," he proclaimed, "I blame Fidel Castro!" Immediately, the rest of the family implored Mr. Garcia to stop blaming Fidel if the New Jersey property taxes went up or if it snowed. That wasn't easy for him, but gradually he began looking inward at the rigidity of his outlook on the way women were supposed to behave. Only then could the Garcias talk constructively about making plans for Alex to visit them. Please note that as soon as Mr. Garcia and Maria, who was definitely her father's daughter, stopped placing the blame on someone else, compromises were developed, and conflicts became less severe. The Garcia family was now moving at a steady clip on the voyage to change.

As you can see, you need to be alert to determine if you or others are playing the blame game. If so, you've got to neutralize it as quickly as possible. One sure clue that it's been put into play is denial in yourself and others. Once you recognize the denial for what it is, resistance, you'll be back on course in no time.

The Sickness Ruse

In earlier chapters of this book, we gave you examples of Latinas who were referred to therapy by physicians because of physical complaints with no medical basis—conditions such as headaches, backaches, intestinal problems, asthma and allergies. There is good reason to believe that to a certain degree, somatic illness may be used as a lull on the voyage to change.

Be aware that as long as you continue to focus your attention exclusively on the physical aspect of yourself while ignoring or denying your emotional and spiritual components, you're not going to heal and/or change—just as Mrs. Garcia did not get rid of her headaches permanently when she took aspirin. Unfortunately, there are physicians who will collude with the antichange, *marianista* elements in you by not alerting you to possibly psychological linkages. We're thinking here of physicians like the one who gave Gloria from Chapter 9 all the Valium she wanted without a second thought.

The Sacrifice Excuse

As we discuss various forms of resistance to change, it's impossible to overlook the beliefs and principles of *marianismo*. Early in the Garcias' therapy, you'll recall, Mrs. Garcia confessed she thought Maria had a right to be heard but didn't think she had the right herself to express her feelings to her husband. At the time, she added that *la mujer tiene que sacrificarse*—women are expected to sacrifice their own desires and needs—for the sake of family harmony. This is unmistakably an articulation of the principle of self-denial, and the role of *mártir* who blames herself for everything, that is the very heart of *marianismo*.

When this issue was raised, Maria insisted her mother could maintain harmony in the family and still be able to express her opinions, even if they differed from Mr. Garcia's or *la abuela's*. *La abuela* immediately countered that since the beginning of the world, women's function was to stay at home and men's to be *en la calle*, on the street, working to support their women and children. She added that men knew what was best *para las mujeres*, and informed her granddaughter that to be obedient and respectful of Papa's *autoridad* was what God intended. This naturally caused Mr. Garcia to nod his head affirmatively with great force.

Change, as we've said, is painful, and some Latinas feel threatened by it. Such was the case with *la abuela*, who zealously guarded her matriarchal role and intended to fight with her last breath to maintain the status quo which bequeathed household authority to her and her son. Here again, it was Tía Fila who put things in perspective. "In the days of the *conquistadores* that might well have been true," she began, "but it doesn't work anymore." As she pointed out, all the Garcia women except Maria and *la abuela* worked outside the home and contributed to the welfare of the family. "If women are working *en la calle*," she asserted, "they are entitled to their opinions *en la casa*!" Blanca concurred by respectfully suggesting to *la abuela* that the ideas she'd expressed were *creencias muy viejas*, which have no relevance to modern life.

Many sessions passed after this discussion without *la abuela* voicing those thoughts again, which in itself was progress—especially when it came to talking about the prom. Here is a good example of how a cultural value was modified to meet a family's specific needs. Always respectfully, several family members openly disagreed with *la abuela*, without condemnation but emphasizing the need for change because of greatly altered circumstances. It is important for Latinas to be aware that *marianismo* is ingrained in us, and that when a proposed change is threatening, some of our old beliefs surface as a rationalization for not changing.

The Destiny Diversion

Now we come to the last lull on our voyage, but a force of resistance which is very powerful—*la voluntad de Dios*, the will of God, or *el destino*. As we've just seen, *la abuela* often invoked these celestial powers to explain both why we shouldn't institute change and why Maria should accept the status quo. However, it was Mrs. Garcia who cited the proverb *"ayúdate que Dios te ayudara,"* God helps those who help themselves—as justification for resolving her family's conflicts.

That said, the spiritual power of traditional beliefs does offer great comfort to many Latinas, particularly those who have experienced the death of a loved one and can accept a loss as an inexplicable "act of God." Therefore, in deciding which cultural values to keep and which to discard from your belief package, the one under examination must be evaluated in terms of the specific circumstances to which it pertains. Here again, it's not an either/or situation. As we all know, there are infinitely more shades of gray than of black and white. Our object is not to have you discard every traditional Hispanic value from your life. We have already referred to the many wonderful cultural values that most Latinas want to keep, for example *familismo*. These values, which have a soothing and positive side, will provide you with great comfort, support, and enhanced self-esteem at necessary times in your life.

Now, using what you've just learned, let's go back to the hypothetical problem we stated before—confronting your husband over selecting your vacation house—and see how you press ahead and resolve it. First you review your problem—fears of incurring his anger and of being considered selfish, followed by your feeling that he's the one who's thinking only of himself. After exploring your emotions, you realize that you are trying to contain your anger rather than risk the consequences of your husband's thinking you are a bad person. You then tell yourself you are an adult and should stop feeling like *una niña*. And as a grown woman, you admit that it's better to risk the consequences than to keep your anger bottled up.

As a result of this internal dialogue, you find the perfect opening: On a Saturday night your husband suggests driving to the country the next day to visit the proposed vacation area. You take a deep breath and tell him that you appreciate how much he's doing to make the summer wonderful for the entire family, but wouldn't it be possible to look into a beach community as well? He seems surprised and confesses that option just never occurred to him. You tell him, "If the choice were solely yours, you'd prefer the ocean to the country." And he says, "Of course. Let's drive to the shore tomorrow. The kids would love being near the water, and I would too. And it isn't even as far away. Next year," he adds, "maybe we'll try the mountains. What do you think?" And you say, "Fine."

As you see, you expressed yourself, even got what you wanted, and nothing disastrous happened. There's a lesson to be learned here— that sometimes our worst fears occur only in our minds, because very often others don't judge us as harshly as we judge ourselves. Having confronted your resistance, you're back on course to permanent change.

LA NUEVA MARIANISTA: FINAL LEG OF THE VOYAGE TO CHANGE

Throughout this book you have read about Latinas suffering with low self-esteem expressed through feelings such as incompetence, dependency, self-denial, depression, self-doubt, anxiety, and physical complaints. You have come to see that in many Latinas, depressed self-esteem is the result of centuries of the belief system called *marianismo*, which defined the worldview of the Hispanic woman—including self-image, interpersonal relationships at all levels, and place in society. You must by now be asking yourself, "Why have we allowed

these beliefs and practices which have been so detrimental to our well-being to go on for so long without overturning them?" Evelyn Stevens made a similar observation when she noted that women placed a key role in perpetuating their own subservience. "Why," she writes, "would they work against their own interests?"

Stevens's question assumes that Hispanic women have options other than the ones they choose to exercise, whereas the social reality in traditional Latin societies is that women had no choices. Social and economic determinants made them absolute subordinates to men, maintaining them in service tasks and in the ideal feminine roles of giving, nurturing, caring, submission, dependence, selflessness, femininity, inferiority, powerlessness, and intimidation. Indeed, the inability to freely express anger is still perceived as a sign of virtue, and a healthy response to the *marianismo* mandate. Therefore, it should come as no surprise that even today in the United States many Hispanic women suffer from depression, anxiety, and physical illness. How can this in fact be changed? What must you consider to promote change in yourself and your *amigas*?

As we've stressed, all women living in the United States, including Latinas, have more role choices available to them than women in Latin America. Although we still have a long way to go before we bring about justice and equity for all women, we've made substantial progress on the change continuum. If that's the case, then you are in a fertile environment, a place where you can become *una nueva marianista*. Furthermore, if we change, we'll bring about changes in Latino men which will eventually produce *un macho liberado*. But now let's talk more about what this *nueva marianista* will be like.

Her femininity will not be stereotyped. She will experience healthy self-esteem, will love herself for what she is, will freely demand and receive the social and emotional support of others, will express herself without fear of social castigation or ostracism, and will develop to her fullest potential.

Such Latinas will be confident and proud of being the fusion of the best values of two cultures. They will have a choice of performing whatever roles they wish, wife and mother among them, optional but not mandatory. They will have the right, along with men, to express the full range of human emotions and behaviors—including assertiveness, independence, self-fullness, activity, and sexuality—without being labeled sick. They will participate in all spheres of human activity they choose to, and their contributions will be welcomed and valued in public as well as private life.

These women will not be relegated to taking care of the house simply because it is perceived to be their assigned gender role. They will not allow themselves to be formally or informally prevented or discouraged from performing any work in the public arena which they themselves consider an enhancement of their well-being. They will be fully enfranchised to make decisions affecting their present and future lives.

Each Latina will stride toward these goals in her own way, but the one lesson we must all bear in mind is that —socially, individually, culturally, psychologically, physically, and spiritually—true and permanent change will not come until we have full awareness of the conditions and circumstances of the problem *con un deseo intenso*, with a burning desire, to change. Fear may well set in, yet knowing that we are not sick or crazy, or guilty or *malas*, but yearning to be a whole person will give us the will to continue on our voyage. Remember, above all, that change is always possible if you are committed to it with all your heart and soul. If you doubt our word, ask the Garcias.

By the time the Garcias bade the therapist *adiós*, they had brokered a domestic compromise and had made great strides across the acculturation continuum together. In the course of treatment, even Mr. Garcia and *la abuela* were able to relax some of their traditional Hispanic beliefs and behaviors, which freed all family members to select the aspects of American culture they would integrate into their daily lives. Once this happened, the Garcia women began to assert themselves both within the family and in the workplace, with both women and men. Everyone felt better about themselves, about each other, and about being Cuban-American. Only as their ship of change sailed to-

ward the harbor did they realize that what at first had seemed a tempestuous crossing had turned into a marvelous voyage of discovery for them all.

In the years that followed, the Garcias kept in contact with the therapist and informed her of all important family events. Mr. Garcia called when Maria was accepted at Radcliffe, and admitted that although Harvard was full of communists, he was thrilled by the prospect of his *niña* attending such a prestigious university.

Blanca checked in when she became engaged to an American stockbroker. She mentioned that *la abuela* had at first vowed to remain in her room when he was being presented to the family. Finally, however, curiosity got the better of her, and she made quite an entrance, very late but all dressed up. While still not overjoyed, *la abuela* was coping.

Mrs. Garcia reported to the therapist that she and Tía Fila had acted upon her suggestion and started a *tertulia* group. Over time, it evolved into 100 Hispanic Women—a popular and important organization dedicated to advancing the well-being and empowerment of Latinas in the New York area. Mrs. Garcia became widely known for her patience and enthusiasm, and Tía Fila for her kindness and superb fashion sense.

Maria followed in her father's footsteps by earning a law degree from Yale after graduating from Radcliffe with honors. She was now an assistant district attorney in New York, where she had her own apartment—to Mr. Garcia's disapproval, but with her mother's, her aunt's, and her sister's support. Alex, who had also earned a law degree, was still in the picture but across the country. With so much distance between them, Maria and he had both agreed to date other people.

And every once in a while, the therapist got a call from *la abuela*, informing her she continued to keep harmony in the family through the tireless exercise of her Cuban values, wisdom, and widely praised domestic skills.

✳ EMPOWERMENT:
THE PLEASURE AFTER THE PAIN

Using the eminent Brazilian educator Paulo Freire's concept of consci-
entization—which means the development of critical awareness of
one's own circumstances and actions in order to change personal reality—we can say that the Garcia women opened themselves to questioning their realities, including the pain and unhappiness of their
lives, and mobilized their inner strengths to change. To different degrees, each of them was awakened to a critical awareness of the subju-
gations, miseries, and longings which they were experiencing. Only
after fully confronting the extent of their unhappiness and dissatisfaction could they begin exercising a new power within themselves—the
power to act with others to effect change. That process is empowerment.

You can experience these powerful feelings. We've told you all
along that change isn't easy or painless, but if you are hurting and have
a burning desire to relieve your suffering, there is no question in our
minds that you can develop the critical awareness you need to take actions to vastly improve your circumstances. Once you do, your self-
esteem will be enhanced as others perceive you in a new light, and
acknowledge and respect your new strength. That's exactly what happened with the Garcias.

The fact is people don't change drastically. *La abuela* will always
be bossy, and Mr. Garcia will always be a bit of a bully, but if *you*
change, you'll change the way people relate to you. If you don't merely
cry, scream, or slink off, they'll take you more seriously as a needed
component in the decision-making process. Likewise, if you don't hide
behind *marianismo*, you'll be well on your way to having a rich and fulfilling life.

As you read these lines, *mujer*, gather the strength to become *una
nueva marianista*. Determine what you need to discard in your cultural
belief package, and what you want to keep with all your heart—price-

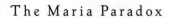

less values like cooperation and loyalty. Indeed, it was through so traditional a value as *familismo* that the Garcia women were empowered. Likewise, there are North American values you will want to integrate, such as individualism and innovation, because they will enable you to function better in your personal and business life. And don't fear losing your ethnic identity by acculturating. You won't. In fact, integrating the two cultural systems will actually enhance who you are.

So here is where our voyage together ends and yours begins. We have taken you through the rough seas experienced by other Latinas as they became empowered and claimed their right to be *nuevas marianistas*, women who treasure their *herencia cultural latina* and the rich heritage of America in equal part. They are women who understand how fortunate they are to be able to enjoy the best of both worlds, *lo viejo y lo nuevo*, the old and the new. You can be one of this strong new breed with a unique and special identity full of assertiveness, enthusiasm, and success. Never forget that *marianismo*, the Maria Paradox, dictates that you can only gain empowerment through submission. Now, in the United States of America, you have the opportunity to resolve that paradox once and for all.

Comadre, open your heart, your mind, your soul, and your spirit to the winds of change as you travel from *marianismo* through acculturation to self-esteem—and become your own woman at last.

References

Adler, A. (1979). *Superiority and Social Interest*, Ansbacher, H. L., and Ansbacher, R. R., eds. and trans. New York: Norton.

Ainsworth, M. D. S., Blehar, M. C., Waters, E., and Wall, S. (1978). *Patterns of Attachments: A Psychological Study of the Strange Situation.* New York: Wiley.

Alberti, R. E., and Emmons, M. E. (1993). *Yo Soy Dueño de Mi Vida: Triunfa con Estima y Confianza.* Mexico, D. F.: Editorial Pax Mexico.

Bailey, R. H. (1976). *Violence and Aggression.* New York: Time-Life Books.

Basaglia, F., and Basaglia, F. (1984). *La Mayoría Marginada.* Mexico, D.F.: Fontamara.

Bernal, G. (1982). "Cuban Families," in McGoldrick, M., Pearce, J. K., and Giordano, J., eds., *Ethnicity and Family Therapy.* New York: Guilford.

Berry, J. W. (1990). "Psychology of Acculturation: Understanding Individuals Moving Between Cultures," in Brislin, R. W., ed., *Applied Cross-Cultural Psychology.* Newbury Park, Cal.: Sage.

Blizard, R., and Bluhm, A. (1994). "Attachment to the Abuser: Integrating Object-Relations and Trauma Theories in Treatment of Abuse Survivors," *Psychotherapy*, vol. 31, no. 3 (Fall 1994).

Bosch, J. (1984). *Composición Social Dominicana: Historia e Interpretación.* Santo Domingo, República Dominicana: Alfa y Omega.

Bowlby, J. (1969, 1973). *Attachment and Loss. Separation: Anxiety and Anger,* 2 vols. New York: Basic Books.

Branden, Nathaniel (1992). *The Power of Self-Esteem.* Deerfield Beach, Fla.: Health Communications.

References

Brischetto R. (1994). "Women Professionals Take the Growth Lead," *Hispanic Business*, vol. 16, no. 2 (February 1994).

Canino, G., Rubio-Stipec, M., Shrout, P., Bravo, M., Stolberg, R., and Bird, H. (1987). "Sex Differences and Depression in Puerto Rico," in Amaro, H., and Felipe, R., eds., *Psychology of Women Quarterly*, Cambridge University Press for Division 35, American Psychological Association, vol. 11, no. 4 (December 1987), pp. 443–59.

Caplan, P. J. (1989). *Don't Blame Mother: Mending the Mother/Daughter Relationship*. New York: Harper.

Cooley, C. H. (1902). *Human Nature and the Social Order*. New York: Scribners.

Comas-Diaz, L. (1987). "Feminist Therapy with Mainland Puerto Rican Women," in Amaro, H., and Felipe, R., eds., *Psychology of Women Quarterly*, Cambridge University Press for Division 35, American Psychological Association, vol. 11, no. 4 (December 1987), pp. 461–74.

———— (1989). "Culturally Relevant Issues and Treatment Implications for Hispanics," in Koslow, D. R., and Salett, E., eds., *Crossing Cultures in Mental Health*. Washington, D.C.: Society for International Education Training and Research.

———— (1991). "Feminism and Diversity in Psychology: The Case of Women of Color," *Psychology of Women Quarterly Special Issue Hispanic Women and Mental Health*, vol. 15, pp. 597–609.

Cortes, D. E., Rogler, L. H., and Malgady, R. G. (1994). "Biculturality among Puerto Rican Adults in the United States," *American Journal of Community Psychology*, vol. 22, no. 5.

Davis, S. K., and Chavez, V. (1995). "Hispanic Househusbands," in Padilla, A., ed., *Hispanic Psychology: Critical Issues in Theory and Research*. Thousand Oaks, Cal.: Sage.

De la Cancela, V. (1986). "A Critical Analysis of Puerto Rican Machismo: Implications for Clinical Practice," *Psychotherapy*, vol. 23, no. 2 (Summer 1986).

Diagnostic and Statistical Manual of Mental Disorders, Fourth Edition (DSM IV) (1994). Washington, D.C.: American Psychiatric Association.

Diaz-Guerrero, R. (1970). "Adolescence in Mexico: Some Cultural, Psychological and Psychiatric Aspects," *International Mental Health Research Newsletter*, vol. 12, no. 4 (Winter 1970).

Diccionario Manual e Ilustrado de la Lengua Española, Segunda Edición (1950). Madrid: Calpe, S.A.

"Domestic Violence," *Journal of the American Medical Association*, vol. 267 (1992), pp. 3109–3240.

Ehrenberg, O., and Ehrenberg, M. (1994). *The Psychotherapy Maze: A Consumer's Guide to Getting In and Out of Therapy*. Northvale, N.J.: Jason Aronson.

Escobar, J. I., Gomez, J., and Tuasson, V. B. (1983). "Depressive Phenomenology in North and South American Patients," *American Journal of Psychiatry*, vol. 40, pp. 47–51.

Espin, O. M. (1984). "Cultural and Historical Influences on Sexuality in Hispanic/Latin Women. Implications for Psychotherapy," in Vance, C., ed., *Pleasure and Danger: Exploring Female Sexuality*. London: Routledge and Kegan Paul.

———— (1987). "Psychological Impact of Migration on Latinas: Implications for Psychotherapeutic Practice." *Psychology of Women Quarterly*, vol. 11, no. 4 (December 1987), pp. 489–504.

————, and Gawalek, M. A. (1992). "Women's Diversity: Ethnicity, Race, Class and Gender in Theories of Feminist Psychology," in Brown, L., and Ballow, M., eds., *Personality and Psychopathology: Feminist Reappraisals*. New York: Guilford.

Ferre, R. (1990). "La Cucarachita Martina," in Sola, M. M., ed., *Aquí Cuentan Las Mujeres: Nuestro Estudio de Cinco Narradoras Puertorriqueñas*. Rio Piedras, Puerto Rico: Ediciones Huracan.

Freire, P. (1994). *Pedagogy of the Oppressed*. New York: Continuum.

Garcia, G. (1994). "Tropical Tycoon Nelly Galan," *New York Times Magazine*, December 11, 1994, pp. 59–61.

Gies, J., and Gies, F. (1978). *Women in the Middle Ages*. New York: Harper.

Ginorio, A. (1979). "A Comparison of Puerto Ricans in New York with Native Puerto Ricans and Caucasian and Black Americans on Two Measures of Acculturation. Gender Role and Racial Identification." Doctoral dissertation, Fordham University. *Dissertation Abstracts International*, vol. 40, pp. 983–84.

Goleman, D. (1994). *New York Times*, June 12, 1994.

Gordon, L. H. (1993). *Passage to Intimacy*. New York: Simon and Schuster.

Greeley, A. M. (1969). *Why Can't They Be Like Us?* New York: Institute of Human Relations Press.

Grosjean, F. (1982). *Life with Two Languages: An Introduction to Bilingualism*. Cambridge, Mass.: Harvard University Press.

Guntrip, H. (1989). *Schizoid Phenomena, Object Relations and the Self*. Madison, Conn.: International Universities Press.

Hakuta, K. (1986). *Mirror of Language: The Debate on Bilingualism*. New York: Basic Books.

References

Harlam, S. L., and Berheide, C. W. (1991). "Barriers to Workplace Advancement Experienced by Women in Low-Paying Occupations." University at Albany, State Univesrity of New York, Center for Women in Government, January 1991.

James, W. (1981). *Principles of Psychology*. Cambridge, Mass.: Harvard University Press. (Original work published 1980.)

Jordan, J. V., Kaplan, A. G., Miller, J. B., Stiver, I. P., and Surrey, J. L. (1991). *Women's Growth in Connection: Writings from the Stone Center*. New York: Guilford.

Kaplan, H. I., and Sadock, B. J., eds. (1989). *Comprehensive Textbook of Psychiatry*. Baltimore: Williams and Wilkins.

Kernberg, O. F. (1984). *Object Relations Theory and Clinical Psychoanalysis*. Northvale, N.J.: Jason Aronson.

———— (1985). *Internal World and External Reality: Object Relations Theory Applied*. Northvale, N.J.: Jason Aronson.

———— (1986). *Severe Personality Disorders: Psychotherapeutic Strategies*. New Haven: Yale University Press.

Kilborn, P. K. (1965). "For Many in Workforce, Glass Ceiling Still Exists," *New York Times*, March 16, 1995.

Lagarde, M. (1993). *Los Cautiverios de las Mujeres: Madresposas, Monjas, Putas, Presas y Locas*. Mexico, D.F.: Universidad Nacional Autónoma de Mexico.

Luborsky, L., Crits-Christoph, P., Mintz, J., and Auerback, A. (1988). *Who Will Benefit from Psychotherapy? Predicting Therapeutic Outcomes*. New York: Basic Books.

McGinn, N. F., Harburgh, E., and Ginsburg, P. (1965). "Dependency Relations with Parents and Affiliative Responses in Michigan and Guadalajara," *Sociometry*, vol. 28 (September 1965), pp. 304–21.

McGoldrick, M., Pearce, J. K., and Giordano, J., eds. (1982). *Ethnicity and Family Therapy*. New York: Guilford.

McKay, M., and Fanning, P. (1972). *Self-esteem*. Oakland, Cal.: New Harbinger.

Masterson, J. F. (1976). *Psychotherapy of the Borderline Adult: A Developmental Approach*. New York: Brunner/Mazel.

———— (1981). *The Narcissistic and Borderline Disorders: An Integral Developmental Approach*. New York: Brunner/Mazel.

Mead, G. H. (1934). *Mind, Self and Society*. Chicago: University of Chicago Press.

Meloy, J. R. (1992). *Violent Attachments*. Northvale, N.J.: Jason Aronson.

Mezzich, J. E., and Raab, E. S. (1983). "Depressive Symptomatology Across the Americas," *Archives of General Psychiatry*, vol. 37, pp. 818–23.

Miller, J. B. (1986). *Toward a New Psychology of Women*. Boston: Beacon.

Minuchin, S., and Fishman, H. C. (1982). *Family Therapy Technique*. Cambridge, Mass.: Harvard University Press.

Mizio, E. (1981). "Puerto Rican Culture," in Mizio, E., and Delaney, A. J., eds., *Training for Service Delivery to Minority Clients*. New York: Family Service Association of America.

Mones, G., and Panitz, P. (1994). "Marital Violence: An Integrated Systems Approach," *Journal of Social Distress and the Homeless*, vol. 3, no. 1.

New York State National Woman Abuse Prevention Project. *General Facts About Domestic Violence: New York State Domestic Violence Fact Sheets.*

Nunberg, H. (1955). *Principles of Psychoanalysis*. Madison, Conn.: International Universities Press.

Nyamathi, A., and Vasquez, R. (1995). "Impact of Poverty, Homelessness and Drugs on Hispanic Women at Risk for HIV Infection," in Padilla, A., ed., *Hispanic Psychology: Critical Issues in Theory and Research*. Thousand Oaks, Cal.: Sage.

Ogbu, J. U. (1981). "Origins of Human Competence: A Cultural-Ecological Perspective," *Child Development*, vol. 52, pp. 413–29.

Ogden, G. (1990). *Sexual Style and Creating Intimacy*. Deerfield Beach, Fla.: Health Communications.

O'Leary, K. D., & Vivian, D. (1990). "Physical Aggression in Marriage," in Fincham, F. D., and Bradbury, T. N., eds., *The Psychology of Marriage: Basic Issues and Applications*. New York: Guilford.

Olivier, C. (1984). *Los Hijos de Yocasta: La Huella de la Madre*. Mexico, D.F.: Fondo de Cultura Económica.

Padilla, A. M., ed. (1980). *Acculturation: Theory, Models and Some New Findings*. Boulder, Co.: Westview.

Padilla, A. M. (1986). "Acculturation and Stress among Immigrants and Later-Generation Individuals," in Frick, D., Hoefert, H., Legewie, H., Mackensen, R., and Silbereisen, R. K., eds., *The Quality of Urban Life: Social, Psychological, and Physical Conditions*. Berlin: de Gruyter.

Peal, E., and Lambert, W. (1962). "The Relation of Bilingualism to Intelligence," *Psychological Monographs* 76, no. 546.

Phinney, J. S. (1995). In Padilla, A., ed., *Hispanic Psychology: Critical Issues in Theory and Research*. London: Sage Publications, International Educational and Professional Publisher.

Queralt, M. (1984). "Understanding Cuban Immigrants: A Cultural Perspective," *Social Work*, vol. 29, no. 2, pp. 115–21.

Ramos-McKay, J. (1977). "Locus of Control, Social Activism and Sex Roles among Island Puerto Rican College and Non-college Individuals." Unpublished dissertation, University of Massachusetts.

References

Robins, L., and Regier, D. (1991). *Psychiatric Disorders in America*. New York: Free Press.

Rogler, L. H., and Cooney, R. S. (1984). *Puerto Rican Families in New York City: Intergenerational Process* (Monograph no. 11). New York: Hispanic Research Center, Fordham University.

Rosenfield, S. (1980). "Sex Differences in Depression: Do Women Always Have Higher Rates?" *Journal of Health and Social Behavior*, vol. 21, pp. 33–42.

Secunda, V. (1990). *When You and Your Mother Can't Be Friends: Resolving the Most Complicated Relationship in Your Life*. New York: Delacorte.

Stevens, E. D. (1973). "Marianismo: The Other Face of Machismo in Latin America," in A. Decastello, ed., *Female and Male in Latin America*. Pittsburgh: University of Pittsburgh Press.

Straus, M. A., and Gelles, R. J. (1986). "Societal Change and Change in Family Violence from 1975 to 1985 as Revealed by Two National Surveys," *Journal of Marriage and the Family*, vol. 48 (August 1986), pp. 465–79.

Stycos, J. M. (1955). *Family and Fertility in Puerto Rico: A Study of the Lower Income Group*. New York: Columbia University Press.

Surrey, J. L. (1991). *Women's Growth in Connection: Writings from the Stone Center*. New York: Guilford.

Szapocznik, J., and Kurtines, W. (1980). "Acculturation, Biculturalism, and Adjustment among Cuban Americans," in Padilla, A. M., ed., *Acculturation: Theory, Models and Some New Findings*. Boulder, Co.: Westview.

Torrey, E. F. (1972). *Witchdoctors and Psychiatrists: The Common Roots of Psychotherapy and Its Future*. Northvale, N.J.: Jason Aronson.

U.S. Department of Labor Women's Bureau. (1989). "Women in Management," *Facts on Working Women*, no. 89-4. Washington, D.C.: U.S. Government Printing Office.

————.(1986). "Women of Hispanic Origin in Labor Force," *Facts on Working Women*, no. 89-1. Washington, D.C.: U.S. Government Printing Office.

Vasquez, M. J. T. (1994). "Latinas," in Comas-Diaz, L., and Greene, B., eds., *Women of Color: Integrating Ethnic and Gender Identities in Psychotherapy*. New York: Guilford.

Webster's Ninth New Collegiate Dictionary. (1991). Springfield, Mass., Merriam-Webster.

Weidman, A. (1986). "Family Therapy with Violent Couples," *Social Casework: The Journal of Contemporary Social Work*, vol. 67, pp. 211–18.

Winnicott, D. W. (1969). "The Use of an Object and Relating Through Identifications," in *Playing and Reality*. London: Tavistock, 1971.

Wolman, B. B. (1973). *Dictionary of Behavioral Science*. New York: Van Nostrand.

Young, G. H., and Gerson, S. (1991). "New Psychoanalytic Perspectives on Masochism and Spouse Abuse," *Psychotherapy*, vol. 28, no. 1, pp. 30–38.

Young, J. G., Brasic, J., Sheitman, B., and Studnick, M. (1994). "Brain Mechanisms Mediating Aggression and Violence," in Chiland, C., and Young, J. G., eds., *Children and Violence*, vol. 11 of *The Child in the Family*, Monograph series of the International Association for Child and Adolescent Psychiatry and Allied Professions. Northvale, N.J.: Jason Aronson.

Zulueta, F. (1994). *The Traumatic Roots of Destructiveness: From Pain to Violence*. Northvale, N.J.: Jason Aronson.

ROSA MARIA GIL, D.S.W., is vice-president of Mental Health and Dependency Services for the New York City Health and Hospitals Corporation, an assistant professor of clinical psychiatric social work in Columbia University's College of Physicians and Surgeons, and a psychotherapist in private practice. She lives in New York.

CARMEN INOA VAZQUEZ, PH.D., ABPP, is the founding direc-tor of the Bilingual Treatment Program clinic (BTP) at Bellevue Hospital, and the director of the NYU-Bellevue clinical internship, a clinical associate professor at New York University School of Medicine, and a psychotherapist in private practice. She lives in New York.